The Co

Sleep Medicine
Handbook

Essential Knowledge for
the Boards & Beyond

6th Edition

David E. Westerman MB.ChB., FCP(SA), FCCP, FAASM

Medical Director, Northside Hospital Sleep Center, Atlanta, GA
Faculty Member, Atlanta School of Sleep Medicine

The Concise Sleep Medicine Handbook
Essential Knowledge for the Boards and Beyond

6th Edition

© Copyright 2021 by David E. Westerman

GSSD Publishers, LLC, Atlanta, Georgia

Design by Craig Moonshower
craigmoonshower@yahoo.com

This edition in memory of

Hymie Phillips
1947-2021

A true and lifelong friend

Preface to the 6th Edition:

The goals of this handbook are unchanged since first published in 2011: (a) as a study aid for the board certification examination in sleep medicine and (b) as a resource for the practicing sleep clinician.

Recent AASM guidelines and practice positions are included and those remaining on the AASM website are retained. The website indicates new guidelines for which the reader is encouraged to review when available. Selected articles relevant to clinical sleep medicine are summarized. The impact of the Covid 19 pandemic on sleep and sleep related disorders remains in evolution. The AASM website contains a link to Covid 19 related articles.

The AASM scoring manual was updated in 2020 and, together with the International Classification of Sleep Disorders (3rd edition 2014) remains essential reading.

David Westerman, MB.ChB., FCCP, FAASM.
Atlanta, Georgia, April 2021.

For the sake of space journal references are sometimes abbreviated; most often *JCSM* for the Journal of Clinical Sleep Medicine, or *AJRCCM* for the American Journal of Respiratory and Critical Care Medicine.

Preface to the 5th Edition:

Ever since the original edition in 2011, the aim of this book remains the same: to be a useful study aid and review for the ABIM sleep medicine board certification examination as well as a clinical resource for the busy sleep physician. The format therefore attempts to remain concise with frequent use of bullet points.

The current blueprint of contents for the ABIM examination consists of nine categories. This book maintains the 12 categories of earlier ABIM examinations with all nine current categories still included. The three additional categories are organ system physiology in sleep, pharmacology and pediatric considerations. While they may be subsumed within other categories, they maintain clinical value independently (especially for pharmacology and pediatric considerations) while in no way diminishing their usefulness for study purposes.

The latest AASM position papers including nightmare disorder and actigraphy are summarized. Old papers dating back to at least 2005 remain on the AASM website and are therefore still included (with appropriate updates) in the various sections.

A brief approach to personalized/targeted therapy for OSA which appears to be the way of the future is summarized in the section on Breathing Disorders. An outline of the association of cancer and sleep is added in section 11 (Sleep in other Disorders). References to important scientific papers since the previous edition are referenced in the appropriate sections.

An appendix towards the end of the book summarizes the AASM Health Advisory recommendations found on the AASM website.

Comments are once again welcome at
david.westerman@northside.com.

David Westerman, MB.ChB., FCCP, FAASM.
Atlanta, Georgia, April 2021.

Preface to the 3rd edition:

Since this book's second edition in 2013, a major development in sleep medicine has been the introduction of the **Third Edition of the International Classification of Sleep Disorders** (ICSD3) in 2014, the first update in nine years. The major sleep disorders affected in the classification include the insomnias, narcolepsy, and sleep-disordered breathing. The other contribution has been the introduction of a new version of the **AASM Manual for the Scoring of Sleep and Associated Events (Version 2.1 2014)**. A thorough review of both these publications is critical for candidates who will be sitting for the upcoming board examinations in Sleep Medicine. A primary aim behind this book is to assist busy physicians in their preparation for the board examinations. The major changes in both of the ICSD3 and the latest version of the Scoring Manual are therefore summarized for rapid review in this edition.

The individual chapters of previous editions of this book were arranged to reflect the ABIM's exam content outlined in 12 sections. The ABIM's website indicates that the content is now compressed into eight sections. For example, there is no longer an independent section for pediatric sleep disorders. The various pediatric sleep disorders are now incorporated into one of the general sections. Since a second purpose of this book is to be a quick reference guide for physicians in clinical practice, it is felt that maintaining the previous outline would be an advantage for the busy clinician while at the same time not losing its value in preparation for the examinations.

As with previous editions, the text will also include certain new advances and treatments as well as summaries of important review articles. Where necessary, information now redundant has been modified or deleted.

David Westerman
Atlanta GA
March, 2015

Another book on sleep medicine? (Preface to 1ˢᵗ edition)

The idea behind this book is to assist busy physicians prepare for their board examinations in sleep medicine. While there are several comprehensive sleep medicine texts with which candidates for the ABIM sleep boards may familiarize themselves, this book aims to summarize the essentials of sleep medicine in a compact volume able to be reviewed over a relatively short period of time.

The format of this book is also geared towards board preparation:

- Sections are arranged to reflect exam content as outlined by the ABIM.

- Official AASM publications and reports are *essential* preparatory reading. The International Classification of Sleep Disorders, 2nd edition, 2005, (hereafter referred to as ICSD2) is a major and authoritative reference source. The AASM Manual for the Scoring of Sleep and Associated Events (2007) as well as position papers and guidelines published in the journals *SLEEP* and *Journal of Clinical Sleep Medicine* are summarized in the appropriate sections for easy reference and compact organization of study material (one-stop shopping!). These pages contain a border for easy identification.

- Data is presented in bullet form wherever possible to facilitate review.

- Gray shaded areas introduced with a " *REMember* " serve to highlight facts and figures needing particular emphasis (and which could easily be material for board questions).

Sleep medicine, of course, does not end with the board examinations. The book's handy size should allow it to fit into most lab-coat pockets and its contents to be a resource in the day-to-day practice of clinical and laboratory sleep medicine. The tables of common psychoactive medications have been included specifically for the benefit of sleep specialists (like me) who may not prescribe these drugs on a regular basis but frequently encounter patients taking these medications.

Key journal references are included both in the body of the text and as "further reading / reference" at the end of several sections. Standard reference books have also provided important information, including prevalence data and are listed at the end of this volume. Any errors are mine alone. — David Westerman, Atlanta, Georgia.

CONTENTS

1. **Normal sleep and variants**   1
   Anatomy and Chemistry of Wakefulness and Sleep
   The Sleep-wake cycle
   Sleep Deprivation
   Normal Sleep Stages in Adults

2. **Organ system physiology in sleep**   11
   Respiratory
   Cardiovascular
   Gastrointestinal
   Endocrine
   Cerebral Blood Flow
   Genitourinary
   Thermoregulation

3. **Sleep evaluation**   17
   Evaluation of Excessive daytime sleepiness
   Evaluation of Insomnia
   Sleep Testing
       Polsomnography and scoring rules
       MSLT
       MWT
       Actigraphy

4. **Pharmacology**   39
   Medications causing sedation
   Sleep-disrupting Medications
   Impact of Medications on REM sleep
   Effects of Alcohol on Sleep
   Table of Psychoactive Medications

5. **Circadian rhythm disorders (CRD)**   53
   Basic Circadian Physiology
   Specific Circadian Rhythm Disorder
       Delayed sleep-wake phase disorder
       Advanced sleep-wake phase disorder
       Jet-lag disorder
       Shift-work disorder
       Irregular sleep-wake rhythm disorder
       Non-24hr sleep-wake rhythm disorder
   Treatment of CRDs

6. **Insomnia**   63
   Overview
       Diagnostic criteria
       Classification
       Demographics
       Pathophysiology
   Acute/adjustment insomnia

Chronic insomnias (primary & co-morbid)
Clinical evaluation
Management
Table of FDA approved hypnotics
Summary of AASM article for Insomnia Evaluation & Management

7. Hypersomnolence unrelated to SDB   77
Narcolepsy.
Idiopathic hypersomnia.
Kleine-Levin Syndrome including menstrual-related hypersomnia.

8. Parasomnias   89
Associated with NREM sleep.
    Confusional arousals.
    Sleepwalking.
    Sleep terrors.
    Sleep-Related Eating Disorder (SRED).
Associated with REM sleep.
    REM Sleep Behavior Disorder (RBD).
    Recurrent Isolated Sleep Paralysis.
    Nightmare Disorder.
"Other" parasomnias (ICSD-2)
    Sleep enuresis.
    Sleep-Related Hallucinations.
Violent parasomnias
Sexsomnia

9. Sleep-related movement disorders   109
Restless leg syndrome
Periodic Limb Movement Disorder
Sleep Related Rhythmic Movement Disorder
Sleep-Related Bruxism

10. Sleep-related breathing disorders   125
Obstructive Sleep Apnea Syndrome (including UARS)
    i. A review of OSA (including pathogenesis, risk factors, complications and management).
    ii. Summaries of Practice Parameters and special articles published in Sleep and the Journal of Clinical Sleep Medicine (JCSM).
Central Sleep Apnea (CSA) Syndromes
    Primary Central Sleep Apnea Syndrome
    Cheyne Stokes Breathing
    Treatment Emergent CSA(Complex Sleep Apnea)
    CSA due to Medication or Substance
    Central Apneas in Hypercapnic Disorders
Sleep Related Hypoventilation/hypoxemic Syndromes
    Idiopathic Central Alveolar Hypoventilation Syndrome
    Obesity Hypoventilation Syndrome
    Post Polio Syndrome
Sleep Related Groaning (Catathrenia)

11. Sleep in other disorders   183

Epilepsy Syndromes
> Nocturnal frontal lobe epilepsy
> Benign Epilepsy of Childhood with Central Temporal Spikes
> Juvenile Myoclonic Epilepsy
> Continuous Spike Waves During Non-REM Sleep
> Temporal Lobe Epilepsy
> Nocturnal Paroxysmal Dystonia
> Absence seizures

Psychiatric Disorders
> Depression
> Bipolar disorders
> Generalized anxiety disorder
> Post-traumatic stress disorder
> Obsessive compulsive disorder
> Schizophrenia

Neurodegenerative disorders
Respiratory Disorders
> Asthma
> COPD
> Interstitial lung disorders
> Pulmonary hypertension

GERD
Fibromyalgia
Pregnancy and sleep
Cancer and sleep

12. Pediatric Considerations and Disorders   209

Development of sleep patterns.
Sleep scoring.
OSA in children
Other respiratory disorders occurring in infants and children.
> Congenital Central Alveolar Hypoventilation Syndrome (CCAHS).
> SIDS.
> Acute Life-Threatening Event (ALTE).
> Primary Central Sleep Apneas of Prematurity and Infancy.

Insomnias in childhood.
> Behavioral insomnia of childhood.
> - Sleep onset association type
> - Limit setting type
> Other childhood insomnias

Points of differentiation in sleep disorders occurring in adults & children:
> Narcolepsy.
> RLS
> Periodic leg movement disorder.

Appendix   234

AASM clinical and public awareness statements summarized.

Section 1:

NORMAL SLEEP AND VARIANTS

ANATOMY AND CHEMISTRY OF WAKEFULNESS AND SLEEP.

A. WAKEFULNESS:

Key anatomic areas.

i.   Brain stem: Ascending reticular formation; nuclei include
   - Raphe nucleus (RN)
   - Locus ceruleus (LC)
   - Substantia nigra (SN)
   - Pedunculopontine tegmental nucleus(PPT)
   - Laterodorsal tegmental nucleus (LDT)

ii. Thalamus.

iii. Hypothalamus (posterolateral nuclei).

iv. Basal forebrain (BF).

Note: **The ascending reticular activating system** (ARAS) is the route by which the ascending reticular formation sends projections to the cerebral cortex via the thalamus (dorsal pathway) and via the posterior hypothalamus and BF (ventral pathway). The primary neurotransmitter for the ARAS is **glutamate**.

NEUROTRANSMITTERS OF WAKEFULNESS

Neurotransmitter	Location	Actions
Glutamate	• Reticular formation	• Primary neurotransmitter of ARAS (critical for cortical activation)
NE	• LC	• NE, DA and 5-HT project to cortex through either dorsal or ventral pathways of ARAS; (activity decreased in NREM and inactive in REM) • Inhibit VLPO during wake
DA	• SN	
5-HT	• Dorsal and medial raphe nuclei	
Histamine	• TMN(posterior hypothalamus).	• Projects to virtually entire cortex and brainstem (BS). • Inhibits VLPO.
Hypocretin/ orexin	• Lateral & posterior hypothalamus	• Projects to cortex and wake- promoting BS nuclei (LC,TMN,PPT,LDT) • Orexin neurons are activated by glutamate.
ACh	• BF • PPT and LDT (pons)	• ACh in BF projects directly to cerebral cortex. • ACh from PPT and LDT have excitatory action on thalamic relay neurons and inhibit GABA neurons in thalamus.

AD:adenosine; ACh:acetylcholine; BF: basal forebrain; DA:dopamine; GABA:gaba-aminobutyric acid; 5-HT:serotonin;LDT: laterodorsal tegmental nucleus; LC: locus ceruleus; NE:norepinephrine; PPT:Pedunculopontine tegmental nucleus; SN:substantia nigra; TMN:tuberomammillary nucleus; VLPO:ventrolateral preoptic nucleus

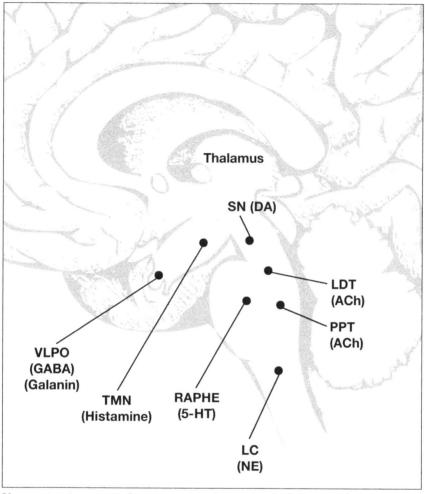

Key anatomic areas and neurontransmitters of wakefulness and sleep.

B. SLEEP:

Key Anatomic Areas

i. Hypothalamus - Anterior and dorsomedial nuclei.

ii. Ventrolateral preoptic nucleus (VLPO).

iii. BF neurons.

NEUROTRANSMITTERS OF SLEEP

Neurotransmitter	Location	Action
GABA	• VLPO • Other regions throughout brain.	• Inhibits ARAS. • Inhibits cerebral cortex via projections to basal forebrain and hypothalamus.
Galanin	• VLPO	• Inhibits ARAS.
AD	• BF	• Accumulates in BF and cortex during wake to promote sleep • Activates VLPO • Inhibits wake ACh neurons. • Levels decrease during sleep
ACh	PPT and LDT (pons).	• Main REM neurotransmitter • Inactive in NREM

REMember:

VLPO and sleep:
• Active during sleep; inhibits arousal systems (GABA and galanin).
• Inhibited during wakefulness by NE, 5-HT, ACh, histamine.

ACh Activity in REM

1. ACh which is active in REM produced by specific population of cholinergic cells in PPT and LDT.
2. REM-active ACh inhibited by NE, 5-HT and histamine during wake and NREM sleep.
3. ACh activity disinhibited when NE, 5-HT and histamine neurons become inactive during REM.
4. ACh activates thalamus to cause cortical dyssynchrony and disappearance of sleep spindles and K-complexes.
5. ACh from second sub-group of pontine cells causes muscle atonia. Activates medial medulla to release glycine producing hyperpolarization and inhibition of motor neurons.

Summary - Main neurotransmitters.

1. Glutamate: Wakefulness.
2. GABA: NREM.
3. ACh: REM.
4. Glycine: REM muscle atonia.

REMember:

Impact of Commonly Used Drugs on Sleep Neurotransmitters

A. Wakefulness enhanced by:
   - Amphetamines .....promote release of DA, 5-HT and NE and block reuptake.
   - Methylxanthines ....antagonize AD.
   - Bupropion ....enhances DA and NE activity.

B. Sleepiness enhanced by:
   - Antihistamines ....block H-1 receptors.
   - BZD's, BzRAs............increase GABA activity.
   - Typical antipsychotics......block DA receptors.

THE SLEEP-WAKE CYCLE

Homeostatic drive for sleep (process S).
   - Homeostatic factor accumulates progressively in wakefulness to promote sleep; declines during sleep.
   - AD accumulating in BF may be neurobiological equivalent.

Circadian drive/rhythm (process C).
   - Regulates timing of sleep/wake cycle.
   - Genetically controlled (e.g., CLOCK, Per and other genes).
   - Circadian pacemaker located in suprachiasmatic nucleus (SCN) of anterior hypothalamus.
   - Synchronized by external cues (zeitgeber) especially light and social activity.
   - SCN promotes wakefulness during the day counteracting homeostatic drive for sleep.
     - Excitatory signals relay to HT and other arousal regions.
     - Inhibitory signals to VLPO.
   - SCN facilitates sleep by regulating the timing of melatonin secretion from pineal gland via signals through the superior cervical ganglion.
   - Internal "clock" is slightly >24hr (24.16hrs).

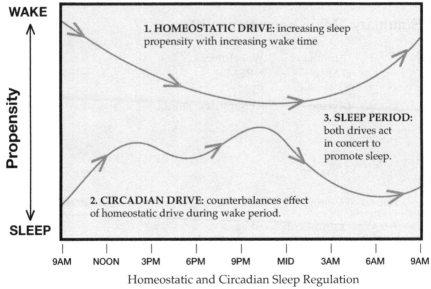

Homeostatic and Circadian Sleep Regulation

(After Roth T. Culpepper L. Insomnia Management in Primary Care. Clin. Symp. 2008; 58(1): 3-32)

SLEEP DEPRIVATION (SD)

<u>Acute SD</u>: Maximum sleep propensity reached after $\pm$ 40 hours of total wakefulness.

<u>Partial SD</u> leads to build up of homeostatic drive resulting in sleep debt; may "make up" over weekends.

<u>Chronic partial SD</u> occurs when sleep is repeatedly reduced to < 5-6 hours per night. May result in the following:

    i. General/cognitive:
- ↑ Sleepiness and motor vehicle accidents.
- ↓ Working memory, ↓ attention, ↓ response time, ↓ concentration.
- Hyperactivity in children.

    ii. Immune responses.
- ↓ Antibodies to flu vaccination at ten days; normal antibody titer at 3-4 weeks.
- ↓ Febrile response to endotoxins.
- ↑ Increased IL-6 and TNF (markers of systemic inflammation).
- ↓ Resistance to infection.

    iii. Psychological effects.
- ↓ Vigor, ↑ fatigue.
- Irritability, hypomania.
- 30-60% depressed patients may become euthymic

    iv. Neurologic changes.
- ↓ Pain tolerance.
- ↓ Seizure threshold.

- Brisk deep tendon and gag reflexes.
- Sluggish corneal reflexes.
- Tremor.
- Nystagmus.
- Slurred speech.

v. Endocrine changes.
- ↓ Growth hormone.
- ↓ Prolactin.
- Insulin resistance/glucose intolerance.
- ↑ Metabolic rate.
- ↓ Leptin →↑ appetite and weight gain.*
- ↑ Ghrelin →↑ appetite.**

vi.
- Cardiovascular morbidity: TST <5-6 hours reported to be associated with ↑ risk of CAD (*SLEEP* 2010;33(8):1037); *Eur J Prev Cardiol* 2014;21(11):1367), hypertension (*Arch Int Med* 2009;169(11);1055) and stroke (*SLEEP* 2010;33(8):1037).
- Excessively shorter (≤ 5 vs 7h) or longer (≥ 9 vs 7h) sleep periods possible risk factors for hypertension (f>m) (Review article: Wang et al *J. Clin Sleep Med*, 2015; 11(9): 1047-1056)
- ↑ A.Fib with short sleep duration (ave 4.7h). (Genuardi et al *CHEST* 2019; 156(3): 544-552.

vii. Dementia and all cause mortality.
- < 5hrs TST →↑risk dementia and all cause mortality. Study of 2812 adults >65 yrs, average 76.9 yrs, published in *Aging* 2021; 13(3): 3254-68).

REMember:

*Leptin secreted by adipose tissue (adipocytes); rises after meals to produces satiety. Lower levels with sleep deprivation increases appetite. Levels higher in obesity (?leptin resistance). Diurnal variation: 20-40% higher levels middle of night. Acts on hypothalamus (HT) and satiety centers in the nucleus of the solitary tract.

**Ghrelin "hunger hormone" produced by gastric epithelium; levels rise prior to mealtime causing hunger sensation. Levels fall after eating and are low in obesity. Levels ↑ with fasting, weight loss, cachexia or anorexia. Elevated levels with sleep deprivation increases appetite. Acts on HT as well as other CNS nuclei. Note: Variable impact of OSA and PAP on leptin & ghrelin (See review article *J Clin Sleep Med* 2019; 15(7): 1037-1050.

Recovery after acute sleep deprivation.

After 24-48 hours of wakefulness:
First recovery night:
- ↑ SWS.
- ↓ REM.

Second recovery night:
- Most SWS regained.
- ↑ REM.

Third night: sleep architecture normalizes.

REMember:
- Equal amounts of sleep are not necessary to replace sleep loss.
- After 2-4days of continuous wakefulness performance recovery may occur after a single night of sleep lasting about eight hours.

Recommended Amount of Sleep for a Healthy Adult (Consensus Statement).
J Clin Sleep Med 2015; 11 (6): 591-592; *SLEEP* 2015;38(6):843-844

- ≥ 7 hours nightly sleep recommended.
- < 7 hours may result in adverse outcomes including cardiovascular and cerebrovascular disease, weight gain/obesity, diabetes, depression ,increased risk of death and impairement of immune and cognitive function.
- > 9 hours nightly sleep appropriate in young adults or following sleep deprivation e.g. recovery from illnesses. Uncertain whether regular sleep > 9 hours per night in adults results in adverse health risks.

NORMAL SLEEP IN ADULTS

(for sleep in infants and children see section 12)

Sleep stages vary between younger and older adults.

Stage	Younger Adults	Elderly
N1	2 - 5%	5 - 8%
N2	45 - 55%	57 - 67%
N3	15 - 20%	6 - 17%
REM	20 - 25%	17 - 20%

REMember:
- Sleep efficiency at age 45 ± 86%. ↓ with age: ± 79% age 70.

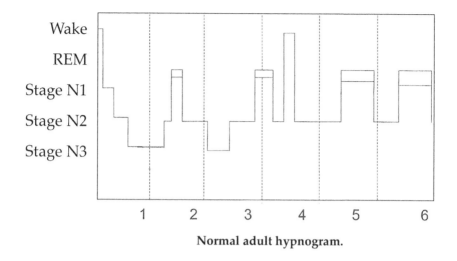

Normal adult hypnogram.

Sequence of Sleep Stages

1. Usually enter sleep through N1 within 10 to 20 minutes after lights out; lasts 30 seconds to 7 minutes.
2. N2 follows N1 and precedes N3; usually recurs to precede REM sleep.
3. N3 occurs 35 - 45 minutes after sleep onset in young healthy adults
4. REM occurs 75 - 90 minutes after sleep onset.
   a. The first REM episode least intense, may last 5 - 10 minutes.
   b. Alternates with NREM at ±90 minutes intervals; usually 4 - 5 REM - NREM cycles.
   c. Increased REM and more intense REM towards the end of sleep period (last REM period may last from 30 to 60 minutes).
   d. N3 sleep gets progressively less during the night and the final sleep period is composed mainly of N2 and REM sleep.

REMember:
- Subjective perception of sleep onset may be different from PSG criteria.
- PSG criteria for sleep onset include slowing of EEG activity, reduction in muscle tone and rolling eye movements (see section 3).

Further reading/references:
Espana RA , Scammell TE: Sleep Neurobiology for the Clinician
SLEEP 2004; 27(4):811-820

Test Your Memory (Section 1):

1. Which of the following neurotransmitters is not associated with promoting wakefulness?

    a. Histamine.
    b. Acetylcholine.
    c. Hypocretin.
    d. Galanin.
    e. Glutamate.

2. Which of the following agents promotes wakefulness by antagonizing adenosine?

    a. Methylphenidate.
    b. Theophylline.
    c. Modafinil.
    d. Bupropion.
    e. Amphetamine.

3. The suprachiasmatic nucleus is located in the:

    a. Thalamus.
    b. Posterior hypothalamus.
    c. Anterior hypothalamus.
    d. Basal forebrain.
    e. Pons

4. Which of the following is not seen with sleep deprivation?

    a. Hyperactivity in children.
    b. Brisk tendon reflexes.
    c. ↑ seizure threshold.
    d. ↑ metabolic rate.
    e. ↓ leptin levels.

5. With regard to REM sleep, which statement is incorrect?

    a. Consists of ± 20% of total sleep time.
    b. REM latency ± 90 minutes after sleep onset.
    c. Is more intense in the second half of sleep period.
    d. First REM period usually immediately preceded by N3 sleep.
    e. Cycles with NREM at ± 90-minute intervals.

6. Which neurotransmitter is responsible for the disappearance of sleep spindles and K-complexes in REM?

    a. Adenosine.
    b. Norepinephrine.
    c. Histamine.
    d. Dopamine.
    e. Acetylcholine

Answers: 1d, 2b, 3c, 4c, 5d, 6e.

Section 2:

ORGAN SYSTEM PHYSIOLOGY IN SLEEP

A. RESPIRATORY PHYSIOLOGY:

Control of breathing is influenced by the following factors:
a. Metabolic.
b. Neurologic.
c. Behavioral/voluntary influences.
d. Waking neural drive.

CONTROL OF BREATHING

Input	Sensor/modulator	Impact of Sleep on Sensor/Modulator
a. Metabolic PaO_2 $PaCO_2$	Carotid bodies Central chemoreceptors	Blunted especially in REM Blunted especially in REM
b. Neurologic	Stretch receptors (lungs and intercostal muscles)	
c. Behavioral/voluntary	Respiratory center in brain stem	Quiescent
d. Waking neural drive	Serotonergic/noradrenergic afferents	Abolished

Respiratory Physiology Changes During Sleep

- ↓ Tidal volume ($\pm10\%$).
- ↓ Minute ventilation (0.4-1.5 L/min.).
- ↓ PaO_2 (3-9 mmHg).
- ↓ Oxygen saturation (~2%).
- ↑ $PaCO_2$ (2-6 mmHg).

Breathing Patterns During Sleep

a. NREM.
- Periodic breathing at sleep onset (instability of respiratory control system prior to established sleep).
- Regular breathing pattern latter part N2 and in N3 sleep.

b. REM.
- Irregular breathing pattern especially in phasic REM.
- Intercostal muscle atonia.
- ↓ Upper airway muscle tone (causes upper airway resistance).
- Diaphragmatic function maintained.

Other Pulmonary Reflexes During Sleep

- Blunted cough reflex.
- Blunted arousal response to hypoxia.
- An arousal response occurs when $PaCO_2 > 15$ mmHg above waking level.

The Apneic Threshold:

The apneic threshold is a level of $PaCO_2$ below which a central apnea occurs during NREM sleep. The apneic threshold is state related and rapidly increases with sleep onset to above the $PaCO_2$ level. Central apneas may therefore be seen physiologically at times of sleep transition whether at sleep onset or during sleep (e.g., after an arousal). The difference between eucapnic $PaCO_2$ and the apneic threshold is usually only 2-5 mmHg during NREM (see *J Clin Sleep Med* Commentary 15 Dec 2020 p1999).

REMember:

Drugs Influencing Respiratory Drive (RD)

- RD↓ by EtOH, narcotics, BZDs, barbiturates (also cause ↑ upper airways resistance).
- RD↑ by progesterone, theophylline, acetazolamide.

B. CARDIOVASCULAR RESPONSES IN SLEEP

a. NREM.
- Parasympathetic tone predominates: ↓ in HR, BP, cardiac output, systemic vascular resistance and coronary artery blood flow.
- Respiratory sinus arrhythmia/heart rate variability (HRV); loss of HRV may occur with ↑ age or cardiac pathology.

b. REM.
- Phasic REM: ↑ sympathetic activity → ↑ in HR, CO, BP, coronary artery blood flow & cardiac metabolic activity. Respirations variable.
- Tonic REM: ↑ parasympathetic and ↓ sympathetic activity → ↓ in CO, BP & HR.

C. GASTROINTESTINAL CHANGES

- Esophageal acid clearance prolonged (due to ↓ in swallowing frequency and salivation).
- Gastric acid secretion peaks between 10pm & 2am; lowest levels 5-11am.
- ↓ Gastric motor function and delayed stomach emptying.
- Intestinal motility generally decreases but may be unchanged.
- Splanchnic circulation unchanged.

D. ENDOCRINE PHYSIOLOGY AND SLEEP

 *REMember:*

- Cortisol and TSH secretion are *circadian* modulated (inhibited by sleep).
- Growth hormone (GH) and prolactin (PL) secretion are *sleep* modulated.

Hormone	Peak/Trough level
Cortisol	• Peaks 8-9 AM; nadir at midnight. • Nocturnal sleep inhibits release.
Thyroid stimulating hormone(TSH)	• Low daytime level; ↑ evening level. • Peaks prior to sleep onset. • Gradual decline during sleep. • ↑ with sleep deprivation.
Growth hormone(GH)	• Peaks ~90 minutes after sleep onset (usually in N3) especially in men. • In females, daytime GH pulses may be more frequent.
Prolactin (PL)	• ↓ during wakefulness. • lowest level around noon. • ↑ begins ±1hour after sleep onset. • Peak usually 5 AM-7 AM.
Testosterone	• Increases during sleep; highest levels in early am (in young healthy males). • Lowest levels 7-10pm.
Melatonin	• Increases in evening. • Suppressed by light. • Peaks early morning then declines.
Leptin	• ↑ during sleep (peaks midnight-4am).
Ghrelin	• ↑ during early part of sleep (but not in obesity).

REMember:

Leptin & ghrelin levels both increase in sleep even though they have opposite effects on satiety (leptin decreases appetite; ghrelin increases).

E. CEREBRAL BLOOD FLOW

- Decreases in NREM
- Increases in REM

F. GENITOURINARY CHANGES

- Renal function: ↓ GFR, ↑ renin, ↑ water reabsorption→ ↓ urine production in sleep.
- During REM: penile tumescence; vaginal/clitoral engorgement.

G. THERMOREGULATION DURING SLEEP

- Core body temperature highest late pm/early evening (± 6-8pm) then declines.
- Sleep onset usually occurs during declining phase of temperature rhythm.
- Nadir in temperature occurs ±4-5am (about 2hrs before wake time).
- Awakening from sleep usually occurs after temperature nadir and during the rising phase of temperature cycle.
- NREM: Thermoregulation present but diminished compared with wakefulness.
- REM: Thermoregulation markedly blunted or absent. Shivering and heat production lost.

REMember:

A strategy in treating sleep onset insomnia includes an evening hot bath. Elevation in core body temperature with subsequent accentuation of diurnal temperature decline may promote sleep onset.

Test Your Memory (Section 2):

1. Which statement is true?

   a. Parasympathetic tone predominates in NREM and tonic REM.
   b. Sympathetic tone predominates in phasic REM.
   c. Both are true.
   d. Neither is true.

2. Which hormones are circadian modulated (inhibited by sleep)?

   a. Growth hormone (GH) and prolactin.
   b. Cortisol and TSH.
   c. GH and TSH
   d. Cortisol and prolactin

3. Peak cortisol production occurs at:

   a. 8:00 am. - 9:00 am.
   b. 8:00 pm. - 9:00 pm.

4. With regard to temperature regulation in sleep, which statement is incorrect?

   a. Sleep onset occurs during the declining phase of temperature rhythm.
   b. Nadir in temperature usually occurs about two hours before wake time.
   c. Heat production is lowest in REM.
   d. Wakefulness usually coincides with temperature nadir.

5. Respiratory changes in sleep include all of the following except:

   a. ↓ minute ventilation.
   b. ↓ $PaCO_2$.
   c. ↓ PaO_2.
   d. ↓ cough reflex.
   e. ↓ arousal response to hypoxia.

Answers: 1c, 2b, 3a, 4d, 5b.

Section 3:

SLEEP EVALUATION

This section includes

1. An approach to the clinical evaluation of **excessive daytime sleepiness** (EDS) and **insomnia** (among the most commons sleep-related symptoms).

2. An overview of **laboratory procedures** for sleep testing based on standard **AASM guidelines and recommendations**.

EVALUATION OF EDS: A PRACTICAL APPROACH

A. History

1. Evaluate for

    - **Medical causes** (e.g., chronic renal failure, hypothyroidism, CNS disease, fibromyalgia).
    - **Psychiatric causes** (e.g., mood disorders).
    - **Medication effects/substance abuse** (e.g., antihistamines, antiseizure mediations, sedating antidepressants, opioids, BZDs, alcohol and drug abuse).

2. Evaluate for **sleep related disorders/problems**

    a. Too little sleep.
    - Poor sleep hygiene, economic or social factors.
    - Chronic insomnia (see approach below).
    - Circadian rhythm disorders (e.g., delayed sleep-wake phase disorder- DSWPD).

b. Poor quality sleep.
- Medical causes (e.g., asthma, CHF, GERD, pain, nocturia).
- Effects of drugs and alcohol.
- Sleep apnea syndromes.
- RLS/PLMS.

c. Hypersomnias independent of sleep time or quality.
- Narcolepsy.
- Idiopathic hypersomnia.
- Other causes of hypersomnia (e.g.menstrual-related).

B. Physical Examination:

Depends on underlying condition; may be normal.

In patients with *sleep apnea*, may find the following:

- Obesity (BMI $\geq$ 30 kg/m^2).
- Neck circumference >17 inches males, >16 inches females.
- Oropharyngeal appearance
  - Modified Mallampati classification (see section 10 for details)
  - Tonsillar size (see section 10)
- Retrognathia/micrognathia.

C. Epworth Sleepiness Scale (ESS):
(Johns MW; *Sleep* 1991; 14 (6); 540-545).

Assesses the propensity to sleep in eight situations.
- Maximum score 24/24.
- Score $\leq$ 10 normal.
- In original article:
    OSAS patients scored 11.7
    narcolepsy 17.5
    idiopathic hypersomnia 17.8
    insomnia 2.2.
- Studies have not shown a good correlation with MSLT.
- ESS remains a good screening tool.

EVALUATION OF INSOMNIA

Background

Basic approach: evaluation of insomnia should include
- The *psychodynamics* involved, and then
- The *specific cause* of insomnia.

Psychodynamics:

The "3 P" model (Spielman AJ et al, *Psychiatr Clin North Am* 1987;10:541-553)

1. **P**redisposing factors (e.g., personality traits, "light sleepers," "night owls").

2. **P**recipitating factors - usually acute stress (e.g., illness, bereavement, job loss, divorce, etc).

3. **P**erpetuating factors (e.g., conditioned anxiety regarding sleep, ruminating thoughts, abnormal coping skills, persistence of precipitating factor).

Specific causes:

Note: The 2014 ICSD3 classification of insomnia has combined the 11 etiological subgroups of ICSD2 into 2 subtypes of insomnia, namely Chronic Insomnia Disorder and Short-Term Insomnia Disorder. All subtypes (except acute insomnia) are now described within the broad group of chronic insomnia since, despite etiologic differences, patients may share similar symptoms and outcomes. Nevertheless, from a diagnostic standpoint, it may still be useful to conceptualize chronic insomniacs into those whose insomnia is co-morbid with other disorders and those whose insomnia is the primary issue. Approaching the individual patient in this manner may enhance both the diagnostic and therapeutic processes while still having the new ICSD3 classification as the basic reference point.

i) **Insomnia secondary to, or comorbid with**
- psychologic/psychiatric disorders.
- medical disorders (e.g., chronic pain, asthma, GERD).
- drug/substance abuse.
- specific sleep disorders
    - ~ PLMS
    - ~ CSA>OSA
    - ~ circadian rhythm disorders eg delayed sleep-wake phase disorder (DSWPD).

ii) **Primary insomnias**
- Adjustment (acute insomnia)
- Psychophysiological (conditioned insomnia)
- Paradoxical (sleep-state misperception)
- Idiopathic (childhood onset)
- Poor sleep hygiene

History (clues to nature of insomnia):

1. Duration of insomnia.
   a. Short term (adjustment insomnia) e.g., emotional stress, medical conditions, jetlag.
   b. Chronic: primary or co-morbid insomnia (see above).

2. Age of onset.
   a. Childhood: e.g., idiopathic insomnia (*"never* slept well"),?PTSD (h/o abuse).
   b. Teens: e.g., sleep hygiene, drug/alcohol abuse, depression, DSWPD.
   c. Elderly: circadian rhythm (e.g., advanced sleep-wake phase disorder), depression, dementia, medical conditions.

3. Sex: higher incidence in females; impact of menopause (Note: in postmenopausal females insomnia may be the presenting symptom for OSA).

4. Assess patient's insight into total sleep time (e.g., "I never sleep" may give clue to paradoxical insomnia)

5. Stressful precipitating event (e.g., illness, job loss, bereavement) often signals start of psychophysiological insomnia. Constant focus on inability to sleep and its consequences typical in this condition.

6. Review ability to nap during the day.
   a. "Cannot nap": patients with psychophysiological insomnia are frequently hyperaroused and cannot nap even though sleepy.
   b. If *significant EDS*, consider presence of co-morbid sleep disorder (e.g., OSA).

7. Review sleep hygiene
   ~Caffeine, alcohol, large meals near bedtime
   ~Stimulating activities close to bedtime (e.g., exercise, computer)
   ~Non-sleep related activities in bed (e.g., telephone calls, balancing checkbook).

8. Medication & alcohol history.

Physical examination:

- Often normal unless associated co-morbid disorder present.
- Flat affect of depression or unkempt appearance due to drug or alcohol abuse.

Investigations:

- Sleep diary (two weeks).
- Screening tests for depression (e.g., Beck Depression Scale).
- Actigraphy.
- PSG usually not indicated unless to detect comorbid disorder e.g., OSA, CSA, PLMS, fibromyalgia (alpha intrusions). May also be useful in confirming paradoxical insomnia.
- MSLT if narcolepsy as a cause of disrupted sleep is suspected.

LABORATORY SLEEP EVALUATION: SLEEP TESTING

Sleep testing includes:

Polysomnography (PSG).
Multiple sleep latency test (MSLT).
Maintenance of wakefulness testing (MWT).
Actigraphy.

POLYSOMNOGRAPHY (PSG)

The basis for PSG scoring is found in the *AASM Manual for the Scoring of Sleep and Associated Events* of which the latest version 2.6 was published in January 2020. The following summarizes several technical essentials found in the latest version, but the reader is strongly encouraged to refer to the new manual for comprehensive details.

REMember.

- A derivation is the selection of a pair of EEG electrode inputs.
- Left sided electrodes designated by odd numbers; even numbers for right sided electrodes.
- Mastoid electrodes (M) are reference electrodes.
- Alternative derivations may utilize midline placement, designated with a Z.

Variables recorded during a PSG include:

1. EEG.

a. EEG electrodes are positioned according to the International 10-20 system. Recommended EEG derivations:
- F_4-M_1.
- C_4-M_1.
- O_2-M_1.

b. Backup electrodes should also be placed at F_3, C_3, O_1, and M_2.

SCALP ELECTRODE PLACEMENTS FOR PSG

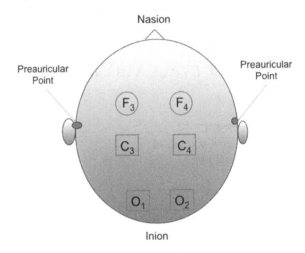

2. Recommended EOG derivations:

a. E_1-M_2.

b. E_2-M_2.
- E_1 - 1 cm lateral to and below outer canthus of left eye.
- E_2 - 1 cm lateral to and above outer canthus of right eye.

NOTE: If M_2 electrode fails, reference E_1 and E_2 to M_1.

REMember:

- Movement *towards* an electrode creates positive voltage (deflection is *down*).
- Movement *away* from an electrode creates *negative* voltage (*upward* deflection).
- *Conjugate* eye movements therefore produce out of phase (*opposite*) deflections in left and right derivations.

3. Chin EMG (three electrodes).

- In midline 1 cm above the inferior edge of the mandible (Chin Z).
- 2cm below inferior edge of the mandible and 2 cm to right of midline (Chin 2).
- 2cm below inferior edge of the mandible and 2 cm to left of midline (Chin 1).
- Masseter electrodes may also be placed to assist with bruxism detection.

EYE AND CHIN PLACEMENTS

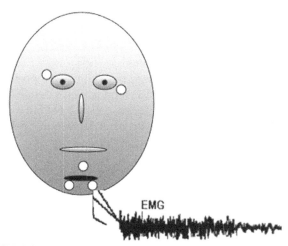

4. Leg EMG.

- Two electrodes placed over both left and right anterior tibial muscles, or 1/3 of the muscle length, whichever is shorter.
- Electrodes placed longitudinally 2 to 3 cm apart at $\pm$ middle of muscle or 1/3 of the muscle length, whichever is shorter.
- Leg movements should be recorded on separate channels for each leg.

5. EKG.

6. Respiratory parameters.

- Nasal pressure transducer - identifies hypopneas.
- Oronasal airflow (thermistor) - detects apneas.
- Respiratory effort (inductance plethysmography).
- O_2 saturations (pulse oximetry; maximum signal averaging 3 secs).
- Snoring microphone.
- CO_2 monitoring (end tidal or transcutaneous) as indicated.

7. Video Monitoring.

Sleep Staging (Adults).

For pediatric scoring, see section 12.

A. Sleep staging is defined by EEG, EMG, EOG.

EEG frequencies used in scoring:
- Alpha 8-13 Hz (Hz = cycles per second or cps). Maximum over occipital region.
- Beta > 13 Hz.
- Theta 4-7.99 Hz.
- Delta 0-3.99 Hz.
- Slow wave activity 0.5-2.0 Hz and peak-to-peak amplitude of > 75 µV over frontal regions.

Other EEG changes used in scoring:
- K complexes: Negative followed immediately by positive component; total duration ≥ 0.5 seconds (helps define N2 sleep).
- Sleep spindle: Burst of 11-16 Hz (usually 12-14 Hz), with duration ≥ 0.5 seconds and maximum in central derivations (helps define N2 sleep).

SUMMARY OF SLEEP WAVEFORMS

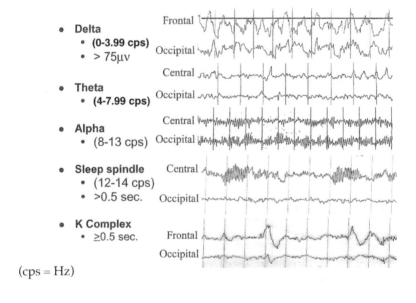

- **Delta**
  - **(0-3.99 cps)**
  - **> 75µv**

- **Theta**
  - **(4-7.99 cps)**

- **Alpha**
  - (8-13 cps)

- **Sleep spindle**
  - (12-14 cps)
  - >0.5 sec.

- **K Complex**
  - ≥0.5 sec.

(cps = Hz)

REMember:

    Spindles originate from reticular nucleus of thalamus.

B. Key EEG, EOG, EMG Components:

Stage W

- Alpha rhythm (8-13 Hz); maximum over occipital region, occurs with eye closure and attenuated with eye opening.

- Eye blinks, reading eye movements, rapid eye movements.

- Score stage W when:
    - \> 50% of epoch has alpha rhythm over occipital region (posterior dominant rhythm).

REMember:

- Sleep onset scored when the first epoch is scored other than stage W (usually N1).

- If ≥ 3 sleep segments present in 30 sec epoch which includes stage W, score epoch as sleep if combined sleep segments comprise majority of epoch.

- If ≥ 2 sleep stages in single epoch, designate sleep stage for epoch according to stage comprising majority of epoch.

Stage N1

- Slow eye movements.
- Low amplitude mixed frequency activity - predominantly 4 - 7 Hz (theta).
- Vertex sharp waves (V waves). < 0.5 seconds and maximal over central regions.
- **Score N1** when alpha attenuated and replaced by theta waves for more than 50% of epoch.

Stage N2

- **K-complexes.**
- Sleep spindles.
- **Score N2** when K-complexes (unassociated with arousals) and/or sleep spindles occur in the first half of a particular epoch or in the last half of the preceding epoch.

Stage N3

- Defined by the presence of slow wave activity (SWA): 0.5-2 Hz with amplitude of > 75 μV over the frontal region.
- **Score N3** when 20% or more of epoch consists of SWA.
- Sleep spindles may be seen in N3; eye movements not usually present.

Stage R

- REMs.
- ↓ chin EMG.
- Low voltage, mixed frequency EEG (may also have sawtooth waves 2-6Hz).
- **Score stage R** when all the above present:

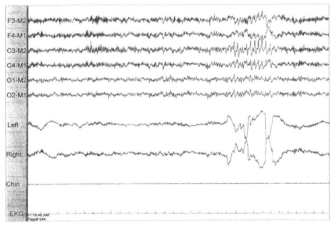

30 sec epoch of REM sleep. Note saw-toothing, REMs and flat chin EMG.

Additional REM characteristics (unrelated to scoring):

- Diaphragmatic, extraocular and sphincter muscles are not atonic.
- Penile tumescence in men; vaginal vascular engorgement and clitoral erection in women.
- Dreaming in stage R more frequent and more complex compared with dreaming in NREM.

REMember:

SYNCHRONIZED sleep implies similar EEG wave forms at the same time over all areas in scalp recordings.
DESYNCHRONIZATION occurs when SWS is interrupted by low voltage fast activity.
PARADOXICAL SLEEP (synonymous with REM sleep): EEG tracing shows low voltage and desynchronization resembling wakefulness but the patient is asleep with muscle atonia and phasic events with REMs.

PSG Scoring Rules (Adults) Essentials:

Reference: AASM Manual for the Scoring of Sleep Associated Events (Version 2.6; 2020).

A. Respiratory:

1. Apnea.
- Identified during **diagnostic study** with *oronasal thermal sensor.*
- Use alternative signal if thermal sensor signal malfunctioning:
  - ~ Nasal pressure transducer.
  - ~ Respiratory inductance plethysmography (RIP).
- Score apnea if peak signal excursion ↓ by ≥ 90% of baseline, **AND** duration of ≥ 90% drop lasts 10 seconds or more.
- Identification of apnea does *not* require minimum oxygen desaturation.
- **Obstructive apnea** scored when absence of airflow is associated with persistent inspiratory effort for the whole period of absent airflow.
- **Central apnea** scored when there is no inspiratory effort throughout the period of absent airflow.
- **Mixed apnea** scored when initial absent inspiratory effort is followed by inspiratory effort during the apnea.

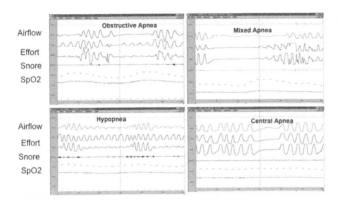

2. Hypopneas.
- Preferably detected during a diagnostic study with *nasal pressure transducer*.
- Alternate signals include oronasal thermal sensor or RIP.
- Score hypopnea when the following criteria met:
  - ~ Pressure or flow signal ↓ by ≥ 30% from baseline and lasting ≥ 10 seconds.
  - ~ Event is associated *either* with a desaturation of at least 3% from pre-event baseline *or* with an arousal.
- Alternative is to use a 4% desaturation (rather than 3%). Interpretation should indicate which criterion used.
- Note that for Medicare or Medicaid patients to qualify for PAP reimbrsement, hypopneas need to meet the criteria of a ≥ 30% drop in flow and a 4% or more desaturation from pre-event baseline.
- Classification of hypopneas into obstructive or central is optional.
- Supplemental oxygen used during a PSG may result in attenuation or elimination of potential desaturations and result in underestimation of the number of hypopneas and of the AHI/RDI.

Summary of AASM special article:
Polysomnography for OSA should include arousal-based scoring: An AASM Position Statement. *J. Clin. Sleep Med* 2018; 14 (7): 1245-7.

This position statement emphasizes the recommended rule for scoring hypopneas as stated in the latest AASM manual for scoring of sleep associated events (version 2.6; 2020). See page 28 opposite.

Unless obligated by payer policy requirements (e.g., MCR which requires a 4% O_2 desaturation for scoring hypopneas), hypopneas should be scored when diminished airflow (≥ 30% from baseline) is associated with a ≥ 3% oxygen desaturation **or** an arousal. The aim of this approach is to capture those patients who c/o neurocognitive symptoms and who would be "missed" as having OSA if the only the 4% desaturation criterion is used. Since a HSAT does not allow for the scoring of arousals, negative HSAT for patients at "increased risk for OSA" should be followed by a PSG. (A PSG should also be performed in patients strongly suspected of having OSA who have a normal AHI (or REI) on a HSAT. (Clinical Practice Guideline *JCSM* 2017; 13 (3): 479–504)

Note:
- During a **positive airway pressure (PAP) titration**, the PAP device flow signal should be used to identify apneas or hypopneas.
- **Oxygenation:**
  - ~ Pulse oximetry with a maximum acceptable signal averaging time of ≤ 3 seconds at a heart rate of 80 beats per minute.

3. Respiratory Effort-Related Arousals (RERA): (see p.31 for definition of arousal)
- RERA scored when an arousal is preceded by a series of breaths lasting ≥ 10 seconds that do not qualify for hypopnea by virtue of the absence of a 3% desaturation.

Note: MCR does not regognize RERAs for scoring purposes.

4. Hypoventilation Rule.
- Hypoventilation scored if there is an ↑ $PaCO_2$ to > 55 mmHg for ≥ 10 minutes, OR
- There is ≥ 10 mmHg ↑ $PaCO_2$ above awake supine value to > 50 mmHg for ≥ 10 minutes.
- End tidal CO_2 or transcutaneous CO_2 monitoring may be used as alterative measurements for $PaCO_2$.
- O_2 saturations are **not** criteria to diagnose hypoventilation.
- Monitoring of hypoventilation is *optional* recording.

5. Cheyne-Stokes Breathing (CSB).
CSB scored when:
- At least 5 central apneas and/or central hypopneas per hour of sleep associated with a cresendo – decrescendo breathing pattern and having a cycle length of at least 40 seconds.
- There should be at least 3 concecutive central apneas or hypopneas separated by the cresendo – decrescendo breathing pattern to be included in scoring.

(Respiratory rules for children are found in section 12.)

B. Periodic Limb Movements of Sleep (PLMS):

- The leg movement (LM) lasts 0.5 -10 seconds. The amplitude is at least 8 μV ↑ in EMG voltage above resting EMG.
- The length of time between individual LMs is from 5 to 90 seconds.
- LMs from different legs separated by < 5 seconds counted as one movement.
- There should be at least four consecutive LMs in order to define a PLM series.
- LMs within 0.5 seconds before or after an apnea, hypopnea, or RERA are not scored.
- Attribute an arousal to a LM if < 0.5 seconds between the LM and the arousal regardless of which comes first, or if the arousal and LM occur simultaneously.

Note:
There are specific EMG bursts of activity to define **Alternating Leg Muscle Activation, Hypnagogic Foot Tremor, and Excessive Fragmentary Myoclonus.** However, all of these phenomena with their characteristic EMG patters have no reported clinical consequences and may be merely benign movement phenomena. Reporting is optional and the reader is referred to the official AASM Scoring Manual for specific criteria.

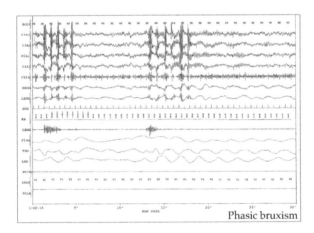

Phasic bruxism

C. Bruxism:

- Bruxism may be brief (phasic) or sustained (tonic) increases in chin EMG 2+ the amplitude of the background EMG.
- Brief/Phasic bruxism scored if ≥ 3 elevations in EMG lasting 0.25 - 2 seconds occur in sequence.
- Sustained/tonic bruxism scored when the chin elevation lasts for > 2 seconds.
- ≥ 3 seconds of stable EMG activity needed prior to a new episode of bruxism.

D. REM Without Atonia (RWA); (optional scoring):

— See page 55 AASM Scoring Manual

E. Arousal Rule:

- Abrupt shift of EEG frequency ≥ 3 seconds.
- 10 sec of stable sleep should precede the arousal.
- Arousals scored in *any* sleep stage; if in REM sleep, there should be simultaneous ↑ submental EMG activity ≥1 sec.
- Δ EEG frequency may include α, θ, and freq > 16 Hz (*not* spindles).

F. Scoring Epochs with Major Body Movements (MBM):

- Definition: MBM is a movement/muscle artifact obscuring > half of an epoch's EEG so sleep stage can't be determined.
- The epoch with the MBM is scored as *stage W* if alpha rhythm is present for *any* part of the epoch. If no alpha rhythm then the epoch in question is scored as the same stage as the epoch that *follows* it.

For Home Sleep Apnea Testing Rules see AASM Scoring Manual version 2.6, 2020 pp69ff.

PSG: INDICATIONS
Summary of: *Practice Parameters for the Indications for Polysomnography and Related Procedures; an update for 2005 (SLEEP* 2005, 28(4); 499-521).

A. PSG routinely indicated for:
  1. Diagnosis of sleep-related breathing disorders.*
  2. CPAP titration.
  3. Assessment of treatment results.*
  4. With a MSLT in the evaluation of suspected narcolepsy.
  5. Violent or otherwise potentially injurious sleep behaviors.
  6. Atypical or unusual parasomnias.
  * HSAT an alternative

B. PSG is NOT routinely indicated in the following situations:
  1. Diagnosis of chronic lung disease.
  2. Cases of typical uncomplicated and noninjurious parasomnias.
  3. Seizure disorder without sleep related symptoms.
  4. Diagnosis or treatment of restless leg syndrome.
  5. Diagnosis of circadian rhythm disorders.
  6. To diagnose of depression.
  7. Diagnosis and management of insomnias (Clinical Guideline, *J Clin Sleep Med.* 2008;4(5),487-504).

MULTIPLE SLEEP LATENCY TEST (MSLT)

Indication

- Measures propensity for daytime sleepiness.
- Indicated as part of the evaluation for narcolepsy or idiopathic hypersomnia.
- **Not** routinely indicated in the initial evaluation for OSA, insomnia, circadian rhythm disorders or EDS in conjunction with medical and neurological disorders.

Protocol — see Practice Parameters for the Clinical use of the MSLT and MWT (*SLEEP* 2005; 28:113-121).

Essentials include:

a. Five nap opportunities at two-hourly intervals. The initial nap opportunity should begin 1.5 to 3 hours after a nocturnal polysomnogram in which the TST is at least 6 hours. MSLT should not be performed after a split night study.

b. Stimulant and REM-suppressing medications should be stopped two weeks before the MSLT. Drug screening may be useful.

c. Conventional recording montages include frontal,central and occipital derivations, left and right EOGs, a mental/submental EMG, and an EKG.

d. The patient is instructed to lie quietly and to **try to fall asleep**. Between naps, the patient should be out of bed and prevented from sleeping.

e. **Sleep onset** is defined as the first 30-second epoch with more than 15 seconds of cumulative sleep. If **no sleep occurs**, the nap opportunity is **terminated after 20 minutes**, the sleep latency is considered to be 20 minutes and is included in the calculation of the mean sleep latency.

f. If **sleep occurs**, the test should be continued for a **further 15 minutes**, determined by **"clock time"** (not sleep time) in order to allow time for REM sleep to occur.

g. **REM latency** is the time taken from the first epoch of sleep to the beginning of the first epoch of REM sleep (defined as greater than 15 seconds of REM sleep in a 30-second epoch).

Interpretation

The sleep latencies for all naps are documented. *A mean sleep latency (MSL) of <8min is regarded as evidence of excessive daytime sleepiness.* The presence or SOREMPs on two naps is regarded to be specific for a diagnosis of narcolepsy. (It is, however, important to exclude other causes of SOREMPs such as sleep deprivation, shift-work disorder or OSA).

Note: • ICSD3 guidelines permit a diagnosis of narcolepsy where only one SOREMP present on MSLT and REM latency on preceding PSG is <15min.
• If 2 SOREMPs occur during the first 4 naps, nap 5 may not be necessary.

Limitations of the MSLT:

• Lack of validation in children less than eight years of age.
• Absence of validation outside usual testing hours of 8 a.m. to 6 p.m.
• A MSL of <8 min is not necessarily diagnostic of a sleep condition and may be seen in 30% of healthy individuals.

MAINTENANCE OF WAKEFULNESS TEST (MWT)

Indication

• The MWT is a validated objective measure of the ability to stay awake.
• MWT used in conjunction with a clinical history to *assess the ability to maintain wakefulness.*

Protocol Essentials: (See detailed protocol *SLEEP* 2005; 28: 113-121).

a. **Four trials of 40 minutes** each performed at two-hourly intervals, beginning at about 1.5 to 3 hours after the patient's usual wake time. **Neither a sleep log nor a PSG are routinely required prior to the MWT** (may be decided on individual cases).

b. The conventional recording montage is identical for that of the MSLT (see above).

c. For each trial, the patient is asked to **"please sit still and remain awake for as long as possible."** The patient should not use extraordinary measures to stay awake.

d.   Sleep onset is defined as the first epoch of greater than 15 seconds of cumulative sleep in a 30-second epoch period.

e.   **Unequivocal sleep is defined as three consecutive epochs of N1 sleep or one epoch of any other stage of sleep.** The trial ends after unequivocal sleep has been documented or after 40 minutes if no sleep occurs.

Interpretation.

- The strongest evidence of an individual's ability to remain awake is wakefulness during all 40 minute MWT trials.

- A mean sleep latency of less than eight minutes is regarded as an indication of excessive daytime sleepiness.

- Values between 8 and 40 minutes are of "uncertain significance" (*CHEST* 2008; 134: 854-861).

- The MWT is often used in individuals whose jobs require a high level of alertness, particularly when public safety issues are involved.

Limitations of the MWT.

Does not necessarily correlate with on-the-job ability to stay awake since testing conditions differ from that of the workplace.

References:
Practice Parameters for Clinical Use of the MSLT and the MWT (*SLEEP* 2005; 28:113-121).
Sullivan S and Kushida C: MSLT and MWT(*CHEST* 2008; 134: 854-861).

ACTIGRAPHY

Special article: Use of Actigraphy for the Evaluation of Sleep Disorders and Circadian Rhythm Sleep-Wake Disorders: an AASM Clinical Practice Guideline. *J. Clin. Sleep Med* 2018; 14 (7): 1231-1237.

This guideline would seem to replace the *SLEEP* 2002 and 2007 practice parameters.

General comments from all articles remain valid:

- An actigraph measures limb movement/activity which reflects the level of alertness (minimal movement should occur during sleep).

- Device usually worn on wrist (or leg); data stored then downloaded.

- Studies should ideally be conducted over three consecutive nights (2002, 2007) though the length of time may be individualized, e.g., one night when in conjunction with a HSAT; 7-14 nights prior to a PSG/MSLT; 2-3 weeks or more in a patient with suspected insufficient sleep syndrome (2018).

- A sleep diary should be completed simultaneously.

The latest (2018) guideline mostly suggests application of actigraphy as *CONDITIONAL* where there is only a low degree of certainty regarding outcome. The only *STRONG* recommendation is that actigraphy not replace EMG for the diagnoses of PLMD in adults or children.

The following, then, are all the *conditional* suggestions: Actigraphy suggested for assessment of:
- Sleep parameters in adult insomnia patients.
- Pediatric patients with insomnia disorders.
- Adults with circadian rhythm sleep wake disorders (CRSWD).
- Pediatric patients with CRSWD.
- Total sleep time (TST) during a HSAT.
- TST prior to a MSLT in adults with and children (over 1-2 weeks).
- TST in adults with suspected insufficient sleep syndrome (over 2-3 weeks).

Suggestions in the previous practice parameter papers not included in current guidelines but which may be clinically useful include actigraphy to monitor response to treatment for insomnia or CRSWD.

Test Your Memory (Section 3):

1. Typical ESS scores may include all except:

   a. 18/24 in narcolepsy.
   b. 8/24 in normals.
   c. 15/24 in insomniacs.
   d. 13/24 in OSA.
   e. 17/24 in idiopathic hypersomnia.

2. Investigations in the evaluation of insomnia may include all of the following except:

   a. Sleep diary.
   b. Actigraphy.
   c. Urine testing for substance abuse.
   d. Maintanence of wakefulness test.
   e. Beck depression inventory.

3. With respect to EEG frequency bands useful for sleep staging, which of the following is incorrect?

   a. alpha = 8-13 Hz.
   b. beta = > 13 Hz.
   c. theta = 4 - 7.99 Hz.
   d. delta = 2 - 3.99 Hz.
   e. sleep spindle = >18 Hz.

4. Hypopnea rules (2014) include all of the following except:

   a. Signal ↓ by ≥ 30% from baseline.
   b. Preferred signal is nasal pressure transducer.
   c. Event is associated with at least a 3% ↓ in oxygen saturation.
   d. Medicare criteria include at least a 4% ↓ in oxygen saturation from pre-event baseline.
   e. Event must be associated with an EEG arousal.

5. With reference to Cheyne-Stokes breathing, a typical cycle length is:

   a. ≥ 40 seconds.
   b. 20 - 40 seconds.

6. In scoring PLMS, which of the following is correct?

    a. The leg movement (LM) should last 10 seconds or more.
    b. Time between LMs varies from 5 - 90 seconds.
    c. PLM series requires at least three consecutive LMs.
    d. Count LMs from different legs as one LM if separated by 5 - 10 seconds.
    e. LMs occurring within 5 seconds before or after an apnea are not scored.

Answers: 1c, 2d, 3e, 4e, 5a, 6b.

Section 4:

PHARMACOLOGY
(EFFECTS OF MEDICATIONS ON
VARIOUS ASPECTS OF SLEEP)

This section includes:

- Medications causing sedation including effects on sleep archicture

- Medications disrupting sleep including effects on sleep architecture

- Medication effects on REM sleep

- Effects of alcohol on sleep

- Reference table of psycho-active medications

MEDICATIONS CAUSING SEDATION

BZD = Benzodiazepines; SL = Sleep latency; WASO = Wake after sleep onset time; TST = Total sleep time; BzRA = Benzodiazepine receptor agonists; MT = Melatonin; SARI = Serotonin antagonist and reuptake inhibitor; TCA = Tricyclic antidepressants; 5HT = 5 hydroxy tryptamine (serotonin); H = Histamine; ACh = Acetylcholine; DA=Dopamine, GABA=gamma-aminobutyric acid, NE = Norepinephrine.
NOTE: SSRIs/SNRIs have with exceptions generally no sedating effects (see p 42).

Class	Effect on Sleep and Sleep Architecture	Mode of action	Additional Properties
BZDs	$\downarrow$ SL, $\downarrow$ WASO, $\uparrow$ TST $\downarrow$ N1, $\uparrow$ N2, $\downarrow$ N3, $\pm$ mild $\downarrow$ REM, $\uparrow$ REM latency	$\uparrow$GABA activity	• Anterograde amnesia especially if short acting (e.g., triazolam). • Rebound insomnia and $\uparrow$ REM with abrupt discontinuation.
BzRAs	• $\downarrow$ SL, $\downarrow$ WASO, $\uparrow$ TST • Little effect on sleep architecture.	$\uparrow$GABA activity	• Little tolerance or rebound insomnia. • Sleepwalking, sleep driving reported mostly with zolpidem.
MT receptor agonists (ramelteon).	• $\downarrow$ SL • Little effect on sleep architecture.	Binds to melatonin M_1 and M_2 receptors	• Virtually no tolerance. • Use for sleep onset insomnia.
Antidepressants: a) TCAs.	• $\downarrow$ SL, $\uparrow$ TST • $\uparrow$REM latency, $\downarrow$ REM sleep	• 5HT and NE reuptake inhibition. • Block H_1, ACh and alpha 1 adrenergic receptors	• Amitriptyline, doxepin more sedating. • Imipramine, trimipramine less sedating.
b) SARIs. Trazodone, nefazodone	• $\downarrow$ SL, $\downarrow$ WASO, $\uparrow$ TST • Little effect on REM. • Trazodone may $\uparrow$ SWS.	• Both are $5HT_2$ receptor antagonists, weak 5HT reuptake inhibitors • Trazodone also inhibits H_1 receptors • Nefazodone also weak NE reuptake inhibitor	• Trazodone ~extensively used for insomnia though not FDA approved. ~more appropriate use if comorbid depression ~risk of arrythmias • Nefazodone - risk of severe liver damage

Atypical Antidepressants: Mirtazapine (*Remeron*)	• ↑ sleep efficiency • Possible ↑ N3; no effect on REM	Blocks NE, 5HT and H_1 receptors	Not FDA approved for insomnia
Older antiseizure medication: Barbitrates	• ↓SL, ↓WASO, ↑TST • ↑ N2, may↓↓ REM	↑ GABA activity by facilitating chloride entry into cells	• ↑spindle density • Rapid tolerance • High-risk dependency
Newer antiseizure drugs: Gabapentin (*Neurontin*) Tiagabine (*Gabitril*) Pregabalin (*Lyrica*)	• ↓WASO ↑ TST • ↑ N3	Enhance GABA activity (various mechanisms)	• Gabapentin and tiagabine used for insomnia but not FDA approved for this indication
Antihistamines: First generation (*lipophilic*), e.g., diphenhydramine (*Benadryl*), hydroxyzine (*Atarax,Vistaril*)	Subjective improvement in SL,WASO & TST but not confirmed on PSG	• Block postsynaptic H_1 receptors • Also block: ACh, NE, and 5HT receptors	• Often used OTC for insomnia. • Hydroxyzine most sedating. • Second generation antihistamines are hydrophilic; do not cross blood-brain barrier and therefore have little effect on sleep or sleep architecture
Antipsychotics (First and second generation; see list below)	↓ WASO, ↑ TST. Variable effects on SWS and REM (ziprasidone & risperidone →↓ REM)	Block DA & H_1 receptors	• Olanzapine and quetiapine often used off label for insomnia • Clozapine very sedating. • Aripiprazole least sedating

REMember: Mode of Action BZDs and BzRAs:
- GABA most widespread inhibitory neurotransmitter; acts by opening chloride channels and entry of chloride ions into cells causing hyperpolarization.
- Three types of GABA receptors: GABA-A,GABA-B & GABA-C
- GABA-A the major receptor; responsible for hypnotic effects
- GABA-A has several subunits; alpha-1,2,3,4& 5 are BZD sensitive
- alpha-1 subunit is sedating; others are anxiolytic, anti-seizure, myorelaxant & amnesic
- BZDs bind to most GABA-A receptor subunits with variable affinities thus explaining their varied clinical propensities and effects
- BzRAs bind primarily to the alpha-1 receptor subunit with little affinity for the others

SLEEP-DISRUPTING MEDICATIONS (enhance action of wake promoting neurotransmitters)			
Class	**Effects on Sleep and Sleep Architecture**	**Mode of Action**	**Additional Properties**
CNS Stimulants e.g., ritalin, adderall	• ↑ SL, ↑ WASO, ↓ TST • ↑ N1, ↓ N3, ↓ REM	• Block reuptake and promote release of DA, NE and 5HT	Rebound REM after discontinuation.
Methylxanthines (caffeine, theophylline).	• ↑ SL, ↑ WASO, ↓ TST • ↑ N1	Antagonizes AD receptors.	Enhance daytime alertness.
Beta Blockers (*lipophilic* beta-blockers include propranolol, metoprolol, pindolol).	• ↑ Arousals, ↑ WASO, ↓ TST • May ↓ REM, ↑ REM latency	• High 5-HT affinity. • May ↓ melatonin release.	• May cause hallucinations and nightmares in addition to insomnia. • Atenolol (*Tenormin*) and sotalol (*Betapace*) are **hydrophilic** and do not have the same affects on sleep as the lipophilic beta-blockers.
SSRIs	• ↑ WASO, ↓ TST. • ↑ REM latency, ↓ REM sleep	Block serotonin (5HT) reuptake.	• Most SSRIs disrupt sleep and cause insomnia, especially fluoxetine. • Some SSRIs may cause daytime sedation especially paroxetine and fluvoxamine.
SNRIs		Block 5HT, NE reuptake Effexor also blocks DA reuptake.	

REMember:

SSRIs:
- Multiple 5-HT receptor sub-types in CNS.
- Individual SSRIs may interact with different receptor subtypes.
- Effects on sleep and sleep architecture therefore differ between SSRIs.
- Most are alerting and cause insomnia. (Paroxetine, Fluvoxamine →EDS).

SNRIs (Selective serotonin and norepinephrine reuptake inhibitors).
- Similar effects to SSRIs.
- ↑ WASO, ↓ TST, ↓ REM.

See table p47 for list of SSRIs and SNRJs.

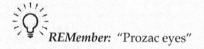

REMember: "Prozac eyes"

Fluoxetine as well as other SSRI's may produce prominent rapid and slow eye movements in all stages of NREM sleep.

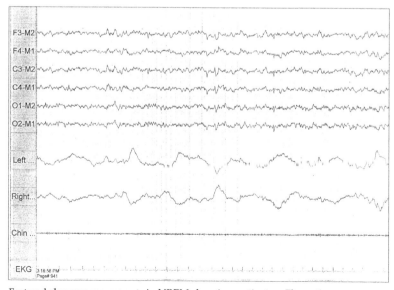

Fast and slow eye movements in NREM sleep in a patient on Fluoxetine.

IMPACT OF MEDICATIONS ON REM SLEEP

A. REM suppressants (may also ↑ REM latency)

Antidepressants
- TCAs (not trimipramine)
- SSRIs
- SNRIs (desvenlafaxine may not ↓ REM %, may ↑ REM latency).
- MAOIs--potent REM suppressors

Lithium

Stimulants

BZDs (REM suppression mild, mainly decrease N3 sleep)

Barbiturates

Opioids

Other psychoactive medications:
- Quetiapine (*Seroquel*)
- Risperidone (*Risperdal*)
- Ziprasodone (*Geodon*)

REMember:
Antidepressants which do *not* ↓ REM sleep or ↑ REM latency include
- Trimipramine
- Bupropion (may ↑ REM).
- Trazodone (sedating; used off label for insomnia; may ↑ TST and SWS).
- Mirtazapine (sedating; used off label for insomnia).
- Nefazodone (sedating; danger of hepatic toxicity).

B. Medications which may increase REM Sleep

- Cholinergics e.g., drugs used in dementia (acetylcholinesterase inhibitors)
- Reserpine
- Bupropion
- Nefazodone
- Gabapentin
- Lamotrigine
- Following discontinuation of REM suppressants (REM rebound)

EFFECTS OF ALCOHOL ON SLEEP

A. Acute intoxication.
- $\downarrow$ Sleep latency.
- During the first half of the night:
  - $\uparrow$ NREM including N3.
  - $\downarrow$ REM.
  - $\uparrow$ TST.
- During second half of night there may be
  - $\uparrow$ wake (withdrawal symptoms due to rapid EtOH metabolism).
  - $\uparrow$ REM (rebound).
  - $\uparrow$ Dreaming.
  - $\uparrow$ Sympathetic arousal.

B. With Alcoholic dependency:
- $\uparrow$ sleep latency
- $\downarrow$ TST.
- Fragmented sleep especially second half of the night.
- $\downarrow$ REM.
- Circadian rhythm disrupted when EtOH consumed throughout day.

C. Acute withdrawal in alcohol dependent subjects.:
- Insomnia.
- $\downarrow$ sleep continuity.
- $\downarrow$ TST.
- $\downarrow$ SWS (N3).
- $\uparrow$ REM (rebound).
- Nightmares.

D. Prolonged effects of withdrawal (may be present for up to 1 - 2 years).
- $\downarrow$ TST.
- $\downarrow$ SWS (N3).
- $\uparrow$ REM.

REMember:

Medications and Sleep: Fact Check
- Barbiturates and BZDs ↑ sleep spindle density.
- BZDs.
  - ~ produce pseudospindles (15 - 16 Hz compared with 12 - 14 Hz of regular spindles).
  - ~ potent N3 suppressors; milder REM suppressors.
- MAOIs - among the most potent REM suppressants.
- Opioids
  - ~ ↓ sleep efficiency, ↑ WASO, ↓ N3 sleep and ↓ REM .
  - ~ may also cause central sleep apneas, obstructive sleep apnea, as well as ataxic breathing
- Corticosteroids
  - ~ cause insomnia, ↑ WASO, ↓ REM
- Bupropion (NE & DA reuptake inhibitor)
  - ~ stimulating; may cause insomnia
  - ~ *may* ↑ REM
- Alpha-2 agonists (methyldopa, clonidine)
  - ~ cause sedation (clonidine also reported to cause insomnia)
  - ~methyldopa → ↓ N3, may ↑ REM
  - ~ clonidine → ↑ N3, ↓ REM

REMember:

- Reports of complex sleep related behaviors such as sleepwalking, sleep driving and sleep eating with hypnotics (mainly zolpidem) resulted in the FDA issuing a class warning labeling recommendation for all FDA approved hypnotics.

Table of Brand and Generic Names of Psychoactive Medications

Note: virtually all have Black Box warnings.

(Important effects on sleep are reemphasized.)

A. Antidepressants

1. SSRIs:
   - *Celexa* (citalopram).
   - *Lexapro* (escitalopram).
   - *Luvox* (fluvoxamine).
   - *Paxil* (paroxetine).
   - *Prozac* (fluoxetine).
   - *Zoloft* (sertraline).
   - *Viibryd* (vilazodone); also partially agonizes 5-HT1A receptors.

2. SNRIs:
   - *Cymbalta* (duloxetine).
   - *Effexor* (venlafaxine).
   - *Pristiq* (desvenlafaxine).
   - *Fetzima* (levomilnacipran).

3. TCAs:
   - *Elavil* (amitriptyline).
   - *Anafranil* (clomipramine).
   - *Tofranil* (imipramine).
   - *Vivactil* (protriptyline).
   - *Surmontil* (trimipramine).
   - *Pamelor* (nortriptyline).
   - Doxepin.

4. Other antidepressants:
   - *Wellbutrin* (Bupropion HCl).
   - *Remeron* (mirtazapine).
   - *Desyrel* (Trazodone).
   - *Serzone* (nefazodone).
   - *Aplenzin* (bupropion HBr).
   - *Trintellix* (USA) / *Brintellix* (vortioxetine).

5. MAOIs:
   - *Nardil* (phenelzine).
   - *Parnate* (tranylcypromine).
   - *Marplan* (isocarboxazid).

REMember: ADs' effect on sleep (selective list):

Sedating ADs include:
- Amitriptyline (*Elavil*)*.
- Mirtazapine (*Remeron*)*.
- Trazodone (*Desyrel*)*
- Doxepin*.
- Paroxetine (*Paxil*).
    * Often used off-label for insomnia. Branded doxepin (*Silenor*) approved for insomnia in 3-6mg strengths.

Alerting ADs (may cause insomnia)
- Fluoxetine (*Prozac*).
- Sertraline (*Zoloft*).
- Venlafaxine (*Effexor*).... may also be sedating.

Effect on REM sleep
- Most ADs ↓ REM and ↑ REM latency.
- MAOIs may cause almost total disappearance of REM.
- REM rebound and ↓ REM latency may be seen for days or weeks after discontinuation of ADs.
- ADs which do <u>not</u> decrease REM include trazodone (*Desyrel*), bupropion (*Wellbutrin*), trimipramine (*Surmontil*), nefazodone (*Serzone*), mirtazapine (*Remeron*).

B. Drugs used for bipolar disorder:

- *Depakote* (divalproex sodium).
- *Eskalith* (lithium).
- *Lamictal* (lamotrigine).
- *Abilify* (aripiprazole*).
- *Risperdal* (risperidone*).
- *Seroquel* (quetiapine*).
- *Zyprexa* (olanzapine*).
- *Tegretol* (carbamazepine).
- *Geodon* (ziprasidone*).
    * 2nd generation anti-psychotics (see below).

C. Antipsychotics - first generation ("conventional or typical"):

- *Compazine* (prochlorperazine).
- *Mellaril* (thioridazine).
- *Thorazine* (chlorpromazine).
- *Trilafon* (perphenazine).

D. Antipsychotics - second generation("atypical").

- *Abilify* (aripiprazole).
- *Geodon* (ziprasidone).
- *Risperdal* (risperidone).
- *Seroquel* (quetiapine).
- *Zyprexa* (olanzapine).
- *Latuda* (lurasidone).
- *Invega* (paliperadone).
- *Clozaril* (clozapine); may cause granulocytopenia, has FDA boxed warning; patient registration required due to severe neutropenia risk
    — All, except clozaril, also used for bipolar disorder.

REMember:

First & second generation antipsychotics:
- block DA and H1 receptors
- sedating effects probably due to H1 receptor blocking activity
- extrapyramidal/Parkinsonian side effects seen (1st gen. >2nd gen.)
- nightmares or disturbing dreams may occur with all antipsychotics

Second generation agents
- also block 5HT, ACh & alpha-1 adrenergic receptors
- risk of severe hypotension
- olanzapine & quetiapine often used off label as hypnotics

E. Drugs used for treatment of dementia/Alzheimer's disease.

- Actylcholinesterase inhibitors
    - *Aricept* (donepezil)... may cause abnormal dreams.
    - *Cognex* (tacrine) (no longer available in USA).
    - *Exelon* (rivastigmine).
    - *Razadyne* (galantamine).
    - Note: Above agents may cause either insomnia or somnolence.

- *Namenda* (memantine).
    - Not a cholinesterase inhibitor.
    - Acts as a N-methyl-D-aspartate receptor antagonist.
    - May cause somnolence.

MEDICATIONS CAUSING SPECIFIC CLINICAL CONDITIONS.

- Sleepwalking - see section 8.
- Nighmares - see section 8.
- REM Behavior Disturbance - see section 8.
- Restless Leg Syndrome / PLMD - see section 9.

Further reading/references:

Roux and Kryger: Medication Effects on Sleep in *Clinics in Chest Medicine June 2010* pp397-405.

Bostwick, J. Michael: A Generalist's Guide to Treating Patients with Depression. Mayo. Clin. Proc 2010; 85(6): 538-550.
(Useful article for the non-psychiatrist and contains excellent review of ADs - use and adverse effects.)

Test Your Memory (Section 4):

1. Benzodiazepines have the following effect on sleep staging except:

   a. $\downarrow$ N1.
   b. $\uparrow$ N2.
   c. $\downarrow$ N3.
   d. $\uparrow$ REM.

2. Which of the following psychoactive agents does not usually suppress REM?

   a. risperidone.
   b. lithium.
   c. bupropion.
   d. barbiturates.
   e. MAOIs.

3. Acute alcohol intoxication usually causes all except:

   a. $\downarrow$ sleep latency.
   b. $\uparrow$ NREM during the first half of the night.
   c. $\downarrow$ REM in the first half of the night.
   d. $\downarrow$ REM in the second half of the night.
   e. $\uparrow$ stage W during the second half of the night.

4. BzRA agents generally having the following effect on sleep architecture:

   a. $\uparrow$ N3.
   b. $\downarrow$ N3.
   c. $\uparrow$ REM.
   d. $\downarrow$ REM.
   e. none of the above.

5. Antidepressants which generally have little effect on REM include all except:

   a. nefazodone.
   b. amitriptyline.
   c. trazodone.
   d. mirtazapine.
   e. trimipramine.

Answers: 1d, 2c, 3d, 4e, 5b.

Section 5:

CIRCADIAN SLEEP DISORDERS

BASIC CIRCADIAN PHYSIOLOGY:

A. Nomenclature
circa = about
dian = day
ultradian = periods or cycles < 24 hours; may recur during
   the day (e.g., hormonal release, appetite)
infradian = cycles longer than 24 hours (e.g., menstrual cycle)

B. The human sleep/wake cycle (see pp 5-6):
Two processes working in concert.
1. *Homeostatic drive for sleep*: depends on the amount of
   wakefulness.
2. *Circadian drive*: promotes daytime wakefulness counteracting
   homeostatic drive for sleep and reinforcing sleep during nighttime.
   Biphasic sleep tendency, 2 to 4 pm ("siesta time")
   and then late evening.

C. Circadian control of sleep/wake cycle:
- Suprachiasmatic nucleus (SCN) in the hypothalamus regulates the
  natural circadian rhythm (CR).
- SCN also synchronizes the body's CR with external cues; sunlight is
  the most potent external cue.
- SCN gets light input from retinal cells containing melanopsin via
  the retino-hypothalmic tract.
- SCN synchronizes oscillations in periferal organs to the light/dark
  cycle (retino-hypothalamic melanopsin system) *J. Pineal Res* 2012;
  53; 47.
- Endogenous CR lasts slightly more than 24 hours.

D. Melatonin:
Derived from tryptophan; immediate precursor is serotonin (5-HT).
- produced by pineal gland during nighttime darkness.
- regulated by SCN via superior cervical ganglion to the pineal gland.
- helps synchronize circadian rhythm by acting on melatonin
  receptors in the SCN.

- levels start to rise about two hour prior to sleep time and maximum levels found around 3 to 5 a.m. (lowest levels are during the day).
- light (even ordinary room light at 100 Lux) may suppress melatonin production; reading in bed may therefore be counterproductive to sleep ..... insomniacs beware!!
- Beta blockers suppress sympathetic signaling to the pineal gland; may suppress MT levels and may cause insomnia.

E. Temperature and sleep
- Core body temperature has a circadian pattern; falls with sleep onset
- Usually lowest between 4 and 6 a.m.
- Thermoregulation present but reduced in NREM; virtually absent in REM with loss of shivering and diaphoretic responses.

REMember:
- The *phase* of circadian rhythm may be assessed using the *nadir* of the core body temperature.
- Circadian phase also assessed by timing of melatonin secretion; dim light melatonin onset (DLMO).

CIRCADIAN RHYTHM SLEEP-WAKE DISORDERS (CRSWDs)

Note: ICSD3 classification virtually identical to ICSD2 except the term "sleep-wake" (instead of "sleep") now used in describing most subtypes.

Essential features
- CRSWDs are due either to an *alteration* in the endogenous circadian timing system or to a *misalignment* between the timing of the individual's circadian rhythm and the 24-hour social and physical environment.
- This leads to symptoms of insomnia, EDS or both with a negative impact on quality of life including work, family and other social interactions.

1. Delayed sleep-wake phase disorder (DSWPD) - (the "night owls").
- Mainly in teens and younger adulthood; 7-16% (ICSD2 & 3).
- Prevalence <1% of general population; 5-10% of insomniacs.
- Family history common.
- Abnormality is *phase delay* of circadian pacemaker.
- May occur after traumatic brain injury and with personality or psychiatric disorders which may lead to subjects lacking motivation to adapt to a regular lifestyle.
- Poor sleep hygiene (e.g. late-night computer games) may perpetuate the problem.

- Genetic factor may be present (eg abnormality of circadian clock genes *hPer3* and *Clock*). Mutation on cryptochrome (a clock protein) recently reported (Proc. Nat. Acad. Sciences, 26 Oct 2020).
- Sleep onset typically delayed until 2am to 6 am.
- Rise time often after 10am-2pm.
- Symptoms reflect difficulty with sleep onset or arising at conventional times with inability to adapt to conventional work/educational schedules (often asymptomatic if allowed to function at own schedule).
- Condition persistent if untreated. Risk of EtOH/hypnotic abuse.
- Evaluation may include sleep diary and actigraphy (7 days).

2. Advanced sleep-wake phase disorder (ASWPD).
- Affects + 1% of the middle aged and elderly.
- Familial pattern in some cases.
- Genetic factor (mutation of circadian clock gene *hPer2*) may be responsible for familial ASPS with younger age onset.
- Get sleepy ± 6-9pm; awaken 2-5am (typically ± 2hrs before "normal" sleep or wake time).
- Condition persistent; aggravated by superimposed conditioned/psychophysiological insomnia.
- EtOH/hypnotic abuse possible.
- Sleep diary and actigraphy may be helpful in diagnosis (7 days).

3. Jet-lag disorder.
- Temporary mismatch between the timing of the sleep and wake cycle generated by the endogenous circadian clock and that of the sleep and wake pattern required by a change in time zone (ICSD).
- Travellers can't rapidly realign their intrinsic CR to the new time zone; CR remains linked to origin time zone.
- Takes approximately one day per time zone to adjust to the destination time.
- Severity depends on the *number* of time zones crossed and the direction of travel.
- Symptoms include insomnia, fatigue, poor concentration, malaise, GI symptoms.
- Eastward travellers
  - phase *delayed* relative to the new clock time
  - need to *advance* circadian rhythm.
  - sleep/wake hrs *more difficult to adjust* to than westward travel (as endogenous clock slightly >24hrs and more difficult to phase advance);
  - c/o difficulty with sleep onset and with rising the next day
- Westward travellers
  - phase advanced relative to new clock time
  - c/o sleepiness in evening and early waking the next morning
  - need to phase delay body clock
    (usually easier than phase advance; see above).

- Travelling >6-8 *time zones* may shift rhythm in the direction *opposite* to the direction of travel and prolong symptoms. Generally shift delay (antidromic shifting).
- Light exposure at *inappropriate* times may also prolong symptoms.

4. Shift-work disorder.

- SWD occurs when a there is a mismatch between subject's body clock and work schedule.
- Approximately 15m shift workers in US. (US Dept of Labor, Bureau of Labor Statistics, 2011).
- Highest prevalence for alternative shift work ages 18-29.
- SWD estimated to affect 20-25% of shift workers; M=F.
- Subjects c/o excessive sleepiness during work shifts with trouble focusing, reduced work performance and ↑ accidents.
- Aggravated by inability to sleep during the daytime.(Continued mismatch between CR and environmental cues, light exposure at the inappropriate times and social pressures all play a role).
- Irritability, malaise, fatigue, systemic symptoms (exacerbation of GI or cardiovascular disorders) and social/family problems common .
- Risk of drug and alcohol dependency present.
- Sleep diary and actigraphy may be helpful in diagnosis.
- SWD patients have an increased risk for CV disease, cancer and depression (Wickwire et al *CHEST* 2017; 151(5); 1156-1172).

5. Irregular Sleep-Wake rhythm disorders (ISWRD).

- Seen mainly with mental retardation, dementia, head trauma, institutionalized individuals.
- Rare in general population.
- Absence of external synchronizing cues especially light and lack of social activities often responsible.
- If seen in cognitive normals, poor sleep hygiene with almost total lack of environmental and social cues responsible (e.g., hermits).
- Sleep schedule is disorganized and sleep occurs in short periods over a 24 hour period; total sleep time may be relative normal.
- Sleep diary and actigraphy may be helpful in diagnosis.

6. Non-24-hour Sleep-Wake Rhythm disorder (N24SWRD).
(Free running (nonentrained) type CRD)

- Found mainly in sight-impaired individuals who depend on intrinsic CR for sleep-wake cycle
- Sleep cycle therefore shows periodicity of about 24.2 hours.
- Sleep and wake times slightly delayed each day leading to complaints of insomnia or sleepiness depending on clock time.
- Seen rarely in sighted patients, mainly with mental retardation, dementia or psychiatric disorders who ignore synchronizing cues.
- Sleep diaries and actigraphy may be useful in diagnosis.

General Treatment Principles for CRD

1. Chronotherapy.

- Progressive adjustments in bedtime so that sleep onset ultimately coincides with societal times.
- Easier to phase delay.
- Compliance with chronotherapy usually difficult.

2. Phototherapy (timed light exposure).

- Light therapy is administered at appropriate times relative to nadir in core body temperate in order to phase advance or delay circadian clock.
- Phototherapy *after* core body minimum temperature *advances* internal clock.
- Phototherapy *before* core temperature minimum *delays* internal clock.
- **Caution**: avoid phototherapy in patients on photosensitizing drugs or with ocular or retinal pathology. Phototherapy may precipitate manic episodes in patients with bipolar disorder.

3. Melatonin (MT).

- Opposite phase response to light therapy.
- MT in the morning shifts circadian rhythm later.
- MT in the evening shifts rhythm earlier.
- Dosing not well established. OTC products 1mg, 3mg, 5mg. Most references suggest 3-5mg doses.
- The *timing* of melatonin administration may be more important than the dose.

4. Awake Enhancing Medications for Shift Work Disorder

Management of the CRD's

DSWPD.

1. Chronotherapy.

- Sleep time progressively delayed 2 -3 hours a day; often impractical.

2. Phototherapy.

- Exposure to morning bright light; avoid bright light in the evenings.
- Morning light given shortly after minimum core body temperature; practically this involves exposure usually after habitual awakening.
    - Direct sunlight in summer.
    - Artificial light exposure of ±30 minutes at an intensity of 10,000 lux (longer times for light of less intensity).

- Shorter wave length light in the blue-green spectrum may be more effective.

3. **Melatonin- evening dosing (3-5mg).** Reported dosing time 1.5-6hr HS.

ASWPD

1. Chronotherapy: advance bedtime gradually (limited success).
2. Phototherapy: bright light exposure in the early evening (coincides with dim-light melatonin onset); avoid bright light in early morning.
3. Melatonin: ?early morning dosing (weak evidence).

Jet Lag

1. General advice.
   - Consider adapting schedule to the destination time several days before departure (may be difficult to coordinate with usual activities).
   - Adapt schedule at destination as soon as possible to the new clock time.
   - Avoid light exposure at inappropriate times at destination (e.g. by wearing sunglasses).
   - Morning bright light and advancing bed-time one hour earlier for 3 days before eastbound travel may be helpful.
   - Sleep hygiene before and after arrival.

2. Phototherapy.
   Timing of phototherapy depends on *direction* of travel and the number of times zones crossed.
   - **Eastward travel.**
     - If < 6 time zones crossed, morning light exposure at destination.
     - If > 6 times zones crossed, afternoon light exposure.
   - **Westward travel.**
     - If <6 times zones crossed, afternoon light exposure.
     - If >6 six times zones crossed, morning light at destination.

3. Melatonin 3 to 5 mg at bedtime for three to four nights at destination.

4. Short-term hypnotics.

5. ? Armodafinil; not FDA approved for jet-lag. (Rosenberg RP et al; *Mayo Clin Proc* 2010;85(7):630-638)

NOTE:
The only *standard* option from the Practice Parameters for the Evaluation and Treatmnt of CRSD, *SLEEP* 2007; 30 (11): 1445-1459 is the use of melatonin "at the approriate time" following travel across multiple time zones.

Shift Work Disorder

- Nightime alertness enhanced by evening bright light exposure and planned napping prior to (or during) night shift.

- Avoid bright light towards the end of the shift.

- Avoid bright light exposure while driving home (use of sunglasses).

- Insomnia management as appropriate (e.g. sleep hygiene, avoid caffeine and alcohol prior to bedtime, judicious use of hypnotics and possibly melatonin).

- Coordinating social interactions; eliciting family co-operation.

- Modafinil or armodafinil both FDA approved for SWD; take $\pm$ 1 hour before shift work begins.

- Create an "anchor" sleep period that partially overlaps sleep on both work and non-work days (see Wickwire et al *CHEST* 2017; 151 (5) p1156)

- Fatigue risk management program involving employers and employees (Wickwire et al, *CHEST*, 2017)

- Most of above measures included as *guidelines* in Position Paper in *SLEEP* 2007; 30(11): 1445-1459.

Irregular Sleep-Wake Rhythm Disorder

- Structured activities/social interventions during the day.

- Morning bright light exposure.

- Melatonin, (some benefit in children with ISWRD).

- Sleep hygiene.

Non-24-hour Sleep-Wake Rhythm Disorder

- Regulate/ scheduling social events with appropriate sleep times.

- Evening melatonin ($\pm$ 3mg).

- If light perception, consider morning bright light exposure.

- Tasimelteon (*Hetlioz*) a melatonin MT1 and MT2 receptor agonist FDA approved for blind individuals with N24SWRD. Side effects include headache, abnormal dreams, abnormal LFTs.

Key points from the special article:

Clinical Practice Guidelines for the Treatment of Intrinsic Circadian Rhythm Sleep-Wake Disorders: An update for 2015 *(J Clin Sleep Med* 2015; 11(10): 1199-1236).

> Replaces/updates previous AASM practice parameters for treatment of intrinsic CRSWDs *(SLEEP* 2007; 30: 1445-59). Virtually all recommendations are WEAK (low degree of clinical certainty for net benefits whether for or against) vs no treatment. This includes use of melatonin and light therapy (at appropriate times) for any of the CRSWDs. Only STRONG recommendation is *against* using sleep-promoting medications in demented elderly with ISWRD.

Note: No recommendations for using sleep promoting medications or wakefulness promoting medications in any of the above disorders. Also no recommendations for strategic light avoidance, prescribed sleep/wake scheduling or timed physical activities.

(Personal comment: Latest guidelines do not appear to negate current/usual strategies in treating patients with intrinsic CRSWDs but lend perspective into expectations for successful outcomes. DW)

Further reading/references:

- Lu BS, Zee P, Circadian Rhythm Sleep Disorders - *CHEST,* 2006; 130: 1915-1923.

- Gulyani et al. Sleep Medicine Pharmacotherapeutics Review *CHEST* 2012; 142(6): 1659-68.

1. The most potent external cue (Zeitgeber) in the regulation of the sleep/wake cycle is:
   a. Social cues.
   b. Sunlight.
   c. Mealtimes.
   d. Regular bedtime.
   e. Regular wake time.

2. With regard to melatonin, which statement is incorrect?
   a. Highest levels 3-5 a.m.
   b. Production suppressed by B blockers.
   c. Acts on melatonin receptors in the pineal gland.
   d. Can be suppressed by relatively low light intensity.

3. With respect to jet-lag syndrome, which statement is correct?
   a. Eastward travel easier to adapt to compared with westward travel.
   b. Westward travel is more difficult to adapt to than eastward travel because the endogenous clock is slightly < 24 hours.
   c. Eastward travel is easier to adapt to because the endogenous clock is slightly > 24 hours.
   d. Eastward travel is more difficult to adapt to because the endogenous clock is slightly > 24 hours.

4. In shift work disorder, which of the following medications is FDA approved?
   a. Zolpidem.
   b. Methylphenidate.
   c. Melatonin.
   d. Caffeine.
   e. Modafinil.

5. Phototherapy administered after core body minimum temperature delays circadian clock?
   a. True.
   b. False.

6. Treatment of shift work disorder may include all of the following except:
   a. Evening bright light exposure (before shift).
   b. Avoiding bright light exposure after shift completed.
   c. Modafinil taken as soon as sleepiness occurs during the shift.
   d. Ensuring adequate sleep during the day.

7. The AASM 2015 guideline regarding treatment of CRSWD's has as its only STRONG recommendation:

    a. Melatonin for non-sighted adults.
    b. Melatonin for adults with DSWPD
    c   Hypnotics for demented elderly with ISWRD.
    d. Avoiding hypnotics in demented elderly with ISWRD.
    e. Light therapy in adolescents with DSWPD.

8. Tasimelteon for N24SWRD is a:

    a. Melatonin MTI and MT2 receptor agonist.
    b. Melatonin MTI and MT2 receptor antagonist.
    c. Norepinephrine reuptake blocker.
    d. Dopamine reuptake blocker.

Answers: 1b, 2c, 3d, 4e, 5b, 6c, 7d, 8a

Section 6:

ADULT INSOMNIA

(For childhood insomnia, please see section 12.)

BACKGROUND

A. Diagnostic criteria: The 3 D's:

Difficulty initiating or maintaining sleep.......

Despite adequate opportunity for sleep, resulting in.......

Daytime impairment (e.g., sleepiness, fatigue, cognitive, memory problems, etc.).

B. Classification (after ICSD3)

A major change in the ICSD3 is that the 11 categories of insomnia (ICSD2) have been condensed into two major categories:

1. Chronic Insomnia Disorder (present for at least 3 months) and
2. Short-term Insomnia Disorder (present for less than 3 months).

Classification updates:
Most of the 11 categories defined in ICSD2 have been subsumed in ICSD3 as subtypes within Chronic Insomnia Disorders. The section indicates that "the current global classification promotes a generic approach to insomnia therapy" and that as a result an unresolved issue may be that this "ultimately fails to benefit some insomnia subgroups."

Of interest is that the American Psychiatric Association's 2013 fifth edition of the **Diagnostic and Statistical Manual of Mental Disorders (DSM-5)** has a single diagnostic category for "Insomnia Disorder." It recognizes that insomnia may occur as an independent condition or be comorbid with a mental disorder, medical condition, or another sleep disorder. The temporal course of insomnia may be (a) episodic (symptoms last at least one month but less than three months), (b) persistent (symptoms last three months or longer) or (c) recurrent (two or more episodes within the space of one year).

DSM-5 does not include those subtypes found in both ICSD2 and ICSD3, viz, psychophysiological insomnia, idiopathic insomnia, sleep-state misperception and inadequate sleep hygiene, indicating that "there is limited evidence to support these distinct phenotypes" even though they may have "clinical appeal and heuristic value."

[Authors note: In view of the above, it may therefore be clinically/diagnostically useful and hence of therapeutic benefit to bear in mind the major subtypes of insomnia when approaching the individual patient (see section 3, evaluation of insomnia).]

From an **Etiologic** standpoint insomnia may therefore be:

- *Co-morbid/Secondary*: associated with a medical or mental disorder, due to substance abuse or occurring in the course of another sleep disorder.

- *Primary*
  - Adjustment (acute insomnia)
  - Psychophysiological (conditioned insomnia)
  - Paradoxical (sleep-state misperception)
  - Idiopathic (childhood onset)
  - Poor sleep hygiene

REMember:

NIH State of the Art Conference Consensus Statement (2005) views "secondary" insomnia as *comorbid* insomnia, since BOTH the primary disorder and the insomnia may need to be treated in parallel rather than as a single condition.

C. Demographics:

- 30 - 50% of American adults experience insomnia during a one-year period.
- 10 - 15% of the general population may have chronic insomnia.
- Females have increased risk for chronic insomnia compared with males (factors may include the menstrual cycle, pregnancy, postpregnancy, perimenopausal, and postmenopausal issues).
- Increase risk of insomnia in the economically disadvantaged, single and unemployed populations.
- Insomnia is both a risk factor for depression and a consequence of depression.
- 40-55% of outpatients and ±90% of inpatients with a major depression episode have insomnia.
- Insomnia is a risk factor for substance abuse
  - almost 30% of chronic insomniacs may develop alcohol abuse
- Covid19 Pandemic: Insomnia prevalence ↑ significantly.

D. Pathophysiology:

- Insomnia associated with perpetual state of hyperarousal
- Suggests persistent ↑ SNS stimulation
- Hyperarousal results in
  - inability to relax
  - exaggerated reactions to environmental stressors
  - heightened awareness of bedtime associations and potential sleep disruptions which creates anxiety and frustration leading to sleep impairment
- Hyperarousal shown to be associated with
  ↑ brain metabolic activity (RothT et al, *Sleep Med Rev* 2007;11:71-79)
  ↑ BMR, ↑ body temperture, ↑ HR
  ↑ cortisol & ACTH in sleep

FEATURES OF INDIVIDUAL SUBTYPES

Short-term (Acute/adjustment) insomnia:

- Precipitated by an identifiable stressor.
- One year prevalence in general population + 15 -20%.
- More common in women and in older adults.
- By definition, lasts no more than 3 months.
- Usually remits after adaptation to or reduction in stressor.

Chronic Insomnias (subtypes subsumed within general body of Chronic Insomnia Disorder in ICSD3).

A. Primary Insomnias

1. **Psychophysiological insomnia:**

   - Learned sleep-preventing associations.
   - Extreme concern with inability to sleep and consequences which follow.
   - Heightened state of arousal during the day (frequently unable to nap). Often sleep better away from home.
   - Inability to relax prior to bedtime.
   - Estimated to affect 1 - 2% of the general population.
   - Not due to psychiatric or medical condition, or substance abuse.

2. **Paradoxical insomnia (sleep-state misperception).**

   - Daytime impairment much less severe than expected from the patient's report of extreme sleep deprivation.
   - Mismatch between PSG or actigraphy and subjective sleep estimates.
   - ↑ risk from depression/anxiety, hypnotic use/abuse.

3. **Idiopathic insomnia.**

   - Onset during childhood with lifelong sleep difficulty and often no identifiable precipitating event.
   - Periods of sustained remission not reported.

4. **Inadequate sleep hygiene.**

   - Patients adopt living activities inconsistent with quality sleep.
   - Activities may include:
     - Varying bedtimes.
     - Frequent napping, especially evenings.
     - Abuse of substances interfering with sleep, especially close to bedtime (e.g., alcohol, caffeine, nicotine).
     - Engaging in stimulating activities close to bedtime.
     - Sleep environment not conducive to sleep (noise,light,etc).

B. Insomnias secondary to comorbid with:

- Medical conditions (e.g., pain, asthma, GERD).
- Specific sleep-related disorder (e.g., RLS, OSAS, DSWPD).
- Psychiatric disorders (e.g., anxiety or depression).
- Drug or alcohol abuse.
- Medications causing insomnia may include:
  - Antidepressants (e.g., fluoxetine, venlafaxine, phenelzine).

- Beta-blockers, especially propranolol.
- Bronchodilators (e.g., theophylline, long-acting beta agonists).
- Decongestants.
- Corticosteroids.
- Stimulants (e.g., methylphenidate, dextroamphetamine).
- Certain anticonvulsants (e.g., lamotrigine).

ICSD3 indicates that insomnia may be a secondary symptom in conditions listed above. However, as previously stated, insomnia may have its own independent clinical course and may therefore exist in a comorbid fashion with these varying clinical conditions.

DSM-5 also points out that persistent insomnia may be a risk factor for depression and is a common residual symptom after treatment for depression.

(for childhood insomnia, please see section 12)

CLINICAL EVALUATION

See Section 3: Sleep Evaluation.
Brief recapitulation:

1. Evaluate psychodynamics (3P Model):
   - **P**redisposing factors (e.g., patients who are light sleepers, tendency to anxiety, tendency to relationship problems).
   - **P**recipitating factors: an event/stress which overwhelms coping mechanisms (e.g., bereavement, loss of job).
   - **P**erpetuating factors (e.g., maladaptive behaviors and misconceptions regarding sleep, persistent sleep hygiene issues, persistence of precipitating factor(s), or **learned** sleep-preventing associations).

2. Evaluate for a specific cause:
   - Primary or
   - Co-morbid/secondary insomnia

3. Investigations
   - Sleep diary: may over-estimate sleep latency and underestimate total sleep time but should be collected prior to and during the course of insomnia management.
   - Actigraphy (may be useful in some cases).
   - PSG and MSLT not indicated in the routine evaluation of chronic insomnia.
   - Screening tests for anxiety or depression as applicable.

MANAGEMENT

REMember:
- If insomnia is due to a co-morbid condition (e.g., medical, psychiatric or a specific sleep disorder), first treat the underlying condition.
- Management approaches for insomnia per se may include both **nonpharmacologic/behavioral therapy** and **pharmacotherapy**.
- Aim is to reduce anxiety/tension/hyperarousal prior to bedtime and simultaneously increase sleepiness.

Cognitive-behavioral therapy for insomnia (CBT-I) strategies:

a. Stimulus-control therapy: attempts to reassociate the bedroom environment with healthy sleep. Recommendations include:
- Bedtime only when sleepy.
- Using the bed only for sleep and intimacy.
- Curtail time spent awake in bed e.g., if unable to sleep within 15 - 20 minutes (estimate) of nocturnal wakening, relax or engage in quiet activity in another room and return to bed when sleepy.
- Avoid clock watching (turn clock face around).

b. Sleep-restriction therapy:
- Aim is to improve sleep onset through partial sleep deprivation.
- Begin by reducing the time in bed according to the estimated time spent asleep (sleep diary).
- Establish a regular wake time and advance bedtime by 15-30 min when 90% sleep efficiency is achieved.

c. Cognitive therapy:
- Re-educates patient's faulty beliefs and attitudes to sleep.
- Correct irrational fears, unrealistic expectations, and excessive concern about the amount of sleep time needed for adequate daytime function.

d. Relaxation therapy:
- Aims to decrease anxiety and lower arousal threshold.
- Hot bath prior to bedtime (helps relaxation and also increases core temperature to promote sleep during its subsequent decline).
- Breathing exercises, meditation, modified yoga, guided imagery (may be useful for both sleep-onset and sleep-maintenance insomnia.).

e. Progressive muscle relaxation (PMR):
Patient taught to systematically relax each part of the body; (experience needed in conducting PMR).

f. **Sleep hygiene education:**
  - Often ineffective *on its own* in chronic insomnia but a necessary component of insomnia management.
  - Recommendations include:
    - Adjusting the bedroom environment conducive to sleep (cooler rather than warmer temperature).
    - Establish a regular "wind down" routine.
    - Avoid stimulating activities preventing sleep onset, e.g., computer games, emailing, paying bills.
    - Reduce or eliminate products which interfere with sleep (caffeine, nicotine, alcohol).
    - Avoid napping especially in evenings
    - No exercising or large meals close to bedtime (±3hrs)
    - Establish a regular wake time.

g. **Biofeedback:**
  - Complex procedure, may need many sessions, needs experienced operator.

h. **Paradoxical intention:**
  - Persuades subject to confront fear of staying awake.
  - Aims to eliminate performance anxiety associated with insomnia.

NOTE: ASSM practice parameter report on the Psychological and Behavioral Treatment of insomnia lists CBT, stimulus control therapy and relaxation training as *standard* recommendations (high degree of clinical certainty). Other approaches are mostly guidelines (moderate degree of certainty). *SLEEP* 2006; 29 (11): 1415-1419.

 *REMember:*

Meta-analysis of treatment efficacy of non-pharmacological treatments indicated that sleep restriction, multicomponent programs, stimulus control, and cognitive relaxation showed the greatest improvements for sleep-onset and maintenance insomnia. Sleep hygiene not effective when used alone. (Morin, Culbert, and Schwartz· Am. J. Psych., 1994; 151: 1172-1180).

2012 study showed that 3 week trial of melatonin in atenolol or metoprolol induced insomnia resulted in sleep improvement. *SLEEP* 2012; 35(10): 1395-1402.

Self-help: CBT-I available as interactive web-based training programs. Self-help CBT-I programs also available as apps on smart phones.

Pharmocatherapy
FDA APPROVED MEDICATIONS FOR INSOMNIA

Drug	Approximate Half life (hours)	Dose Range (mg)
Benzodiazepines (BZDs)		
Temazepam (*Restoril*)	9.5-12.5	7.5 - 30
Triazolam (*Halcion*)	1.5 – 5.5	0.125 - 0.5
Estazolam (*ProSom*)	10 - 24	1 - 2
Flurazepam (*Dalmane*)	40-100*	15-30
Quazepam (*Doral*)	39-73	7.5-15
Nonbenzodiazepines (*Benzodiazepine Receptor Agonists-BzRAs*)		
Eszopiclone (*Lunesta*)	6	1 - 3
Zolpidem (*Ambien*)	2.5-3	5-10
Zolpidem ER (*AmbienCR*)	2.5 -3**	6.25-12.5
Zolpidem sublingual (*Edluar*)	2.5-3	5-10
Zolpidem sublingual (*Intermezzo*)	2.5-3	1.75female / 3.5male
Zolpidem spray (*Zolpimist*)	2.5-3	5-10 (5mg / spray)
Zaleplon (*Sonata*)	1	5 - 10 (max20)
Melatonin Receptor Agonist		
Ramelteon (*Rozerem*)	2 - 5	8
Antidepressants Doxepin (*Silenor*)	15.3	3 - 6
Dual Orexin Receptor Agonist (DORA) Suvorexant (*Belsomra*) Lemborexant (*Dayvigo*)	12 12	5,10,15,20 5, 10

*Active Ingredient
** AmbienCR contains immediate and delayed release zolpidem resulting in longer duration of action than ambien though active ingredients themselves have same half lives.

NOTE:
    On 1/10/13 FDA issued a safety announcement advising lower recommended doses for zolpidem in women: 5mg for IR zolpidem and 6.25mg for extended release forms due to apparant slower elimination compared with men.
    On 5/14/14 FDA advised a 1mg starting dose of eszopiclone (*Lunesta*); 3mg dose shown to cause impairment of driving and of memory for up to 11 hours post dose.

To refresh your memory: **Mode of Action BZDs and BzRAs**:
- GABA most widespread inhibitory neurotransmitter; acts by opening chloride channels and entry of chloride ions into cells causing hyperpolarization.
- Three types of GABA receptors: GABA-A, GABA-B & GABA-C.
- GABA-A the major receptor; responsible for hypnotic effects.
- GABA-A has several subunits; alpha-1, 2, 3, 4 & 5 are BZD sensitive.
- alpha-1 subunit is sedating; others are anxiolytic, anti-seizure, myorelaxant & amnesic.

- BZDs bind to most GABA-A receptor subunits with variable affinities thus explaining their varied clinical propensities and effects.
- BzRAs bind primarily to the alpha-1 receptor subunit with little affinity for the others.

Note: DORAs act by reducing the wake - enhancing activity of orexins. They are contraindicated in narcolepsy.

Summary of special article: **Clinical Practice Guideline for the Pharmacologic Treatment of Chronic Insomnia in Adults.** *J Clin Sleep Med* 2017; 13 (2): 307-349.

Note: All recommendations are WEAK (vs. no treatment), indicating a lower degree of certainty in the outcome.

- For **sleep onset insomnia**: zaleplon, triazolam, ramelteon.

- For **sleep maintenance insomnia**: suvorexant, doxepin.

- For **sleep onset insomnia and sleep maintenance insomnia**: eszopiclone, zolpidem, temazepam, lemborexant (*Dayvigo* website).

- Weak recommendations *against* using the following medications: trazodone, tiagabine, diphenhydramine, melatonin, tryptophan, valerian.

- No recommendations were made for the following medications due to inadequate data for statistical analysis: estazolam, quazepam, flurazepam, oxazepam, quetiapine, gabapentin, paroxetine, trimipramine.

REMember:
- Hypnotics should not be used with alcohol.
- Caution patients re risk of amnesia and complex behaviors such as "sleep-driving", sleep walking & sleep eating. Risk ↑ with alcohol and/or other CNS depressants, ↑ doses of hypnotic, history of parasomnia.
- BzRAs have rapid onset of action; should be taken at bedtime.
- Doxepin (Silenor) should be avoided in patients on MAOIs. Acts as a histamine H1 receptor antagonist.

A new approach to insomnia therapy?

Roth et al: A novel forehead temperature-regulating device for insomnia: a randomized clinical trial. *SLEEP* May 2018. Study reports on a thermal approach for insomnia acting to cool the forehead with the aim of reducing frontal lobe activity. Temperatures maintained at 14-16°C/57-61°F. Study over two nights showed variable improvements in PSG sleep indices though main endpoints of absolute sleep latency and sleep efficiency did not show statistical significance compared with sham controls.

Summary of Special Article: **Clinical Guideline for the Evaluation and Management of Chronic Insomnia in Adults** (*J Clin Sleep Med* 2008; 4(5): 487-504).

A. Evaluation includes:

- A diagnosis of insomnia requires *both* complaints of insomnia and symptoms associated with daytime dysfunction.

- PSG and MSLT testing is not routinely indicated (*standard*).

  PSG may be indicated if
  - suspicion of associated sleep breathing or movement disorder,
  - the initial diagnosis is uncertain,
  - treatment failure or violent/injurious behaviors in sleep.

- Actigraphy useful to characterize circadian rhythm disturbances or sleep disturbances associated with insomnia, including depression (*option*).

B. Management

- Psychological and behavioral interventions are effective and recommended in the treatment of chronic, primary, and co-morbid (secondary) insomnia (*standard*).

- Initial treatment should utilize at least one of behavioral interventions (CBT-I) (*standard*). (Components of CBT-I include sleep restriction therapy, relaxation therapy and stimulus control therapy and have been found to be effective in adults of all ages, as well as chronic hypnotic users).

- All patients should adhere to sleep hygiene rules. Insufficient evidence to indicate that sleep hygiene on its own is effective (*consensus*).

- Pharmacologic treatment:

  - Supplement short-term hypnotic treatment with CBT-I. (*consensus*).

  - Recommended *sequence* of medication trials:(*consensus*):
    - Short-intermediate acting BZDs eg temazepam or newer BzRAs (zolpidem, eszopiclone, or zaleplon) or ramelteon.

    - If initial agent fails,use alternate short-acting BzRA or ramelteon.

- Sedating antidepressants, especially if patient has comorbid depression/anxiety (e.g., trazodone, amitriptyline, doxepin, mirtazapine).

- Combined BzRA or ramelteon with sedating antidepressant.

- Other sedating agents: e.g., antiepilepsy medications (gabapentin, tiagabine) and atypical antipsychotics e.g., quetiapine (*seroquel*) and olanzapine (*zyprexa*). Use primarily for patients who could benefit from the primary action of these drugs (for schizophrenia or bipolar disorder), as well as for their sedating effects.

- OTC sleep aids, as well as herbal/nutritional substances (e.g., valerian and melatonin.) are *not recommended* due to the lack of efficacy and safety data (consensus).

- Older approved drugs including barbiturates and chloral hydrate are *not recommended* (*consensus*).

- Chronic hypnotic medications may be indicated for long-term use; the patient should also receive an adequate trial of CBT-I.

CBT-I vs Pharmacotherapy vs Combination therapy :

The review summarizes the literature examining the issue of pharmacotherapy or CBT-I vs a combination of these approaches and concludes as follows:

- Short-term pharmacological treatments *alone* are effective during the course of treatment for chronic insomnia but *do not provide sustained improvement following discontinuation.*

- CBT-I provides significant improvement of chronic insomnia in the short term and these improvements appear sustained at follow up for up to two years.

- Studies of combined treatment show mixed and inconclusive results.

2021 AASM Guideline (*J Clin Sleep Med* Feb 2021)

Behavioral and psychological treatments for chronic insomnia disorder

Strong recommendation: Multi-component cognitive behavioral therapy (CBT-I) over 4-8 sessions by a trained professional.

Conditional recommendation: Brief therapies for insomnia (BTIs) over 1-4 sessions which may be multicomponent or single component and which may include stimulus control, sleep restriction therapy and relaxation therapy to reduce somatic tension (e.g., breathing training) and cognitive arousal (e.g., guided imagery training)

Conditional *against* use of sleep hygiene as single - component therapy; (forms part of multicomponent CBT-I).

REMember:
- Diphenhydramine, an antihistamine
  - active ingredient in most OTC sleep aids
  - anticholinergic side effects e.g., dry mouth, urine retention, constipation
  - long half-life (8-9hrs) → a.m. grogginess/drowsiness
- Trazodone
  — Causes sedation by antihistamine effect.
  — Adverse effects (AE's):
    - hypotension
    - cardiac arrhythmias, QT prolongation
    - priapism (rare)
    - common AE's: blurred vision, drowsiness, fatigue, light headedness, dry mouth
- In patients with comorbid depression and insomnia, resolution of the sleep disorder may enhance resonse to AD therapy:
  - combination of SSRI and BzRA may improve relapse rate (e.g., fluoxetine with hs eszopiclone) Fava et al., *Biol Psych* 2006; 59(11):1052-60.

FYI:

Natural history of insomnia: Population study in recruited good sleepers showed high 1 year incidence of 27% for acute insomnia (3+ nights/week for 2-12 weeks), but only 1.8% for chronic insomnia, suggesting that most incident cases resolve and only ± 2/100 individuals become chronic. (Perlis et al *SLEEP* 2020; 43(6):1-8.

Insomnia, hypnotic use and road collisions: 40% of reported road accidents over a 5 year period found to be associated with both insomnia and the use of sleep medications. Young females with insomnia and EDS are a newly reported at-risk group. (Morin et al: *SLEEP* 2020; 43(8): 1-7.

Further reading/references:

1. Michael H. Silber: Chronic Insomnia, *NEJM* 2005; 353: 803 - 810.
2. Gulyani et al: Sleep Medicine Pharmacotherapeutics Overview. *CHEST* 2012; 142(6): 1659-68.
3. Williams J. et al: Cognitive Behaviorial Therapy of Insomnia. *CHEST* 2013; 143(2): 554-565.

Test Your Memory (Section 6):

1. With respect to psychophysiological insomnia, which statement is not correct:
    a. Bedtime focus is on obtaining adequate sleep.
    b. Affects <5% of general population.
    c. General anxiety disorder (GAD) not a cause.
    d. Planned napping during the day helps symptoms such as fatigue, tiredness, etc.
    e. Polysomnogram usually not recommended.

2. Half life of zolpidem is:
    a. 1 - 1.5 hours.
    b. 2.5 - 3 hours.
    c. 4 - 5 hours.
    d. 6 - 8 hours.

3. Half life of temazepam is approximately:
    a. 4 - 5 hours.
    b. 6 - 8 hours.
    c. 10 - 12 hours.
    d. 12 - 14 hours.

4. Clinical guidelines for management of insomnia include the use of sedating antidepressants, especially where co-morbid depression is present. Such agents may include all of the following except:
    a. trazodone.
    b. amitriptyline.
    c. doxepin.
    d. mirtazapine.
    e. bupropion.

5. FDA guidelines published on 01/10/2013 recommends reducing dosing of which hypnotic in women because of slower elimination of the drug?
    a. eszopiclone.
    b. temazepam.
    c. zolpidem.
    d. zaleplon.
    e. triazolam.

6. Which of the following hypnotics in contraindicated in narcoleptic patients?
    a. Doxepin (*Silenor*).
    b. Ramelteon (*Rozerem*).
    c. Triazolam (*Halcion*).
    d. Suvorextant (*Belsomra*).

    Answers: 1d, 2b, 3c, 4e, 5c, 6d.

Section 7:

HYPERSOMNOLENCE UNRELATED TO SLEEP-RELATED BREATHING DISORDERS.

This section deals with the following conditions:

1. Narcolepsy.
2. Idiopathic hypersomnia.
3. Kleine-Levin Syndrome. (formerly Recurrent Hypersomnia)

(Other hypersomnias in the ICSD-3 include those associated with medical conditions, drug or substance abuse, insufficient-sleep syndrome, or psychiatric conditions.)

NARCOLEPSY

Background

1. Definition:
    *   NL is a hypersomnia in which there is unusual proclivity to transition rapidly from wakefulness into REM sleep and to experience dissociated REM sleep events (ICSD2).
    *   NL may occur with or without cataplexy.

2. Classification.
    *   Narcolepsy Type 1 (NL-1): EDS with diagnostic MSLT (see below) and either a history of cataplexy or abnormal CSF hypocretin (HCR) levels. (CSF HCR levels in NL-1 are ≤ 110 pg/ml or $< 1/3$ of normal mean values.)
    *   Narcolepsy Type 2 (NL-2): EDS with diagnostic MSLT but no cataplexy. CSF HCR not checked or do not meet criteria for NL-1

3. Demographics.
    a. M slightly >F.
    b. Onset usually from teens to early 20's with EDS; rarely <5yrs. Occasionally may present as adult (usually ±35 yrs).

    c.   Prevalence
- Affects 0.02-0.05% of U.S. population.
- Similar in Europe.
- Higher in Japan, ±0.16–0.18% of population.
- Rare in Israel (0.002%).
- NL-2 ± 15-25% of all narcoleptic patients.

4. Pathology.
    a.   In NL with cataplexy (NL-1) there is loss of hypocretin containing hypothalamic neurons possibly on an autoimmune basis.
    b.   The minority of NL without cataplexy (NL-2 patients) have loss of hypocretin neurons.
    c.   Lack of measurable hypocretin (also known as orexin) in CSF (<110 pg/ml, or absent) in NL-1.

5. Predisposing/precipitating factors.
    a.   Genetic susceptibility present: NL with cataplexy strongly associated with human leukocyte antigen (HLA) subtypes **DQB1*0602 and DR2/DRB1*1501**; association less strong in NL without cataplexy. See also review: Narcolepsy type 1: What have we learned from genetics (*SLEEP*, v 43, Nov 2020).
    b.   Onset may follow head trauma, viral infections or sleep deprivation. Cases of NL-1 reported following streptococcal infections (Aran et al, *SLEEP* 2009;32:979-83). Zhang et al (*SLEEP* 2021; 44(2): 1-10) reports on ↑ peak in DQB1*0602 childhood NL1 in 2013 suggesting a possible viral trigger and an immune-mediated response.
    c.   Familial association present in 1 - 2% of first-degree relatives.

6. Autoimmune basis for Narcolepsy:
    The increase in NL following the H1N1 vaccination campaigns in Finland (↑16x) and Sweden and the upsurge following H1N1 infection in China suggests that an H1N1 virus derived antigen may have triggered the disorder in predisposed individuals (*Pharmacological Research* Feb 2015, *Lancet Neurology* June 2014). Studies have shown that triggered autoreactive T cells cause direct injury to hypocretin neurons resulting in Narcolepsy 1. ↑ incidence in Germany also seen post 2009 H1N1 pandemic and vaccination (*SLEEP* 2015; 38(10): 1619-28). Article entitled Narcolepsy Type 1: What have we learned from immunology? (*SLEEP* v.43.Oct 2020) postulates that narcolepsy type 1 still lacks criteria to be classified as an immunological disorder but "more and more results are pointing in that direction."

Clinical features.

    a.   Excessive daytime sleepiness (EDS), hallmark of NL; may be pervasive sleepiness, irresistible sleep attacks or "micro sleeps" lasting split seconds occurring several times daily. Naps transiently refreshing. EDS may precede REM phenomena by years.

b. REM-associated events:
  - Hypnagogic and/or hypnopompic hallucinations (usually visual; may be auditory, tactile or olfactory).
  - Sleep paralysis
    — last seconds to minutes
    — patient is conscious, attacks are frightening
    — may occur with hypnagogic or hypnopompic hallucinations
  - Cataplexy (60 - 90% of narcoleptics)
    — Usually presents in 1st year of onset but may occur many years later. Rarely precedes symptoms of EDS.
    — Loss of bilateral muscle tone precipitated by an emotional response (usually positive e.g., laughter).
    — Due to excessive activation of descending motor inhibitory pathways.
    — Most common muscles affected include the knees, face, neck.
    — Muscles of breathing not involved.
    — Lasts seconds to minutes. Recovery immediate.
    — Subject remains conscious during episode.
    — Status cataplecticus:
      • repetitive episodes of cataplexy lasting minutes to an hour.
      • episodes usually precipitated when ADs such as SSRI's or TCA's abruptly discontinued (rebound cataplexy).
      • treatment with SSRI's or TCA's usually terminate episode.

REMember:

Mechanism of cataplexy:
  - inhibition of motor neurons and of tendon reflexes.
  - muscarinic cholinergic regions of pontine reticular formation and basal forebrain involved through a multisynaptic descending inhibitory pathway.

Other clinical features.
  - "Automatic" behavior: performing activities without awareness (20-40%).
  - Sleep-maintenance insomnia (± 50%); fragmented sleep, multiple arousals.
  - ↓ Memory/concentration; ↓ school/work performance; depression-like symptoms.

Laboratory findings:

a. HLA subtypes.
- HLA genes may promote susceptibility to NL by increasing risk of an autoimmune disturbance targeting HCR hypothalamic neurons.
- Narcolepsy *with cataplexy* strongly associated with HLA DQB1*0602 and DR2/DRB1*1501subtypes.
- DQB1*0602 prevalence data
  - DQB1*0602 present in 85 - 93% of NL with cataplexy.
  - DQB1*0602 in 35 - 56% in NL without cataplexy
  - DQB1*0602 also in 12 - 38% of the *general population*.

b. CSF HCR levels.
- < 110 pg/mL or absent in ± 90% of NL with cataplexy.
- NL with cataplexy and *normal* CSF HCR levels are usually DQB1*0602 *negative*.
- In NL without cataplexy10-20% have CSF HCR levels < 110 pg/mL; may have to reclassify some patients from NL-2 to NL-1 once CSF HCR levels known. These patients almost all DQB1*0602 positive.
- CSF HCR level measurements may be useful in difficult-to-diagnose cases.
- Low CSF HCR levels occasionally found in other CNS disorders such as Guillain-Barré Syndrome, diencephalon strokes, acute head trauma or Creutzfeldt-Jakob disease.

Diagnostic testing

a. MSLT "gold standard" test (For MSLT procedure see section 3).
b. PSG should always precede MSLT; rules out other causes of EDS; may show short sleep latency and short REM latency; may also show ↓ sleep efficiency, ↑ WASO, ↑ N1 sleep.
c. HLA typing (not diagnostic on own; DQB*0602 seen in 12-38% normals).
d. CSF hypocretin levels useful where diagnosis uncertain
  - pediatric narcolepsy
  - atypical cataplexy
  - absent SOREMPs on MSLT.
e. Other tests
  - ESS or other screen for EDS e.g., Karolinska scale.
  - Sleep diary.
  - Drug screen.
  - Brain MRI (e.g., post-trauma or where associated neurological disease present.)

REMember:

MSLT Facts:.
- Measures the *propensity* for daytime *sleepiness*.
- Mean sleep latency (MSL) of ≤ 8 minutes with 2 or more SOREMPs **or** one SOREMP and a REM latency of < 15 minutes from sleep onset on the preceding PSG is diagnostic for narcolepsy (in the appropriate clinical setting).
- ±15% of NL with cataplexy may have *normal* or *borderline* MSLT with only 1 SOREMP (prevalence increases with age; 25% in patients > 36 years). May need to repeat MSLT.
- MSL < 8 minutes seen in up to 30% in normal population studies.
- 1-3% of adults may have multiple SOREMPs during random MSLTs.
- Nocturnal SOREMP ≤ 15 min on PSG has high specificity in NL-1 in adults and in children 6-18 years (±97%) but only moderate sensitivity (*SLEEP* 2015; 38(6): 859-865).
- SOREMPs may also occur in:
  - Following sleep deprivation.
  - Shift-work disorder.
  - Delayed sleep phase syndrome.
  - OSAS - due to decreased REM during nocturnal sleep
    - after initiation of CPAP therapy (REM rebound)
  - Depression.
  - Following drug and alcohol withdrawal.
  - Withdrawal of REM-suppressant medications (e.g., SSRIs, TCAs).
- Normal/Abnormal sleep latencies on MSLT validated if test administered between 8am-6pm.
- Kolla et al JCSM 2020; 16(11):1921-7 showed that tapering REM suppressing anti depressants before a MSLT had ↑ chance of ≥ 2 SOREMS and ↓ mean sleep latency.

Management (Adult NL)

a. Sleep hygiene, avoid sleep deprivation.
b. Planned napping during the day.
c. FDA approved **medications for EDS** include:

1. Modafinil (*Provigil*)200-400mg or
   Armodafinil (*Nuvigil*) 150, 200, 250mg.
   - Mechanism of action felt to be enhancing dopamine activity by blocking its reuptake.

- CAUTION:
  - Decreases the efficacy of steroidal contraceptives and effect lasts for a month after discontinuing these medications.
  - Rare cause of severe systemic rash (e.g., Stevens Johnson syndrome)

2. Solriamfetol (*Sunosi*), a selective dopamine and norepinephrine reuptake inhibitor to improve wakefulness and reduce EDS in adult patients with narcolepsy and OSA. Once daily dosing for narcolepsy is 75mg and 150mg, and in OSA 37.5mg, 75mg and 150mg. Most common side effects reported in clinical studies ($\geq 5\%$) were headache, nausia, ↓appetite and anxiety. Solriamfetol should not be prescribed for patients on a MAOI.

3. Pitolisant (*Wakix*). MOA: Binds to histamine-3 receptors as antagonist and inverse agonist. Approved for NL types 1 and 2. Dose generally 17.8-35 mg qam (start 8.9mg qam). Approved adults only. May ↑ QT interval. Common S/Es: Nausea, anxiety, insomnia

4. Stimulants: methylphenidate, dextroamphetamine and dextroamphetamine/amphetamine (promote release and block reuptake of DA, 5HT and NE). (High abuse potential + dependency)

5. **(a)** Sodium oxybate (*Xyrem*): sodium salt of gamma-hydroxybuterate(GHB) which is a GABA matabolite; short half-life, taken at bedtime and 2 - 4 hours into sleep; maximum dose 9 gm in adults and children >45 kg.
   - Approved ages 7+ years. Dosing weight based.
   - Risk of respiratory depression with overdose (intentional or unintentional).
   - Concommitant use of alcohol contraindicated.
   - Caution in obesity or OSA even with regular doses.
   - High sodium content; caution in CHF, CRF, HT.
   - Rarely amnesic sleep eating/driving (*J. Clin Sleep Med* 2011; 7(3) 3010-11).
   - Response for EDS and cataplexy usually seen by 2 months; maximum resonse may take longer (*J. Clin Sleep Med* 2015: 11(4): 427-432).
   - Pharmacokinetics:
     - < 1% protein bound
     - elimination half life 0.5-1 hour
     - excreted by biotransformation to CO_2 and then eliminated by lungs
     - mechnism of action uncertain —probably through GABA(b) action at noradrenergic, dopaminergic and thalamocortical neurons.

- GHB illegally manufactured and used as "date rape" drug.

   (b) Xywav (Ca, Mg, K, Na oxybate). $\downarrow\downarrow$ Na$^+$ content. Approved ages 7+ years. Same dosing schedule as *Xyrem*.

d. Cataplexy management
   - *Xyrem, Xywav*, pitolisant (*Wakix*) all FDA approved for cataplexy.
   - TCAs (e.g., desipramine, protriptyline, clomipramine, nortriptyline, imipramine), SSRIs (e.g., fluoxetine, fluvoxamine, citalopram, paroxetine) or venlafaxine (SNRI) used based on their REM-suppressant properties. (AASM guideline, *JCSM* 2007)

e. Other measures:
      Family involvement and support groups.

f. Online case studies report the off-label use of *baclofen*, a centrally acting muscle relaxant, for both EDS and cataplexy in narcolepsy. (Morse et al, *Pediatric Neurol* Nov 20, 2018; Lee & Douglass, *Nat Sci Sleep* July 29, 2015)

g. Pregnancy: Caution advised for all FDA approved medications for narcolepsy. Health Canada advised against the use of modafinil during pregnancy (June 2019).

NL due to medical conditions (after ICSD-2)

a. NL *with* cataplexy may be associated with :
   - Tumors or sarcoidosis of the hypothalamus.
   - Multiple sclerosis - plaques involving the hypothalamus.
   - Paraneoplastic syndrome with anti-Ma2 antibodies.
   - Neiman-Pick type C disease.

b. NL *without* cataplexy associated with:
   - Head trauma.
   - Multiple sclerosis.
   - Myotonic dystrophy.
   - Prader Willi Syndrome.
   - Parkinson's disease.
   - Multiple system atrophy.

Pediatric Narcolepsy (see also Section 12)

- Rarely before the age of 5-6 years.
- Obesity often seen in childhood narcolepsy.
- May present as the reappearance of regular napping.

- EDS at school may be misdiagnosed as ADD, laziness, behavioral problems.
- Hallucinations with napping may lead to psychiatric misdiagnosis.
- Cataplexy may be misdiagnosed as seizure disorder.
- HLA testing usually not recommended because of low specificity.
- MSLT not validated in children < 8 years old.
- *Xyrem* and *Xywav* FDA approved for pediatric narcolepsy age ≥ 7 years.

REMember:

- **REM behavior disorder** (RBD) more frequent in NL with cataplexy than the rest of the population. May manifest with RBD symptoms or as a PSG finding of REM sleep without atonia.

- Additional causes of **sleep paralysis** include.
  a. Sleep deprivation.
  b. Irregular sleep patterns (eg shift work).
  c. Alcohol abuse.
  d. 4% of normal population.

- Narcoleptic patients have higher than expected incidence of sleep apnea (obstructive and central), RLS, PLMS, RBD, sleep walking and sleep talking.

  (See also section 8 : Parasomnias: Recurrant isolated Sleep Paralysis)

IDIOPATHIC HYPERSOMNIA (IH)

- Complaint of EDS despite adequate TST (often > 11 hrs in 24 hr period).
- Subjects awake unrefreshed often with confusion ("sleep drunkenness").
- Naps usually unrefreshing.
- Autonomic dysfunction possible (e.g., orthostatic hypotension, Raynaud's). See *JCSM* 2020; 16(5): 749-756: Frequency and severity of autonomic symptons in IH.
- Onset usually young adulthood (< 25yrs); familial pattern may be present.
- MSLT - mean sleep latency <8 minutes with < 2 SOREMPs.
- 24 hr PSG may be useful to document TST.
- Actigraphy may be useful.
- Drug screening during MSLT recommended.
- Management includes sleep hygiene, stimulants and awake-enhancing medications (modafinil or armodafinil) though response variable.

Flumazenil for idiopathic hypersomnia: Rye et al demonstrated that CSF fluid from some hypersomnolent patients potentiated gamma-aminobutyric acid (GABA)-A receptors and this effect was reversed with flumazenil (*Romazicon*), a GABA-A receptor antagonist used to reverse BZA overdoses (*Sci Transl Med* 2012; 4: 16). Based on this finding, Trotti et al treated 153 patients with idiopathic hypersomnia resistant to several wake-promoting medications with sublingual or transdermal flumazenil prepared specifically for their study. Ninety-six patients (62.8%) showed initial symptomatic improvement and 59 (38.5%) showed further improvement for a mean period of 7.8 months. (*J Clin Sleep Med* 2016; 12 (10): 1389-1394).

Review Article: Billiard M, Idiopathic Hypersomnia *Sleep Med Rev* 2016; 29:23-33.

KLEINE-LEVIN SYNDROME

- Typically seen in boys in their teens (M:F 4:1).
- EDS episodes last days or weeks; appear several times a year.
- Sleep period may last most of day (median duration 18 hrs).
- Mood and cognitive changes (e.g., confusion, hallucinations) may be present.
- Abnormal behaviors (e.g., binge eating, hypersexuality) also seen.
- Episodes usually disappear after about 4 to 8 years.
- Initial episode may follow viral infection.
- Treatment is empiric
  - Stimulants to promote wakefulness.
  - Mood stabilizing agents such as lithium (option teatment *SLEEP* guideline 2007).
  - Anticonvulsants (e.g., carbamazepine and valproic acid) (Carney et al: Clinical Sleep Disorders 2005 p. 355.).
- Trotti et al (*J Clin Sleep Med* 2014;10(4);457-8) report on clarithromycin in 4 KLS patients having a positive effect in either improvement in episodes of KLS or preventing episodes for a period of 10 months in one of the patients.

Menstrual-Related Hypersomnia

- Rare; ICSD3 catagories as a subtype of KLS.
- Usually begins after menarche.
- Episodes usually last one week. Similar symptoms as in KLS.
- May be related to hormonal changes.
- Treatment with oral contraceptives.

Further reading/references:

- Thorpy M, Dauvilliers Y: Clinical and practical considerations in the pharmacological management of narcolepsy. *Sleep Medicine* 2015; 16(1): 9-18.

- Scadding TE: Narcolepsy. *New Eng J Med* 2015; 373: 2654-62 (Good review article).

- Challenges in Diagnosing Narcolepsy without Cataplexy: A consensus statement *SLEEP* 2014: 37(6): 1035-42. Article includes diagnostic algorithm for patients with EDS without cataplexy.

- New AASM guidelines for the **Treatment of central disorders of hypersomnia** released on-line on 4/23/2021 prior to publication in the *JCSM*. The paper contains strong and conditional recommendations for the pharmacological treatment of narcolepsy and idiopathic hypersomnia (I.H.) as well as a variety of CNS conditions causing EDS such as KLS, Parkinson's disease, MS, brain trauma and other medical entities. Of interest is the conditional use of clarithromycin (where not contraindicated) in I.H.. The guideline includes a concise table summerizing the recommendations.

Test Your Memory (Section 7):

1. Cataplexy prevalence in narcolepsy is reported to be as high as:
   a. 10%.
   b. 30%.
   c. 50%.
   d. 70%.
   e. 90%.

2. In narcolepsy without cataplexy, prevalence of HLA gene DQB1*0602 reported to be approximately:
   a. 15% - 25%.
   b. 25% - 35%.
   c. 35% - 55%.
   d. 55% - 75%.
   e. 75% - 95%.

3. SOREMs during a MSLT may be seen in the following conditions except:
   a. Narcolepsy.
   b. Following sleep deprivation.
   c. With initiation of CPAP for OSA.
   d. Within a few days of initiating tricyclic antidepressant therapy.
   e. Shift-work disorder.

4. Which of the following medications is FDA-approved for the management of cataplexy?
   a. Imipramine.
   b. Sodium oxybate.
   c. Fluoxetine.
   d. Modafinil.
   e. Venlafaxine.

5. In the Kleine-Levin Syndrome, which of the following is correct?
   a. Prevalence greater in females.
   b. Typical age onset in teens.
   c. Episodes last well into adult life.
   d. Median duration sleep period usually about 8 to 10 hours.
   e. Abnormal behaviors (e.g., hypersexuality) rarely witnessed.

6. The MSLT:
   a. Measures ability to remain awake.
   b. Measures ability to resist sleep.
   c. Measures propensity for daytime sleepiness.
   d. Measures ability to dream during naps.
   e. None of the above.

7. Diagnosis of narcolepsy may now be made with one SOREMP on MSLT if preceding PSG shows REM latency of less than:
   a. 15 min.
   b. 20 min.
   c. 25 min.
   d. 30 min.

8. Sodium oxybate and Ca, Mg, K, Na oxybate approved for children over the age of:
   a. 5 yrs.
   b. 6 yrs.
   c. 7 yrs.
   d. 8 yrs.
   e. 9 yrs.

9. Potential EKG side effect of pitolisant is a:
   a. PR interval increase.
   b. QT interval increase.
   c. QT interval decrease.
   d. RBBB.

Answers: 1e, 2c, 3d, 4b, 5b, 6c, 7a, 8c, 9b

Section 8:

PARASOMNIAS

BACKGROUND:

Definition: Undesirable behavioral or physical phenomena that occur during sleep or during sleep-wake transition.

Classification ICSD3: Parasomnias classified depending on occurrence in NREM or REM sleep.

    A. Associated with **NREM** sleep.
        1. Confusional arousals.
        2. Sleepwalking.
        3. Sleep terrors.
        4. Sleep-Related Eating Disorder (SRED).
    B. Associated with **REM** sleep.
        1. REM Sleep Behavior Disorder (RBD).
        2. Recurrent Isolated Sleep Paralysis.
        3. Nightmare Disorder.
    C. "Other" parasomnias
        1. Sleep enuresis.
        2. Exploding head syndrome.
        3. Sleep-Related Hallucinations.

Pathophysiology:
Pathophysiology not clear but may involve oscillations between sleep stages with intrusion of one state into another.

CONFUSIONAL AROUSALS
(Sleep drunkenness)

Clinical features:
- Occurs in SWS usually during initial sleep period; episodes usually several minutes but can last hours.
- May even occur with naps.
- Prevalence in children 3-13 yrs ± 17%, in adults ± 3-4% and mainly< 35 years.
- Genetic/familial factors common; no sexual predilection.

- Subject is disoriented/confused; speech and mentation sluggish.
- Violence/aggression unusual; seen usually with attempted awakenings.
- May be associated with inappropriate sexual behavior in adults (see sexsomnia below).
- Retrograde and anterograde amnesia common.
- Episodes disturbing for parents/caregivers.
- Confusional arousals may be associated with/precipitated by:
  — forced awakening
  — stress/anxiety
  — sleep deprivation
  — drug/alcohol abuse
  — other sleep disorders: OSA, PLMD, narcolepsy, shift work disorder
  — psychiatric disorders
  — psychoactive drugs e.g., hypnotics, antidepressants
  — encephalopathies due to toxins, fevers, metabolic disturbances
- Outlook good in children; prevalence decreases significantly after five years though sleepwalking may later occur.
- PSG not indicated; would show arousal during SWS in the first third of the night.

Management:
- Avoid precipitating events, drugs, medications, and alcohol.
- Sleep hygiene.
- Treat coexisting sleep disorders.
- Avoid attempt to abort episode, may precipitate aggression; allow the event to run its course unless there is potential for harm.
- Pharmacologic treatment usually unnecessary; if necessary could try TCA (e.g., clomipramine).

SLEEPWALKING
(Somnambulism)

Clinical features:
- Occurs in SWS mostly during the initial portion the sleep period.
- Prevalence similar to confusional arousals: ± 17% children; ± 3-4% adults.
- Reported typical age range 4-12 yrs.
- Previous history of confusional arousals not uncommon.
- Difficult to awaken the patient during the episode; if awakened is confused with amnesia. May react aggressively or violently to attempted awaking.
- Behaviors during episode may be uncomplicated or quite complex including eating or inappropriate sexual behavior (see sexsomnia below).
- Eyes are usually open during the episode though stare may be vacant.

- Risk/precipitating factors
  - Genetic/familial factors increases risk 10x compared with the general population
  - Highest risk (60%) when both parents have a history of sleepwalking; and 45% if one parent affected.(ICSD2)
  - Sleep deprivation (most common risk factor).
  - Medical conditions (e.g., fever especially in children, hyperthyroidism).
  - Neurologic (e.g., migraine, CVA, encephalitis).
  - Sleep disorders (e.g., OSA).
  - Psychologic stress particularly in adults.
  - Premenstrual.
  - Stimuli e.g., noise or light or even a full bladder can precipitate episode.

- Medication/drug induced (mainly psychoactive agents)
  - lithium
  - Major tranquilizers e.g., phenothiazines
  - Hypnotics: BZDs, BzRAs
  - GABA, sodium oxybate (*Xyrem*)
  - antihistamines
  - stimulants
  - anticholinergics
  - Monteleukast (*Singulair*)
  - alcohol

REMember:
Case reports of sleepwalking, sleep driving and sleep eating while on hypnotics (mainly zolpidem) resulted in the FDA issuing a class warning labeling recommendation for all FDA approved hypnotics.

Management:
- Sleep hygiene.
- Avoid/reduce precipitating factors (see above)
- Ensure environmental safety.
- Medications may include:
  - BZDs (e.g., clonazepam; shorter acting BZDs if episodes occur relatively early during sleep).
  - Antidepressants (TCAs or SSRIs).
  - Osmotic release oral system methylphenidate. 2 adults successfully treated. Case report, *JCSM* 2019; 15(11):1683-5.

REMember:
SW may be difficult to distinguish from RBD. Points of diffentiation include:

- Eyes are usually open during SW with a "glassy" stare.
- Eyes usually closed in RBD.
- RBD usually occurs during the second half of the night.
- RBD more frequently in middle-aged or elderly males.

Clinical Review: Harris M, Grunstein R: Treatments for somnambulism: Assessing the evidence. *Sleep Medicine Reviews* 2009;13:295-297.

Standard measures include avoiding sleep deprivation or other priming factors, removing hazards and reassurance.

Medications tried if still distress or danger but literature search did not find any properly powered controlled trials.

Medications used have included

- BZDs (diazepam, triazolam,temazepam,estazolam,clonazopam)
- zolpidem
- TCAs including imipramine
- paroxetine
- trazodone

Hypnosis, guided imagery and relaxing training also used.

SLEEP TERRORS (ST)
(Night terrors, pavor nocturnus)

Clinical features:

- Occurs during SWS during the first third of the sleep period.
- Most frequently between the ages 4 -12years (4-5% prevalence). Laberge et al reported 14.7% prevalence ages 3-10 yrs (*Pediatrics* 2000; 106; 67-74).
- In adults most commonly at 20 - 30 years (±2%; M>F); may occur throughout the sleep period; may have previous history of sleepwalking.
- Arouse from sleep with a piercing scream and fear/panic associated with tachycardia, rapid breathing and diaphoresis.
- Inconsolable; resist external stimuli but if awakened are disoriented.
- May remain in bed but may jump out of bed resulting in physical harm.
- Episodes last 30 seconds to 5 minutes with retrograde amnesia.

Precipitating factors: similar to confusional arousals and sleepwalking (see above). Case report *JCSM* 2021; 17(1): 99-101 reports on cetirizine (H1 antagonist) exacerbating sleep terrors in a 20 yr old male.
- Genetic/familial factors may be present.
- Psychopathology rare in children but may be present in adults.

PSG usually not indicated but PSG with EEG montage may be useful to differentiate from temporal lobe epilepsy in difficult cases.

REMember:

- STs may be associated with violence and may have forensic implications (adults).
- STs differentiated from confusional arousals by the absence of the piercing scream and autonomic activity in the latter.

Management:
- Education/reassurance.
- Ensure a safe sleep environment.
- Improve sleep hygiene.
- Avoid and treat precipitating factors where known (e.g., OSA).
- Medications may be indicated where there are persistent/frequent events or injuries or before anticipated outings (e.g., sleep overs, sports camps).
- Medications used have included BZDs, SSRIs and TCAs (anecdotal).
- Psychotherapy and stress reduction in adults as needed.

SLEEP RELATED EATING DISORDER (SRED)

Diagnostic criteria:
- Involuntary eating and drinking during arousals from nocturnal sleep.
- Foodstuffs mostly unusual, harmful or inedible.
- Episodes have adverse health and psychological consequences.

Demographics:
- ± 4% young adults; most idiopathic; higher if established eating disorder
- Usually begins early adulthood
- F>M

Clinical features:
- Subjects eat/drink unusual foodstuffs (e.g., pet foods) or harmful substances.
- High calorie foods also sought; may result in obesity, hyperlipdemia.
- Recall varies from none to partial to full.
- Sleep disruption causes daytime fatigue and mood changes.
- Injury may occur e.g., while searching for food or while cooking.
- Morning anorexia common.
- Psychological and interpersonal problems may result from SRED.
- F>M

Clinical Associations (ICSD2 & 3)

Sleep disorders:
- Sleepwalking most common; if SRED superimposed becomes part of the complex.
- RLS/PLMD.
- OSA.
- Circadian rhythm disorders.

Medication:
- BzRA's especailly Zolpidem.
- Triazolam as well as BZD's in general.
- Lithium as well as other psychoactive medications including atypical antipsychotic agents.
- Anticholinergics.

Behavioral factors:
- Cessation of cigarette smoking, alcohol, or substance abuse.
- Acute stress.
- Following dieting /weight reduction.
- May be seen with onset of narcolepsy.

PSG findings (ICSD2 & 3):
- Confusional arousals with or without eating, typically during SWS (may also occur in all stages of NREM and occasionally in REM).
- Associated sleep disorder e.g., OSA, PLMD.

Treatment:
a. Treat associated sleep disorders if present.
b. Counseling for precipitating/perpetuating problems .
c. Discontinue causitive medications where possible.
d. Medications empirically used to treat SRED have included:
   - Topiramate (Topamax) 25 - 150 mg at bedtime. See also report of trial using topiramate for SRED (*SLEEP* Sept 2020)
   - Zonisamide (Zonegran) 100 - 400 mg at bedtime.
   - Clonazepam (Klonopin).
   - Dopaminergic agents (especially where co-morbid RLS/PLMD).
   - SSRI's, GABA*, melatonin.*

   *obtained as dietary supplement.

REMember:
Differentiation SRED from nocturnal eating syndrome (NES)
- In NES subject overeats between the evening meal and bedtime
- Full wakefulness and recall present in NES during nightime binges
- Mood disorder more frequent with NES

REM SLEEP BEHAVIOR DISORDER (RBD)

Background:
- Lack of the expected REM sleep atonia in somatic muscles.
- Complex motor activity in response to a dream with violent or injurious consequences.

Demographics/Clinical Associations:
- Prevalence $\pm$ 0.5%.
- Affects mainly males > 50 years.
- Estimated that 2/3 of men with RBD will eventually develop Parkinsonism; 1/3 of newly diagnosed patients with Parkinsonism have RBD.
- Multicenter study of 1280 RBD patients (mean age 66.3 yrs; 82.5% males) showed 6.3% conversion rate per annum to an overt neurodegenerative disorder (*Brain* 2019; 142: 744-759).
- 60% cases idiopathic.
- PTSD (but not other psychiatric disorders) may be associated with RBD.
- Medical/neurologic associations:
    - Synucleinopathies in which insoluble alpha-synuclein protein accumulates in affected neurons:includes Parkinson's disease, dementia with Lewy bodies, multiple system atrophy.
    - Narcolepsy.
    - Other neurological conditions including brain stem neoplasms, ALS, Guillain-Barré syndrome, multiple sclerosis, cerebrovascular disease.

Clinical features:
- Abnormal behaviors during REM sleep associated with *increase* of muscle tone.
- Behaviors often violent and may be injurious to the subject or bedpartner.
- Behaviors usually occur in response to an unpleasant action-filled violent dream in which the subject is being attacked or threatened.
- The subject may awaken abruptly at the end of an episode and report dream recall with his/her action being in response to the observed dream behavior (*isomorphism*).
- The eyes are usually closed during an episode (cf sleepwalking).
- Sleepwalking uncommon during an episode of RBD but actions like yelling, punching, kicking, running etc may occur.

- Episodes of sleep-eating and abnormal sexual behaviors, which may occur with other parasomnias, usually do not occur with RBD.
- The first episode may occur ± 90 minutes into the sleep cycle but more commonly during the second half.
- May occur infrequently or nightly.

REMember:
In narcolepsy-associated RBD, the RBD episode may occur <u>early</u> in sleep cycle.

Pathophysiology:

Not clearly established; in normal REM, cholinergic impulses from pons act on medullary centers via the lateral tegmentoreticular tract to cause hyperpolarization of spinal motoneurons and muscle atonia. In RBD, these mechanisms may be disrupted (see page 4)..

Medication/substance- induced RBD:

- SSRIs.
- SNRIs especially venlafaxine (*Effexor*).
- Mirtazapine.
- MAOIs.
- TCAs.
- Abuse of EtOH, caffeine, amphetamines, cocaine.
- Sudden withdrawal of REM-suppressing agents may precipitate RBD:
  - EtOH
  - Antidepressants (TCAs)
  - SSRIs
  - MAOIs
  - Barbiturates
  - Amphetamines

REMember:
- Bupropion is not felt to be associated with RBD.
- ±75% RBD subjects have PLMS in NREM.
- RBD in children & adolescents usually associated with co-morbid pathology (e.g., narcolepsy, brainstem tumors, autism and psychotropic mediations).

PSG Findings:
- REM sleep without atonia.
- Abnormal REM sleep behaviors (video monitoring).
- Subclinical/preclinical RBD: if REM sleep without atonia detected and no history of RBD
  - 25% eventually manifest clinical RBD.
  - may have a neurodegenerative disorders associated with RBD.
- PLMS during NREM sleep (75%).

Management:
- Environmental safety. Remove dangerous objects from bedroom.
- Discontinue if possible agents which may have caused RBD.
- ? Bedpartner to separate bed till RBD controlled.
- Clonazepam (most widely used); 90% success reported.
- Other helpful agents may include:
  - Imipramine 25 mg h.s.
  - Carbamazepine 100 mg t.i.d.
  - Pramipexole, L-Dopa (especially if Parkinsonism present).
  - Melatonin (IR or SR).
  - Ramelteon (reports more succesful in RBD associated with PD and multiple system atrophy than idiopathic RBD. *JCSM* 2016; 12(5): 689-693).
  - Gabapentin or pregabalin (letter, *JCSM* 2016; 12(8): 1193).
  - Yokukansan (YKS) consisting of 7 herbal ingredients reported 70.6% success as monotherapy for RBD (*JCSM* 2019; 15(8): 1173-8).

Pseudo-RBD diagnosed when RBD - like symptoms caused by OSA with (severe) desaturation. PSG does not show REM atonia. Article in *Sleep Breath*. 2018: 22(3): 825-830 reports on ↑ prevalence of concomitant OSA RBD.

RBD Reviews

J Clin Sleep Med 2010; 6(1); 85-95. **Best Practices Guide for Treatment of REM Sleep Behavior Disorder** (Recommendations based on small case series and case reports; no randomized control trials):
- a Modifying the sleep environment for patients with sleep-related injury (level A).
- b. Clonazepam (level B); caution in patients with dementia, gait disorders, or concomitant OSA.
- c. Melatonin (level B);advantage of few side effects.
- d. Pramipexole (efficacy studies show contradictory results).
- e. Paroxetine -little evidence, success in 1 case series but also 1 report of paroxetine *causing* RBD.
- f. L-DOPA-limited role; little evidence to support use.
- g. Acetylcholinesterase inhibitors - limited data; consider in patients with synucleinopathy (level C).
- h. Very limited evidence, only a few subjects for zopiclone, benzodiazepines other than clonazepam, desipramine, clozapine, carbamazepine, sodium oxyate (levelC).

Rapid Eye Movement Sleep Behavior Disorder, *CHEST* 2017; 152(3): 650-662. Good review includes pathophysiology, clinical features and management.

JCSM 2011; 7(6): 639-644. Customized bed alarm effective in 4 RBD patients. Possible use for medically refractory cases.

RECURRENT ISOLATED SLEEP PARALYSIS

Clinical features:
- Sleep state dissociation with components of REM sleep persisting into wakefulness and resulting in an inability to use voluntary muscles.
- Ocular & respiratory muscles spared.
- May occur once in a lifetime in 40 - 50% of the normal population.
- Usually begins in teens; M=F; may occur several times a year.
- May occur at sleep onset (hypnagogic or predormital form) or on waking from sleep (hypnopompic or postdormital form).
- Episodes often frightening; last seconds to minutes; consciousness maintained.
- Visual, auditory or tactile hallucinations may be present.
- Episodes may end spontaneously or by the subject's own. stimulation (e.g., eye movements) or by being touched or spoken to.

Precipitating events/associations:
- sleep deprivation
- mental stress, social anxiety
- irregular sleep-wake schedules (e.g., jet lag, shift work)
- bipolar disorders
- anxiolytic medications
- poor sleep hygiene
- ↑ with supine sleep position

REMember:
- Sleep paralyses may be part of narcolepsy complex (in which case is not a separate diagnosis).

PSG :
PSG is characterized by dissociation of sleep states with alpha rhythm intrusion into REM sleep and persistence of REM atonia into wakefulness.

Management:
- Reassurance.
- Avoid precipitating factors.
- Medications:
  - anxiolytics prn.
  - REM suppressants (e.g., fluoxetine).

Further Reading: Sharpless & Klikova: Clinical features of Isolated Sleep Paralysis: *Sleep Medicine* 2019; 58: 102-106.

NIGHTMARE DISORDER

Definition
Unpleasant, frightening realistic dreams typically in REM sleep in second half of sleep period; often resulting in wakening oriented and alert with vivid recall and difficulty returning to sleep.

Demographics (ICSD2 & 3)
- 10 - 50% of children ages 3 – 5 years may have occasional nightmares.
- 50 - 85% of adults have occasional nightmares; in 2 - 8% nightmares recurrent.
- PTSD most common reason for recurrent nightmares.
- 80% of PTSD patients have nightmares within three months of the traumatic event; may persist throughout life.
- Nightmares due to Acute Stress Disorder (ASD) or PTSD more likely to occur in:
  – Females.
  – Lower socioeconomic and education levels.
  – History of psychopathology.
  – Personality traits such as schizoid or borderline personality disorder.
- Nightmares may result in mood/behavioral disturbance, cognitive impairment, emotional/social disruption and sleep resistance (e.g. bedtime anxiety/avoidance, fear of the dark).

Medications causing nightmares:
(Seen predominantly with anti-depressants and anti-hypertensives particularly beta blockers. Mechanism unclear but may involve imbalances between neurotransmitter systems.)

Antidepressants:
- TCAs.
- SSRIs
- SNRIs.
- Bupropion (*Wellbutrin*) - NE and DA uptake inhibitor.

Antihypertensives:
- Beta blockers:
    - Cause nightmares more frequently than other antihypertensives.
    - Atenolol may cause less nightmares than other beta blockers.
    - Beta blockers also a cause of insomnia.
- Alpha 2-agonists:
    - Clonidine (*Catapres*).
    - Methyldopa (*Aldomet*).
- Other antihypertensives:
    - Reserpine (blocks monamine neurotransmitters; rarely used today because of side effects).
    - Prazosin (*Minipress*); alpha-adrenergic blocking agent.

Hypnotics:
- BZDs (particularly triazolam).
- BzRAs (more often cause "abnormal dreams.")
- Barbiturates.
- Chloral hydrate.

Stimulant medications - During chronic use and also withdrawal.

Antiparkinsonian drugs (more often "abnormal dreams").
- Levodopa (*Sinemet*).
- Ropinirole (*Requip*).
- Pramipexole (*Mirapex*).

Antipsychotics (first and second generation).

Antimicrobials.
- Erythromycin.
- Hydroxychloroquine (*Plaquenil*).
- Quinolones e.g., levofloxacin (*Levaquin*), ciprofloxacin (*Cipro*)
- Antiviral agents:
    - Zanamivir (*Relenza*); gancyclovir

Withdrawal of REM-suppression agents.
- Barbiturates.
- BZDs.
- Antidepressants (TCAs, SSRIs, MAOIs).
- Stimulants.
- Alcohol (also with acute use).

Miscellaneous:
- Buspirone (*BuSpar*).
- Varenicline (*Chantix*).

- Amiodarone (*Cordarone, Pacerone*).
- Monteleukast (*Singulair*)-may cause "dream abnormalities."
- Donepezil (*Aricept*)-disturbing dreams.

REMember:

- Alcohol and certain medications (e.g. antidepressants) may cause nightmares during use *and* following abrupt withdrawal.

- Nightmares due to PTSD may occur in REM or NREM sleep.

Differential Diagnosis:

Sleep Terrors vs Nightmares

SLEEP TERROR	NIGHTMARE
Aroused from N3 during the first third of sleep.	Associated with REM; latter part of the night.
Vocalizations common and intense.	Vocalizations rare.
Movements (e.g., sitting up, getting out of bed common).	Limited mobility.
Autonomic discharge severe and intense.	Limited autonomic discharge.
Scanty mental content; subsequent amnesia.	Vivid content, clear recall.
Arousal difficult.	Often full awakening with event.
Often usually inconsolable.	Consolable.
Confused/disoriented on waking.	Subject alert and oriented.

Management:

Position paper for the Treatment of Nightmare Disorder in Adults: an American Academy of Sleep Medicine Position Paper *J. Clin Sleep Med* 2018; 14 (6): 1041-1055.

(Note: this position paper replaces the Best Practice Guide for the Treatment of Nightmare Disorder in Adults. *J.Clin Sleep Med* 2010; 6 (4): 389-401. The paper is a Position Paper as opposed to a practice guideline "due to the limited direct evidence for many of the available treatment options.")

Therapeutic approaches include behavioral and psychological approaches as well as pharmacological options. Treatment approaches may also depend on whether nightmares are associated with PTSD.

Summary
- Image rehearsal therapy (altering nightmare content with a set of positive images and daily rehearsing new dream scenarios). Recommended for PTSD-associated nightmares and nightmare disorder.
- Other behavioral therapy is for PTSD-associated nightmares may include CBT, CBT-I, eye movement therapies; exposure, relaxation and reception therapies (see position paper for details).
- Behavioral therapies for nightmare disorder may include CBT, hypnosis, lucid dreaming therapy, desensitization, etc (see position paper for details).
- Pharmacotherapy: Summary of agents used/studied:
  (a) for PTSD-associated nightmares:
    - atypical antipsychotics olanzapine, rispiradone, aripiprazole.
    - clonidine, cyproheptadine, fluvoxamine, gabapentin, nabilone, phenelzine, prazosin, topiramate, trazodone, TCAs.
  (b) for nightmare disorders:
    - nitrazepam, prazosin, triazolam.

Note:

(1) Prazosin only common drug recommended for both PTSD-associated nightmares and nightmare disorder.

(2) See details of each drug's studies with success notes and safety profile in the position paper.

(3) Venlafaxine and clonazepam not recommended for nightmare treatment.

(4) Other measures from 2010 Best Practice Guidelines include:
  - Management of comorbid psychopathology
  - Discontinuation of medications causing nightmares
  - Prazosin (Average dose 3 mg: range 1-10mg) was the only level A recommendation; clonidine (0.2-0.6 mg in divided doses) was level C.
  - Other agents were low-grade due to sparse data.

REMember:

- Nightmares rarely seen in sleep laboratory.
- PSG not usually indicated; may be useful to exclude other disorders such as RBD.
- RBDs seen more frequent in late middle-aged males, associated with violent or explosive behavior and nocturnal injuries which are not usually seen with nightmares.

New approach: FDA approved *Nightware* app for PTSD nightmares. Detection of increased HR and body movement → vibration ↑ to end dream state. Needs prescription and should be used with prescribed medications (i.e., not stand alone Rx).

SLEEP ENURESIS:

Diagnostic Criteria:

Diagnosed if > 5years and nocturnal involuntary voiding at least *twice a week* for $\geq$ 3 months.
- *Primary* if had *never* been consistently dry.
- *Secondary* if *previously* consistently dry during sleep for at least *six months*.

Demographics/Etiology:

- Prevalence $\pm$ 30% in 4 year olds, boys > girls.
- Spontaneous remission 15% per annum (prevalence, 5% age 10 years, and 1 - 2% in 18 year olds).
- More common in ADHD, if recent significant psychological stress and with OSA.
- Suspect organic etiology in children if involuntary voiding also during *wakefulness*.
  - o Diabetes mellitus or insipidus.
  - o Urinary tract disorders.
  - o Nocturnal epilepsy.
  - o Neurologic disorders involving bladder.
- <u>Adults</u>: organic pathology usually present including above causes & also

OSA	Chronic constipation
Prostatism	Caffeine, diuretics
Dementia	Lithium side effect
- Seen in $\pm$ 2% of elderly population (F>M)

PSG not indicated except to rule out associated sleep disorder (e.g., OSA).

Pediatric Management:

A. Nonpharmacologic approaches:
- Motivational therapy (reward commensurate with duration of dryness).
- Bladder training; requires a highly motivated child.
- Fluid management.
- Enuresis alarms.
- Alarm clocks (waking time determined during a 1 - 3 week trial period).

B. Pharmacologic therapy.
- Desmopressin (DDAVP): administered orally in late evening.
- TCAs: imipramine used most frequently, though amitriptyline and desipramine are also prescribed. Use of TCAs no longer recommended by some authorities; carry FDA black-box warning regarding the possibility of increased suicidality.

In adults, management targeted to underlying cause.

VIOLENT PARASOMNIAS

Clinical features:

- Parasomnias causing violence/injuries to self or to others.
- Not a separate ICSD category but acknowledged to affect 2.1% of adolescents and adults with male predominance (ICSD2 p138).
- May be associated with specific sleep disorders, organic neurologic disorders or psychogenic disorders during sleep, or may even be due to malingering.
- Sleep-related violence usually occurs without apparent awareness and could be described as an automatic behavior (automatism).
- Consequences:
    Homicide or attempted homicide
    Murders
    Suicide
    Injury during sleep walking or other parasomnias
    Inappropriate sexual behavior (sexomnia)

Classification:
(modified after *Principles and Practice of Sleep Medicine* 4th Edition p961):

a. Sleep disorders:
    i. Parasomnias –disorders of arousal in NREM.
    ii. RBD.
    iii. Nocturnal seizures.
    iv. Automatic behaviors associated with narcolepsy, sleep apnea, or sleep deprivation.

b. Organic neurologic disorders.
    i. Vascular or mass lesions.
    ii. Toxic/metabolic causes including drugs and alcohol.
    iii. Infections.
    iv. Head trauma.
    v. Seizures.

c. Psychogenic disorders:
    i.   Fugues.
    ii. Multiple-personality disorder.
    iii. PTSD.

d. Malingering.

e. Munchausen syndrome by proxy (child injury induced by an adult).

Further reading/references:
- Cramer Bornemann et al: A review of Sleep Related Violence. *CHEST* 2019; 155(5): 1059-1066. Point made that SRV mostly associated with disorders of arousal and "represent a condition of state dissociation resulting from the simultaneous occurrence of wakefulness and NREM sleep" in different parts of the brain. Stress may be a trigger.
- Cramer Bornemann et al: Parasomnias, Clinical features and Forensic Implications *CHEST* 2006; 130: 605-610

SEXSOMNIA

Not a separate ICSD category but "atypical sexual behavior during sleep" regarded as a subtype of the NREM confusional arousal parasomnia (ICSD3 p. 232). Dubessy et al (*SLEEP* 2017; 40 (2): 1-8) describe **sexomnia** as an "amnestic sexual behavior during sleep." Study included 17 cases, mostly males, having an association with other non-REM parasomnias (sleepwalking and night terrors) and with forensic, personal and interpersonal consequences.

Summary of review article:

Schenck C et al: Sleep and Sex: What Can Go Wrong? A Review of the Literature on Sleep Related Disorders and Abnormal Sexual Behaviors and Experiences *SLEEP* 2007; 30(6):683 – 702. The authors review the current literature on "sexsomnia" and include a proposed classification.

1. **Symptoms** may include painful erections, sleep-related dissociative disorders (see below), nocturnal psychotic disorders, masturbation, sexual vocalizations, fondling, sexual intercourse, sexual assaults/rape, and ictal phenomena (sexual hyperarousal or orgasm).

2. **Classification** (Note: conditions included often based on case reports where sexual behavior described in conjunction with the underlying condition).

I. Parasomnias with abnormal sleep-related sexual behaviors.
   a. Confusional arousals (with or without OSA).
   b. Sleepwalking.
   c. RBD (diagnosis made by history in three cases and not borne out with PSG monitoring).

II. Sleep-related sexual seizures (e.g., masturbation, orgasm, automatisms).

III. Sleep disorders with abnormal sexual behaviors during wakefulness and sleep/wake transitions.
   a. Klein-Levin Syndrome.
   b. Severe chronic insomnia ($\uparrow$ libido, compulsive sexual behaviors).
   c. Restless leg syndrome (masturbation, pelvic thrusting).

IV. Special clinical considerations.
   a. Narcolepsy (perceived sexual assault during hypnagogic or hypnopompic hallucinations; cataplectic orgasm).
   b. Sleep exacerbation of persistent sexual-arousal syndrome: sexual arousals intensified by sleep.
   c. Sleep-related painful erections and increased sexual activity.
   d. Sleep-related dissociative disorders: sexual behavior occurs while actually in an awake dissociative state.
   e. Nocturnal psychotic disorders: sexual delusions and hallucinations which may or may not be sleep related.
   f. Hypersexuality after nocturnal awakenings (single case report).
   g. Miscellaneous e.g., REM-sleep erections and sexual vulnerability; medication induced states: mainly zolpidem and sodium oxybate (*Xyrem*).

3. **Management principles.**
   - Bed partner's evaluation is important.
   - *Careful documentation* important in view of the forensic issues involved.
   - Consider screening psychological testing.
   - Time synchronized video-PSG with seizure montage strongly recommended. (Monitoring for sleep-related erections is not recommended.)
   - Discontinue medications felt to be cause of abnormal sexual behavior.
   - Treat co-morbid seizure or sleep disorders.
   - Hypersexuality in KLS usually no reported effective therapy.

FYI: Case report: Resolution of sexomnia with paroxetine. (JCSM 2020; 16(7) : 1213-4 Mechanism may be due to increase in serotonin which may decrease sexual function.

EXPLODING HEAD SYNDROME:

- Sudden loud noise in sleep-wake transition: "like a bomb, explosion, gunshot etc" → arousal, no pain but often fright.

- Rare, ? ↑ with stress, generally good prognosis → reassurance.

- Treat associated sleep disorders first (see case report- Nagayama et al, JCSM 2021; 1(1):103-6). Report also mentions TCAs, calcium channel blockers and anticonvulsants used effectively in other reports.

Test Your Memory (Section 8):

1. In Recurrent Isolated Sleep Paralysis, which statement is correct?
   a. Not seen in the normal population.
   b. Ocular muscles typically affected.
   c. Associated with prone sleep.
   d. Awareness during episode.
   e. Female predominance.

2. Sleepwalking has many associations. Which statement is incorrect?
   a. May be precipitated by a febrile illness.
   b. Strong association with sleep deprivation.
   c. Family history uncommon.
   d. Psychoactive medications (e.g., lithium) may precipitate an episode.
   e. Eyes are usually open during an episode.

3. RBD has a clinical association with the following except:
   a. PTSD.
   b. Narcolepsy.
   c. Parkinsonism.
   d. Dementia with Lewy bodies.
   e. Depression.

4. Nightmares may be differentiated from sleep terrors by the following clinical features except:

    a. Nightmares usually occur later in the sleep cycle.
    b. Vocalization more common in nightmares.
    c. Recall more frequent with nightmares.
    d. Confusion on waking with sleep terrors; usually not with nightmares.
    e. Autonomic features are more common with sleep terrors.

5. In Sleep Related Eating Disorder (SRED), which statement is true?

    a. Event typically occurs just prior to bedtime.
    b. Subjects typically seek their favorite foods.
    c. Condition may be associated with hypnotic use.
    d. Ready recall of the event.
    e. No association with other sleep disorders.

6. Which medication recommended for both nightmare disorder and PTSD?

    a. triazolam
    b. prazosin
    c. trazodone
    d. clonazepam
    e. fluvoxamine

Answers: 1d, 2c, 3e, 4b, 5c, 6b.

Section 9:

SLEEP-RELATED MOVEMENT DISORDERS

Definition:

Sleep-related movement disorders include conditions which result in relative simple stereotyped movements which disrupt sleep and result in daytime symptoms such as sleepiness or fatigue (ICSD3).

The disorders most often encountered include
- Restless leg syndrome
- Periodic Limb Movement Disorder
- Sleep Related Rhythmic Movement Disorder (body rocking, head banging, etc)
- Sleep-Related Bruxism

See ICSD3 for additional conditions in this category.

RESTLESS LEG SYNDROME
(Willis-Ekbom disease)

Diagnostic criteria

Four essential features:
1. Urge to move the legs, usually associated with paresthesias or dysesthesias described in varying terms (e.g., creepy, crawly sensations, itching under the skin, electric-like shocks. Often difficult to describe sensation. Painful sensations less frequent).
2. Symptoms occur with or exacerbated by rest.
3. Relief with movement.
4. Worse in the evenings or night-time.

Note: With disease progression, symptoms may begin earlier in the day, sometimes progressing to symptoms throughout the day.

Demographics

- Prevalence ±7-10% in U.S. and N. Europe (Caucasians > African-Americans). Less prevalent in Mediterranean, Middle Eastern, and Asian areas.
- 65% subjects age onset <40yrs; symptoms often initially intermittent, become progressive before seeking treatment.
- F 1.5-2x > M.
- Familial predisposition especially with onset < 45 years.
- Genetic risk factors found in both population based and familial studies.
- Onset in older ages is often associated with a neuropathy and faster disease progression.

Pathophysiology

- Abnormalities of cellular iron transport and of dopaminergic function.
- Improvement with iron supplements and dopaminergic agents supports this hypothesis.
- Iron necessary for dopamine synthesis; acts as cofactor for tyrosine hydroxylase, an enzyme needed for dopamine synthesis.
- RLS patients have ↓ iron stores in substantia nigra and ↓ CSF ferritin and ↑ CSF transferrin levels.
- Iron & dopamine levels have circadian pattern falling at night.

Conditions Associated with RLS:

- Pregnancy.
- Iron deficiency.
- Neurologic disorders:
    a. Peripheral neuropathy including diabetic neuropathy.
    b. Spinal stenosis.
    c. Parkinsonism.
    d. M.S. (*JCSM* 2015; 11(5): 553-7).
- End-stage renal disease.
- Venous insufficiency lower extremities.
- Vitamin & mineral deficiencies (e.g., ↓ magnesium).
- Possibly with rheumatoid artritis, Sjogren's syndrome.
- COPD (Lo Coco et al; *Sleep Med* 2009;10:572).
- ↑ prevalence reported in postural orthostatic tachycardic syndrome (POTS). *JCSM* 2021; 17(4): 791-5.

Drugs which may precipitate/aggravate RLS

- Antidepressants.
  - SSRIs.
  - SNRIs.
  - TCAs.
  - Mirtazapine (*Remeron*).
- Lithium.
- Dopamine antagonists:
  - Antiemetics e.g., metoclopramide (*Reglan*), prochlorperazine (*Compazine*)
  - Antipsychotics/major tranquilizers
- Older/sedating antihistamines ~ e.g., diphenhydramine (*Benadryl*)
- Calcium channel antagonists ~ e.g., nifedipine, diltiazem, verapamil
- Tramadol (*Ultram*)
- Methylxanthines
- Corticosteroids
- Opioid, BZD withdrawal
- "Social" agents
  - caffeine
  - nicotine
  - alcohol
- HRT

REMember:
- Bupropion does not cause RLS
- RLS symptoms may be precipitated by medication withdrawal, especially opioids and BZDs.
- ↑psychopathology in RLS patients: depression, GAD, PTSD, ADHD.
- ↑risk CVD, CAD, HT in secondary RLS (associated with anemia, pregnancy, renal failure). *JCSM* 2015; 38(7): 1009-15.

Laboratory testing

- PSG: Not indicated for diagnosis of RLS. May, however, show evidence of PLMs (>15/hr) in up to 80 – 90% of RLS patients.
- Serum ferritin level (<50 μg/L an indication for iron replacement therapy).
- As indicated to evaluate for secondary causes (e.g., renal function, CBC).
- Tests to aid in different diagnosis, e.g., EMG, MRI spine.

Management

- Lifestyle changes: avoid exacerbators/precipitators such as caffeine, alcohol, nicotine, and OTC medications. Avoid sleep deprivation.
- Iron replacement therapy as needed.
- Medications (most used "off-label"). Drugs listed with an * are FDA approved for RLS.
  - a. Dopaminergic agents (90% efficacy).
    - Ropinirole (*Requip**), 0.25-4mg ± 2hr HS. Start low dose; ↑ dose q4-7 days.
    - Pramipexole (*Mirapex**), 0.125-0.5mg ± 2hr HS. Start low dose; ↑ dose q4-7 days.
    - Levodopa/carbidopa (*Sinemet*).
    - Pergolide (ergot derivative with risk of pleural, pericardial, and retroperitoneal fibrosis). No longer available in USA, not recomended.
    - Rotigotine patch (*Neupro*)*; 1-3mg/24hr.
  - b. $\alpha 2 \delta$ Ligands.
    - Gabapentin (*Neurontin*).
    - Pregabalin (*Lyrica*).
    - Gabapentin enacarbil (*Horizant*)* 600mg with food at ±5pm; ↓ to 300mg if renal dysfunction.
  - c. Benzodiazepine receptor agonists.
    - BZDs especially clonazepam (*Klonopin*).
    - BzRAs (e.g. zolpidem).
  - d. Opioids e.g., oxycodone, hydrocodone, codeine, tramadol, methadone.
- Treatment RLS and depression (Picchetti & Winkelman *SLEEP* 2005;28(7):891-898)
  - treat RLS first if depression mild
  - if AD's needed, Rx bupropion (am dosing to avoid insomnia)
  - consider switch SSRI to bupropion
  - if persistent insomnia, Rx trazodone, BzRA or gabapentin
  - if RLS persists on AD's, add standard therapy for RLS (see above)

Summary of Recommendations from the International Restless Legs Syndrome Study Group (IRLSSG) Task Force (2013).

- Initial treatment: dopamine-receptor agonists (pramipexole, ropinerole, rotigotine) or an $\alpha 2 \delta$ ligand (gabapentin enacarbil, pregabalin). Choice of specific agent should be based on individual patients circumstances:

  e.g., For patients who have simultaneous troublesome daytime symptoms, consider initial treatment with a long-acting agent (vs multiple doses of a short-acting agent).

e.g., For patients who have severe co-morbid insomnia (disproportionate for their RLS), co-morbid pain or an impulse control disorder consider an α 2 δ ligand.

- If loss of efficacy:

  - Review and correct lifestyle changes or new medications that could aggravate or precipitate RLS.
  - Check serum ferritin level (if not yet done) for concentration < 75 mcg/mL supplement with iron (other authorities recommend supplemental iron for ferritin levels < 50 mcg/ml).
  - Increase dose (with careful monitoring for side effects or augmentation) or add or substitute with an alternative medication.

- Augmentation:

  - Progressive, symptomatic worsening of RLS symptoms.
  - Onset may occur earlier during the day.
  - Occurs with prolonged use of medications, particularly the dopaminergics and especially with levodopa.
  - Previously uninvolved body parts may be affected (e.g. arms).
  - IRLSSG Task Force suggests that if the patient is on a short-acting dopaminergic medication, an earlier dose could be added or the medication switched to a single dose of a longer-acting dopaminergic or other medication. Close monitoring for increased augmentation advised, particularly if dopaminergic medication increased.
  - For persistent augmentation, switch to an alternative medication.
  - Supplemental iron if ferritin <75mcg/ml.

- If comorbid insomnia persists, consider adding a short-acting GABA-active hypnotic or an α 2 δ ligand (if not yet used).

- For severe refractory RLS: low dose methadone.

- If impulse control disorder occurs on a dopaminergic agent, reduce dose or switch to alternative medication.

- Pregnancy: avoid all pharmacologics; replenish iron stores.

From The AASM Clinical Practice Guideline *SLEEP* **2012; 35(8): 1039-1062**

Comments Regarding Individual Agents:

1. Pramipexole (*Mirapex*).
   - Common side effects include nausea and somnolence which decrease over time.
   - Augmentation reported to occur in up to one third of patients with extended use, although other studies have reported no augmentation after 9 to 12 months use.

2. Ropinirole (*Requip*).
   - Augmentation reported between 0% and 2.3%.

3. Levodopa/carbidopa (*Sinemet*).
   - High risk of augmentation.
   - Levodopa/carbidopa may be the most advantageous for those patients with intermittent RLS symptoms that do not require daily therapy.

4. Cabergoline (*Dostinex*).
   - Cabergoline primarily indicated in treatment of prolactinoma with associated risk of visual field loss.
   - Risk also includes valvular heart disease; use only where other agents have been tried and failed.
   - Average effective dose 2 mg - 3 mg before bedtime. Studies show significant improvement.

5. Opioids.
   - May be effective where other agents have failed.
   - Abuse potential; could worsen OSA.

6. Gabapentin (*Neurontin*).
   - May be useful in patients with both RLS symptoms and pain.

7. Clonidine (*Catapres*).
   - Data not strong; risk of side effects (e.g., dry mouth, lightheadedness, hypotension, somnolence, headache, decreased libido).
   - May be appropriate to treat hypertension and RLS concomitantly.

8. Iron supplementation.
   - May be effective in patients with iron deficiency or refractory RLS.
   - IV iron dextran reported to "dramatically improve refractory RLS" but with inconsistent results and risk of anaphylactic reaction.
   - Oral iron replacement preferentially recommended.

Antidepressants and RLS:

- Studies show conflicting data.
- One study found men to have increased risk of RLS, particularly with citalopram, paroxetine, and amitriptyline.
- Fluoxetine found to show increased risk for RLS in women.
- Higher odds ratio when tramadol and dopamine-blocking agents used concomitantly.
- 8% - 28% RLS with mirtazapine use in two separate studies.
- Two studies with 243 and 200 patients in each study showed no significant association with antidepressant use and RLS.

Nonpharmacologic Therapy:

- "Insufficient evidence to evaluate use of strategies including sleep hygiene, behavioral and stimulation therapies, compression devices, exercise, and nutritional considerations."

Secondary RLS and Special Patient Groups: "Insufficient evidence on the effectiveness of any one therapy or balance of benefits to harm."

1. End-stage renal disease:
   - Agents used have included gabapentin, IV iron dextran, ropinirole, pramipexole, erythropoietin, levodopa, clonidine, clonazepam. Improvement may occur following kidney transplantation.

2. Neuropathy:
   - Pregabalin reported to be successful in one study.

3. Superficial venous insufficiency:
   - Improvement shown in patients with superficial venous insufficiency and severe RLS with endovenous laser ablation.
   - Intravenous sclerotherapy shown to have 98% improvement in RLS symptoms in a second study.

Therapies for PLMD:

- Insufficient evidence to make a recommendation for pharmacological therapy in patients diagnosed with PLMD alone. Agents reported to show improvement in clinical criteria in PLMD (with or without associated RLS and periodic limb movements during wakefulness) include pramipexole, ropinirole, rotigotine, gabapentin, pregabalin, clonazepam 1 mg, melatonin 3 mg 30 minutes prior to bedtime, low-dose valproate (125 mg - 600 mg at bedtime), and selegiline. All of these medications, however, have a NO RECOMMENDATION category.

REMember:

- In refractory cases, **combination therapy** may be necessary.
- Bupropion is dopaminergic and may benefit RLS treatment.
- **Periodic leg movements of wakefulness (PLMW)**
  - document during a 1hr recording prior to a standard PSG.
  - subject sits awake with legs outstretched. (Suggested Immobilization Test.)
  - RLS diagnosis supported by PLMW index of ≥ 40/hour.
- **Compulsive behavior** is an uncommon complication of dopamine agonists. Includes compulsive gambling, shopping, and hypersexuality. F>M. May be dose related. ?↓dose. (± combination therapy) or switch medication (IRLSSG).
- No medication recommendations in children. (For Pediatric RLS see Section 12.)
- RLS in pregnancy: avoid pharmalogic Rx., consider lifestyle issues, (e.g., caffeine consumption), replete iron stores.
- Since $\alpha 2 \delta$ not associated with augmentation, intenational guide-lines suggest an $\alpha 2 \delta$ agent as initial treatment for RLS. Wanner et al; *Adv Phar* 2019;84;187-205

Summary of Recommendations for Prevention and Treatment of RLS Augmentation (Combined Task Force of the IRLSSG, EURLSSG, and the RLS-Foundation). *SLEEP MED* 2016; 21:1-11.

1. May occur with dopaminergic agents over time. Incidence highest with levodopa and possibly higher for short-acting dopaminergic agents compared with longer acting dopamine agonists (cabergoline, rotigotine).

2. For **prevention** of augmentation consider using an alpha-2-delta ligand, use lowest possible dopaminergic dose, consider non-daily treatment if possible (e.g., where symptoms occur infrequently), intermittently attempt to reduce the dose or even discontinue the medication. Avoid exceeding maximum recommended dose. Replenish iron stores if necessary (ferritin level less than 50-75 μg/mL).

3. For **treatment** of augmentation:
   - Evaluate and correct for exacerbating factors including reduced serum ferritin levels, lifestyle changes (e.g., sleep deprivation or

alcohol use), introduction of medications predisposing to RLS (e.g., anti-histamines or anti-depressants), discontinuation of opioid medications or development of anemia.

- For mild augmentation could try splitting the dose, advancing timing or even increasing the dose (usually the earlier dose).

- If above strategy fails, consider switching to an alpha-2-delta calcium-channel ligand (pregabalin, gabapentin enacarbil) or to a long-acting dopaminergic agent e.g., rotigotine which has slightly less risk for augmentation than other dopaminergies. Dopaminergic agents should be tapered before discontinuing.

- Consider a 10-day washout. After weaning off the dopaminergic agent, evaluate response without medications. (Need to be alert for transient extremely severe RLS symptoms and marked insomnia during washout.)

- If all above measures fail and patient continues with severe symptoms, which may be 24/7, consider treating with a low dose opioid (e.g. prolonged release oxycodone or methadone).

- Evaluate for anemia.Consider treating with oral or intravenous iron as appropriate in conjunction with other measures. (Ferritin <50-75μg or transferrin saturation <20%).

Further reading:

• Willis-Ekbom Disease Foundation Revised Consensus Statement on the Management of Restless Leg Syndrome. Silber et al, *Mayo Clin Proc* 2013; 88(9): 977-986.

• Romero-Peralta et al: Emerging concepts of the Pathophysiology and Adverse Outcomes of RLS (*CHEST* 2020; 158(3):1218-1229. (Good review; Includes treatment)

Novel approach: Neuromodulation therapy - A wearable device for refractory RLS. Given FDA Breakthrough Device Designation. (June 2020).

PERIODIC LIMB MOVEMENT DISORDER (PLMD)

Diagnostic criteria

- PLMD is a condition where periodic episodes of repetitive stereotyped limb movements in sleep (periodic limb movements of sleep, PLMS) occur to **cause sleep-related symptoms.** (PLMD not diagnosed if only asymptomatic PLMS).

- Symptoms include insomnia, unrefreshing sleep, and/or daytime dysfunction.

- Symptoms are not explained by another sleep disorder.

Clinical Features:

- Insomnia, unrefreshing sleep and EDS.

- Severity may vary night to night; clinical impact therefore variable.

- Often no clinical correlation with frequency of movements.

- PLMS mainly in lower extremities with extension of the big toe(s) and dorsiflexion ankle(s). Knees and hips may also be affected.

- Movements may disrupt bedpartner's sleep.

- Increased prevalence with age (up to 34% > 60 years); M = F.

- PLMS commonly associated with three primary sleep disorders:
  - RLS: 80 - 90%
  - RBD: ±70%.
  - Narcolepsy: 45-65%.

REMember:

a. Where PLMS found to be co-morbid with the above conditions, daytime symptoms or other cognitive abnormalities should <u>not</u> be ascribed to PLMD. Diagnosis of PLMD is not made unless they persist <u>after</u> treatment for the other sleep disorders.

b. PLMS seen in 80-90% of RLS patients; supports diagnosis of RLS (*SLEEP* 2012; vol 35 p1039)

Other conditions associated with PLMS:

- Pregnancy

- Anemia

- Renal failure

- Neurologic disorders e.g., Parkinsonism, neuropathies, spinal cord injury

- Psychopathology e.g., depression, ADD

- Rheumatoid arthritis

- Drug/alcohol use or withdrawal.

- Medications causing PLMS virtually identical to those precipitating RLS.

REMember:

Bupropion not considered a cause of PLMD.

Pathophysiology:

- Dopaminergic impairment similar to that of RLS.

PSG Criteria:

- Minimum of 4 consecutive leg movements separated by at least 5-90 seconds.

- Leg movements on two different legs separated by < 5 seconds counted as a single movement.

- Minimum duration of a leg movement is 0.5 seconds and maximum duration 10 seconds.

- Minimum amplitude is an 8 μV ↑ in EMG voltage above resting EMG.

- PLMs more frequent in N2 sleep; less in N3, and usually absent in REM, except with RBD.

- Because of variability in PLMS, a single negative PSG does not exclude a diagnosis of PLMD.

REMember:

PLM index ≤15/hr regarded as normal in adults and
≤5/hr in children.

Management:

- Treat the PLMS where unrefreshing sleep and EDS felt to be on the basis of PLMD.
- Treatment for associated RLS as indicated.
- If possible,discontinue medications felt to be responsible for PLMD.
- Supplemental iron as needed (check serum ferritin levels).
- Consider dopamine agonist (FDA approval is however for RLS). No AASM guidleins for treatment PLMS as data scarce (see above, Practice Parameter article for treatment of RLS).

SLEEP RELATED RHYTHMIC MOVEMENT DISORDER (RMD)

(Body rocking, head banging, head rolling, jactatio capitis nocturna)

Clinical features:

- Repetitive stereotyped rhythmic motor behaviors during drowsiness and sleep involving larger muscle groups; usually of head, trunk or extremities.
- Includes body rocking (most frequent), head banging/rolling or combinations.
- Onset infancy or early childhood.
- Prevalence: almost 60% in infants 9 months; declines to 5% by 5 years.
- Persistence into later childhood or adolescence may be associated with mental disorders or emotional disturbances. Persistence into adulthood rare.
- Typically seen near sleep onset/transition; may occur at any time during sleep.
- Movements seen in healthy children; considered a sleep disorder only when sleep impaired, daytime function affected or bodily injury occurs.

Management:

- Ensure a safe sleep envioronment e.g., padded headboard.
- Medications: empiric use of TCAs.

SLEEP-RELATED BRUXISM

Clinical features

- Contractions during sleep of muscles of mastication.
- May be isolated and sustained (tonic), or repetitive (rhythmic).
- Usually begins in childhood ($\pm$15% prevalence); $\downarrow$ with age. Familial pattern may be present.
- May be primary or secondary to conditions such as mental retardation or neurological disease (e.g., cerebral palsy).
- Anxiety/"stress", caffeine or alcohol may increase risk in adults.
- May result in abnormal tooth wear, TMJ pains, or temporal headaches. Insomnia occasionally precipitated.
- Episodes of bruxism may disturb bed partner's sleep.

PSG

- Typical EMG artifact in EEG derivations in either a phasic pattern lasting 0.25 - 2 seconds or tonic activity lasting longer than 2 seconds, or a mixed pattern (see figure page 31).

Management

- Dental evaluation important. Dental appliance/ splints protect teeth and reduce episodes. Correction of malocclusion as indicated.
- Lifestyle changes, stress management as indicated
- Short-term use of medications for muscle spasm or pain.

Review article: Sleep Bruxism in Respiratory Medicine Practice. Mayer et al: *CHEST* 2016; 149 (1): 262-271.

Article reviews sleep bruxism (SB) including its etiology, mechanisms, and diagnosis. The article points out that SB could be primary or comorbid with several sleep related disorders including OSA and RBD. Management is discussed and the article also indicates that "SB management with a maxillary-palatal occlusal splint may aggravate sleep apnea." Where SB is comorbid with SDB, "a CPAP or mandibular advancement appliance in a forward or titrated position are indicated." CPAP treatment may "decrease SB in patients with both OSA and SB."

Further reading/references:

Gamaldo C & Early C: Restless Leg Syndrome; A Clinical Update *CHEST* 2006;130:1596-1604.

Salas RE, et al All the Wrong Moves: A Clinical Review of Restless Legs Syndrome, Periodic Limb Movements of Sleep and Wake, and Periodic Limb Movement Disorder. *Clin Chest Med* 2010;31:383-395.

Silber M et al An Algorithm for the Management of Restless Leg Syndrome *Mayo Clinic Proc* 2004; 79(7): 916-922.

Allen et al Comparison of Pregabalin with Pramipexole for Restless Legs Syndrome *N Engl J Med* 2014;370:621-631.

Test Your Memory (Section 9):

1. Which of the following may be considered a diagnostic criterion for RLS?

   a. Demonstration of PLMS during an overnight PSG.
   b. Demonstration of a PLM of wakefulness index ≥ 40/hr. during a 1 hour recording prior to a standard PSG.
   c. Ferritin level $< 50\,\mu g/L$.
   d. Relief of symptoms following a therapeutic trial of a dopamine agonist.
   e. Relief of symptoms with movement.

2. Lab data in RLS may include:

   a. serum ferritin $\leq 50\,\mu g/L$
   b. ↑ CSF transferrin levels.
   c. ↓ CSF ferritin levels.
   d. a and b.
   e. a, b, and c.

3. Which of the following medications is generally considered not to precipitate symptoms of RLS?

   a. SSRIs.
   b. TCAs.
   c. Lithium.
   d. Bupropion.
   e. Sedating antihistamines.

4. Conditions considered to be associated with PLMS include all of the following except:

    a. Pregnancy.
    b. COPD.
    c. Chronic renal failure.
    d. Anemia.
    e. Rheumatoid arthritis.

5. FDA-approved medications for the treatment of PLMD include:

    a. Gabapentin (Neurontin).
    b. Carbidopa/levodopa.
    c. Gabapentin enacarbil (Horizant).
    d. Clonazepam.
    e. None of the above.

6. Sleep related Rhythmic Movement Disorder in seen most frequently between the ages of:

    a.   3 months - 9months
    b. 6 months - 2 years.
    c. 9 months - 5 years.
    d. 9 months - 10 years.
    e. 18 months - 10 years.

7. Among the following agents, which has the highest propensity to cause augmentation?

    a. levodipa/carbidopa.
    b. pramipexole.
    c. gabapentin.
    d. clonidine.
    e. ropinerole.

Answers: 1e, 2e, 3d, 4b, 5e, 6c, 7a.

Section 10:

SLEEP-RELATED BREATHING DISORDERS IN ADULTS

Section 10 describes:

Obstructive Sleep Apnea Syndrome

- A review of OSA (including pathogenesis, risk factors, complications and management).

- Summaries of Practice Parameters and special articles published in *SLEEP* and the *Journal of Clinical Sleep Medicine* (JCSM).

Central Sleep Apnea Syndromes

- Primary Central Sleep Apnea Syndrome

- Cheyne Stokes Breathing (CSB)

- Treatment-emergent CSA (Complex Sleep Apnea)

- CSA due to Medication or Substance

- Central Apneas in Hypercapnic Disorders

Sleep Related Hypoventilation/hypoxemic Syndromes

- Idiopathic Central Alveolar Hypoventilation Syndrome

- Obesity Hypoventilation Syndrome

- Post Polio Syndrome

Snoring and Catathrenia

The reader is referred to ICSD3 page 49 for an extended classification of the Sleep-Related Breathing Disorders.

Pediatric SDB is covered in section 12.

OBSTRUCTIVE SLEEP APNEA SYNDROME

Definition:
OSA is characterized by repetitive episodes of complete (apnea) or partial (hypopnea) upper airway obstruction occurring during sleep. These events often result in reductions in blood oxygen saturation and are usually terminated by brief arousals from sleep. (ICSD3)

Prevalence (middle-aged adults):
- Young T et al: *NEJM* 1993; 328:1230-1235 (traditional reference study):
  - AHI > 5: 24% males; 9% females.
  - OSA (AHI > 5 with EDS): 4% males; 2% females.
- Estimated that > 75% of OSA patients undiagnosed or untreated.
- Recent studies have indicated an increased prevalence of SDB. Peppard, et al. (*Am J Epidemiol* 2013;177(9):1006-14) reported an apnea/hypopnea index ≥ 15/hr hour in 10% of males and 3% females between the ages of 30 to 49years. In the 50 to 70-year-old age group, the prevalence was 17% in men and 9% in women.
- Heinzer et al in *Lancet Respir Med* 2015; 3:310-318 reported on a population-based PSG study in Switzerland involving 2121 individuals age 40 years or older. The median AHI was 14.9 in men and 6.9 in women. The vast majority of events (75%) in the study were hypopneas. An AHI >5/hr was found in 83.8% males and 60.8% females; AHI $\geq$15/hr in 49.7% males and 23.4% females. Subjects >60 yrs generally had higher AHI's. An AHI > 20/hr was associated with $\uparrow$ prevalence of hypertension, diabetes, metabolic syndrome and depression. High prevalence of SDB in this study compared with older studies may have been due to increased sensitivity of equipment used (nasal pressure sensors) and scoring of hypopneas as recommended in recent AASM guidelines.

Risk factors:
- Obesity (by definition BMI $\geq$ 30 kg/m²; risk OSA $\uparrow$ if BMI $\geq$35). $\uparrow$ fatty tissue in oro-pharyngeal structures including tongue (Kim et al, *SLEEP* 2014;37(10):1639) and also parapharyngeal tissues.
- Oropharyngeal abnormalities (e.g., tonsil enlargement, elongated soft palate and uvula).
- Inferiorly located hyoid bone $\rightarrow$ elongated upper airway.
- Neck circumference >17 inches males, >16 inches females.
- Hormonal (e.g., postmenopausal women but risk $\downarrow$ with HRT).
- Maxillomandibular abnormalities (e.g., retrognathia, micrognathia).
- Endocrine (e.g., acromegaly, hypothyroidism).
- Genetic (e.g., Down syndrome).
- Ethnic factors; usually related to cranial-facial morphology.
- Familial/genetic (*Am. J. Respir. Crit Care Med.* 2006; 173: 453-463). Main familial factors include upper airway and craniofacial

anatomy as well as obesity. Cade et al (*Am. J. Respir. Crit Care Med.* 2016; 194(7): 886-897 identified three gene loci associated with OSA traits in a large population (12,558) among Hispanic/Latino Americans.

- Impact of alcohol, sedative hypnotics, and general anesthesia in predisposed individuals

Pathophysiology:

a. Anatomic factors (e.g., tonsillar hypertrophy, retrognathia, peripharyngeal fat) → ↓ cross section of upper airway.

b. Neuromuscular factors: Inadequate compensation by phasic dilator muscle activity of upper airway and genioglossal muscles during sleep. Most marked in REM sleep.

c. Neuroventilatory control factors: Unstable respiratory control system with abnormal (high) loop gain may cause central apneas. However, in setting of anatomy predisposing to UA collapse, obstructive apneas may instead occur. (May therefore find both central, obstructive and mixed apneas in the same patient).

REMember:

- One or more of the above risk factors may be simultaneously involved in any individual patient. This may be one reason why a UPPP may not be successful. (Another reason is that multiple sites of obstruction may be present).
- Timing of airway collapse may vary from patient to patient (Owens et al, *J. Clin Sleep Med* 2011; 7(1): 23-4).
  (a) during expiration due to passive collapse from extraluminal pressure.
  (b) during inspiration presumably due to "poor upper airway muscle responsiveness."

Sites of Obstruction:

- Major sites of obstruction are retropalatal and retrolingual.
- Equal number of patients may have obstruction at either level (*Laryngoscopy* 1988; 98: 641-647).
- Patients may have obstruction simultaneously at both levels (*SLEEP* 1993; 16: 580-584).
- The nose itself is not a site of obstruction. Nasal obstruction may however act as a Starling resistor to aggravate snoring or obstruction at distal levels (increased resistance upstream creates increased negative intraluminal pressure downstream).

Consequences of OSA:

a. Cognitive impairment
- Excessive daytime sleepiness (EDS). AHI however not a good predictor for EDS.
- Fatigue, tiredness, lethargy, lack of energy, etc common complaints
- Neuropsychological symptoms e.g., depression, irritability, memory loss, poor concentration. In patients with established depression, OSA may aggravate the depression.
- Mild cognitive impairment found in 47.9% of cohort of sleep clinic OSA patients and >55% in older males (mean age 56 yrs) with moderate to severe OSA (*Annals ATS* 2021; 18(5): 865-875).

b. Cardiovascular:
- Coronary artery disease: OSAS may be a direct cause of CAD by way of **oxidative stress** (rapid deoxygenation and reoxygenation) causing **systemic inflammatory changes** leading to **endothetial cell dysfunction** and atherosclerosis. (AHI > 30/hr 2.6x more likely to have an incient coronary disease or CHF compared to no SDB, Wisconsin Sleep Cohort Study *SLEEP* 2015; 38(5): 677-684). Severity and duration of desats rather than AHI related to vascular endothetail dysfunction. ↑ **CRP**, an inflammatory biomarker, noted in OSA.
- Systemic hypertension.
- Diastolic dysfunction.
- Arrhythmias:
  - Nocturnal arrhythmias related to apneas and hypopneas (18x↑ risk compared to non-OSA patients though absolute rate low. *J. Clin Sleep Med* 2015;11(3):274-6; Monahan et al *J Am Coll Cardiol* 2009; 54: 1797-84).
  - ±4.5% prevalence atrial fibrillation in OSA.
  - A.fib may be associated with localized cardiac remodeling and fibrosis which may be due to prolonged or intermittent hypoxia. ↑ CRP also seen in atrial fibrillation/OSA.
  - ↑ risk for recurrent atrial fibrillation following cardioversion or catheter ablation in untreated OSA.
  - Selim et al (*JCSM* 2016; 12(6): 829-837) report on 2x ↑ risk of nocturnal arrythmias including complex ventricular ectopy, atrial fibrillation, SVT, conduction delays and tachyarrythmias in moderate to severe SDB.

c. Cerebrovascular:
- OSAS independent risk factor for stroke (*NEJM* 2005; 353:2034-2041).
- Carotid artery abnormalities (*AJRCCM* 2005; 172: 613-618).
  - Abnormal pulse wave velocity.
  - Changes in intima-media thickness.
  - Abnormal carotid artery diameter.
- Silent brain infarcts on MRI (*AJRCCM* 2007; 175: 612-617; Huang et al *CHEST* 2020).
- Heavy snoring in itself may ↑ the risk of carotid atherosclerosis (*SLEEP* 2008; 31: 1207-1213).

- OSA highly prevalent in asymptomatic caroted stenosis. (Ehrhardt et al *CHEST* 2015; 147 (4): 1029-1036).

d. Endocrine.
  - Insulin resistance (type 2 diabetes) especially with severe OSA. Kent et al *CHEST* 2014; 145(4): 982-990. See also OSA and Diabetes, A State of the Art Review. *CHEST* 2017; 152(5): 1070-1086.
  - Leptin resistance.
  - Aggravating factor for dyslipidemias.

e. Pulmonary hypertension.
  - Usually mild (PA pressure <30mmHg).
  - No correlation with OSA severity.
  - Higher PA pressures if co-morbid disease e.g., COPD, OHS, LV dysfunction.

f. Elevated hematocrit.

g. Increased all-cause mortality:
  - Moderate to severe OSAS independently associated with 33% mortality over 14 years compared with 6.5% and 7.7% mortality in mild or no OSA subjects (*SLEEP* 2008; 31: 1079-1085).
  - The same Australian study group in *J Clin Sleep Med* 2014; 10(4):355-362 report a 20 year follow-up showing that patients with moderate to severe OSA have a "large increased risk of all-cause mortality, incident stroke and cancer incidence and mortality." Other studies have also suggested an association with OSA and cancer (Nieto et al *Am J Resp Crit Care Med* 2012; Campos-Rodrigues et al *Am J Resp Crit Care Med* 2013).

h. Acute CHF due to OSA; (*CHEST* 2012; 141 (3): 798 - 808).
  - In patients with underlying cardiac disease, acute CHF may be precipitated by the negative intrathoracic pressure during an obstructive event causing ↑ LV afterload, ↑ myocardial work, and ↓ SV. O2 desaturations causing myocardial ischemia and arrhythmias may further contribute to LV dysfunction.
  - Acute pulmonary edema also reported in OSA patients with normal LV function. Mechanism unclear; ? "negative pressure edema."

i. Sudden death.
  - OSA patients may have a peak in sudden death in sleeping hours (*NEJM* 2005; 353: 1206 - 1214).
  - Mechanisms may include malignant arrhythmias, extreme hypoxia particularly in the morbidly obese, or a blunted arousal response to pharyngeal closure (*CHEST* 2012; 141 (3): p. 803).

j. Societal/economic impact:
  - ↑ Sick leave, ↓ work performance, ↑ medical costs, ↑ divorce rate (*National Academies Press*, 2006)

k. Relationship of **chronic cough** and OSA: Resolution of chronic cough with CPAP for OSA suggests a direct link between OSA and cough. Review article: **Chronic Cough and OSA: A New Association?** (Sundar & Daly: *J Clin Sleep Med* 2011;7(6):669-677) reviews links between the two conditions (OSA as a cause of lower airway inflammation), potential mechanisms why CPAP may improve cough and also the associations between OSA and other conditions in which chronic cough is common (asthma, GERD and upper airway cough syndrome/post nasal drip syndrome).

l. ? Risk factors for Alzheimer's Disease: markers of ↑ amyloid burden in CSF in cognitively normal elderly. *Am J Resp Crit Care Med* 2018; 197(7): 933-943. See also editorial p855-6.

Further reading:
1. Javaheri et al: Sleep apnea: Types, Mechanisms, and Clinical Cardiovascular Consequences (*J Am Coll Cardiol* 2017; 69: 841-858). This is an excellent review which includes mechanism and impact of sleep apnea on cardiovascular disorders. The article includes the impact of CPAP therapy on cardiovascular outcomes emphasizing the point that to achieve cardiovascular benefit, PAP therapy should be used for at least four hours a night. The review also addresses the results in the SAVE study published in the *New Eng J Med* (2016; 375; 919-31), in which the impact on cardiovascular outcomes was similar in the CPAP and in the control groups. This study appeared, however, to have several limitations that were addressed in this review paper, one of which was an average nightly use of only 3.3 hrs. Study also excluded OSA patients with severe EDS who are those most likely to have CVD.

2. Reutrakul & Mokhlesi: OSA and Diabetes: A State of the Art Review *CHEST* 2017; 152 (5): 1070-1086.

Summary of an Official American Thoracic Society Research Statement: **Impact of Mild Obstructive Sleep Apnea in Adults** *Am J Resp Crit Care Med* 2016; 193: 1044-1057.

The impact of <u>*mild*</u> OSA on neurocognitive and cardiovascular complications remains uncertain. This ATS statement summarizes available evidence regarding both the clinical significance of mild OSA as well as the impact of treatment in these areas. Mild OSA is identified when the AHI, RDI or oxygen desaturation index (ODI) falls between 5 and 14 events/hr.

The findings were as follows:

a. Data regarding the *impact* on *neurocognitive* outcomes such as EDS, memory loss, MVAs, and poor quality of life was in general limited or had conflicting results.

b. Treatment of mild OSA (in comparison to no treatment) suggested only a slight *subjective* improvement in EDS and possibly only in patients with an "elevated level of sleepiness at baseline." There was no impact on objective assessments of EDS. Insufficient data was present to assess other metrics of neurocognitive function.

c. Data regarding the *impact* of mild OSA on *cardiovascular* outcomes such as HT, CAD, CVA events, arrhythmias, and cardiovascular or all-cause mortality were either absent, conflicting or did not support the negative impact of mild OSA on these metrics. The only outcome that mild OSA may have affected was an "increased stroke risk in persons with underlying CAD."

d. In examining whether *treatment* of mild OSA (in comparison to no treatment) could prevent or reduce the adverse outcomes outlined in (c) above, there were either insufficient or no studies to determine the impact of treatment in these areas.

Clinical Evaluation:

a. **Screening Questionaire** (STOP-BANG):
STOP questionnaire (Chung et al; *Anesthesiology*; 2006; 108(5):812-821) developed originally as preoperative assessment to detect OSA. High risk if ≥ 2 positive answers:

STOP:
1. S (snore).
2. T (tiredness/sleepiness).
3. O (observed apneas).
4. P (blood pressure).

BANG: Predictability for OSAS ↑ with the addition of one of the following four factors: High risk if ≥ 3 positive answers to STOP-BANG
1. B (BMI > 35 kg/m²).
2. A (Age > 50).
3. N (Neck circumference >40cm [±16"]).
4. G (Gender - male).
Reference: STOP-Bang Qustionaire. Chung et al *CHEST* 2016; 149(3): 631-638. BMI > 35 and male gender more predictive then neck size or age (Chung et al *JCSM* 2014; 10 (2): 951-958.

b. **History** — include both the patient's <u>and</u> the bed partner's observations
   - Snoring, apneas, choking, gasping, and restless sleep .
   - Unrefreshing sleep.
   - Dry mouth, headache on waking
   - EDS and other cognitive/personality changes (see above).
   - Sexual problems.
   - Nocturnal GERD and nocturnal sweating.
   - Insomnia (especially post-menopausal females).
   - Nocturia and nocturnal enuresis.
   - Chronic cough (see review article *J.Clin Sleep Med* 2011; 7(6); 669-677)

c. **Additional questionaires:** Epworth, Berlin, Funtional Outcomes of Sleep Questionaire (FOSQ)

- OSA associated with 2.5-3x risk of MVA's compared to general population.; (*SLEEP* 2004; 27: 453-458). See also p158.
- Not all studies show correlation between *severity* of OSA and crash risk (*J. Clin Sleep* Med 2006; 2(2): 193-200)

d. **Physical examination:**
- BMI (obesity = BMI $\geq$ 30 kg/m²; BMI $\geq$ 35 kg/m² is high risk factor).
- Oropharyngeal appearance (modified Mallampati score, tonsil size, peritonsillar narrowing, macroglossia, (tongue ridging), elongated uvula, high-arched/narrow hard palate).

Modified Mallampati classification (without tongue protrusion); Friedman M, et al *Laryngoscope* 1999; 109; 1901-1907.

Grade 1: tonsils, pillars, soft palate clearly visible.
Grade 2: uvula, pillars, upper pole (of tonsils) visible.
Grade 3: part of soft palate visible (not tonsils, pillars).
Grade 4: only hard palate visible.

 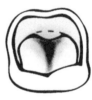 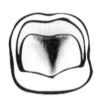

GRADE 1   GRADE 2   GRADE 3   GRADE 4

<u>**Tonsillar size:**</u> (Friedman et al).

Grade 0: S/P tonsillectomy (i.e. no tonsil visible).
Grade 1: Tonsils barely visible behind the anterior pillars.
Grade 2: tonsils (easily) visible behind anterior pillars.
Grade 3: tonsils extend 3/4 of the way to midline.
Grade 4: tonsils completely obstructing airway ("kissing" tonsils).

- Retrognathia/micrognathia. Evaluate for overjet.
- Neck circumference ($\uparrow$ risk if >17inches in men & >16 inches in women).
- Check for complications (e.g., polycythemia, hypertension, edema).

<u>High-risk patients</u> for OSA: (*JCSM* 2009; 5 (3): 263-276).
- BMI > 35 kg/m².
- History of CHF (systolic or diastolic dysfunction).
- History of atrial fibrillation.
- Refractory hypertension.
- Type 2 diabetes.
- Nocturnal dysrhythmias.
- History of stroke.
- Pulmonary hypertension.

- High-risk driving populations (e.g., commercial vehicle operators - CVOs)*.
- Preoperative for bariatric surgery.
- History of coronary artery disease.

* Objective criteria prompting a sleep study in CVOs should include:
- BMI $\geq$ 40kg/m^2
- Neck circumference $\geq$ 17 inches in men, $\geq$ 15.5 inches in women
- BMI $\geq$ 33kg/m^2 with CV disease, treatment-resistant HT, DM type 2 or EDS/EDS-caused accident (*CHEST* 2020; 158(5): 2172-2181).

Sleep Testing (*SLEEP* 2005; *JCSM* 2009)

Types of monitors:
- Type 1: Fully attended in-lab comprehensive PSG.
- Type 2: Comprehensive but unattended (portable) PSG.
- Type 3: Portable study with at least 4 channels (including 2 respiratory channels, heart monitor and oximetry). Referred to as cardiorespiratory study.
- Type 4: one or two channels (O2 saturations $\pm$ airflow).*

* Medicare/Medicaid type 4 monitor definition differs from AASM definition by including minimum of 3 channels.

Sleep studies may be

(a) In-laboratory full-night PSG or PAP titration.

(b) Split-night study (diagnostic PSG followed by CPAP titration).
- AASM Guideline (*JCSM* 2017):
  - Moderate to severe OSA during at least a 2 hour baseline diagnostic portion.
  - CPAP portion should last $\geq$ 3 hours.

REMember:
- If split-night study ordered but OSA not documented during the first portion of the study, the PSG should be converted to a full-night diagnostic study.
- Absence of REM sleep and/or < 3 hr of baseline sleep is associated with significant underestimation of sleep apnea severity.
- Where < 3 hr of CPAP titration, significant difference in final CPAP pressure compared full-night CPAP titration.
- AHI correlation between full PSG and split-night titration is better for severe OSA than for milder sleep apnea(AHI<20/hr).
- Acceptance and adherence rates not statistically different for split-night or full-night CPAP titrations.

Reference: Patil et al: Split-Night Polysomnography (*CHEST* 2007; 131: 1664-1671).

(c) Unattended Portable Monitors
(Type 3 PMs): (*JCSM*, 2009) (Home sleep apnea tests)

- Uses:

  - as an alternative to PSG where there is a high pretest probability of moderate-to-severe OSA.

  - to evaluate the response to non-CPAP treatments for OSA.

  - where the patient is unable to have a laboratory PSG (e.g., immobility).

- Inappropriate use of PMs include the following:

  - Presence of comorbid conditions which may degrade the accuracy of the test (e.g., pulmonary disease, CHF, neuromuscular disease).

  - Presence of comorbid sleep disorders (e.g., PLMD, parasomnias, insomnias, circadian rhythm disorders, narcolepsy).

  - General screening in asymptomatic individuals.

- Technical issues:

  - A minimum recording should include measurements of airflow, respiratory effort, and blood oxygenation. (Ideally PMs should include both an oronasal thermal sensor and a nasal pressure transducer). Type 3 monitors usually include cardiac monitoring.

  - Technically inadequate results or a negative test in patients with a high pretest probability should prompt a laboratory PSG.

The special article **Clinical use of a Home Sleep Apnea Test: an AASM position statement** *J Clin Sleep Med* 2017; 13 (10): 1205-7 reinforces the clinical guidelines outlined in JCSM 2009. Physician involvement in the evaluation for ordering and interpretation of HSATs which should not be automatically scored is emphasized.

Summary of Special 2017 Article:

Clinical Practice Guideline for Diagnostic Testing for Adult Obstructive Sleep Apnea: an AASM Clinical Practice Guideline.
J Clin Sleep Med 2017;13(3):479-504.

The aim of this guideline is to assist clinicians in their approach to diagnose OSA in adults and to be used in conjunction with previously published AASM guidelines regarding the management of SDB in adults (*SLEEP* 2005; *J Clin Sleep Med* 2007). The article indicates that polysomnography (PSG) remains the standard diagnostic test. The alternative is the home sleep apnea test (HSAT). The first 4 guidelines below are recommended as STRONG recommendations and the final two WEAK recommendations.

The following is a summary of the recommendations:

1. A diagnosis of OSA should not be made in the absence of a PSG or HSAT.
2. PSG **or** HSAT should be used for suspected moderate-to-severe OSA in "uncomplicated adult patients."
3. If a HSAT is negative, inconclusive or technically inadequate, a PSG should be performed.
4. A PSG (as opposed to a HSAT) should be performed to diagnosis OSA in patients with significant cardiorespiratory disease, respiratory muscle weakness due to neuromuscular disease, hypoventilation syndromes (awake or asleep), chronic opioid medication, a history of stroke or severe insomnia.
5. If clinically appropriate, a split-night PSG (as opposed to a full night diagnostic study) should be used (WEAK recommendation).
6. If a PSG is negative, consider repeating this study if the suspicion of OSA remains (WEAK recommendation).

Personal comments:

(a) No recommendations made for suspected mild OSA or snoring. Presumably a HSAT would be an acceptable initial study.
(b) Unfortunately, the initial study will depend on what third party payers will cover. Unless there is significant comorbid condition such as COPD, CHF, neuromuscular disease impairing respiration or significant cerebrovascular disease, initial coverage will often be for a HSAT.

REMember:

- Type-3 (&4) PMs are likely to *underestimate* the severity of OSA since respiratory events usually reported for total *recording* time (as opposed to total sleep time).
- Respiratory events with type-3 PMs include only apneas and hypopneas associated with desaturations, ie no *RERAs*. Leads to underestimation of severity.
- ICSD 3 introduces term *"respiratory event index"* to indicate number of events/hour of monitoring time for out of center testing (OCST).
- Use of wrist *actigraphy* in conjunction with PM may be useful in estimating TST but study in *CHEST* (2007:131:725-732) showed only slight improvement in results.
- AASM recommends the term Home Sleep Apnea Test rather than Out of Center Test (OCT) or Home Sleeps Test (HST). The REI (respiratory event index) is also the proposed terminology to quantitate respiratory events on a HSAT (number of events per hour of monitoring time).
- Criteria for severity same as PSG (see below).

HSAT's and night to night variability:

J. Clin Sleep Med (2020); 16 (4): 539-44 and *CHEST* (2020: 158(1): 365-373) articles report on the variability in the AHI (REI) on a night to night basis with HSAT's. Former study found a high negative predictive value for the first study night and the addition of a second HSAT improved diagnostic accuracy. The *CHEST* study found "substantial within-patient variability in the AHI and significant misclassification in sleep apnea severity based on any one night of monitoring." These findings were most applicable to mild and moderate OSA vs those who had a normal study or severe OSA on the first night.

Where significant differences occur between studies could decide to "treat the worst" (see *CHEST* editorial July 2020 p33-4) or use results that best correlates with clinical status.

Note that AASM guidelines (2017) do not advise multiple HSAT's but recommends a PSG where HSAT is "negative, inconclusive or technically inadequate," (see above).

Further reading: Rosenberg et al, The role of home sleep testing for evaluation of patients with EDS. *Sleep Med* 2019; 56: 80-89.

PSG Diagnostic criteria (*ICSD3*)

OSA **confirmed** on PSG if the number of obstructive events [apneas, hypopneas, and respiratory event-related arousals (RERA's)] on PSG is:

> $\geq$ 15 events/hr of sleep OR

> $\geq$ 5 events/hr. in a patient with excessive daytime sleepiness or fatigue, unrefreshing sleep, insomnia, waking up breath holding, gasping, or choking, or bed partner witnesses loud snoring or apneas, or if history of HT, CAD, CHF, CVA, A.fib, DM type2, or mood disorder.

Severity of OSA defined by the number of events (RDI/AHI) per hour of sleep. (see p138 for RDI/AHI definitions).

- Mild: $\geq$ 5 and < 15.
- Moderate: $\geq$ 15 and $\leq$ 30.
- Severe: > 30/hr.

Note: Dependence on the RDI or AHI as a single metric may be insufficient to predict cardiovascular outcomes. Additional endpoints focusing on oxygen desaturation e.g., oxygen desaturation index (ODI), "hypoxic burden" (area under the O_2 desaturation curve) or the total amount of sleep with SpO_2 < 90% or rate of change in SpO_2 during an obstructive apnea may add a greater sensitivity to predict CV events (Commentary *JCSM* 2020; Wang et al *JCSM* 2020; Azarbarzin et al *CHEST* 2020). Castallana et al reported OSA patients with ODI >30 or low O_2 saturation <81% had $\uparrow$dimension of ascending and descending thoratic aorta (*JCSM* 2021: 17(1): 3-11). Kanulainen et al reported $\uparrow$EDS measured by MSLT correlated better with desaturation severity than the AHI (*JCSM* 2019; 15(8): 1135-42).

See also **Metrics of Sleep Apnea Severity: Beyond the AHI** (*SLEEP* 2021): Reviews history of the AHI, its relationship to clinical conditions (e.g., HT, EDS, QOL, CAD, CVA). Additional metrics such as hypoxic burden, arousal intensity and A-H event duration discussed.

Follow-up Studies: (*JCSM* 2009)

Follow up PSG or type 3 PM study indicated for
- Assessment of treatment results including surgery, oral appliances, or significant weight loss (>10% of body weight).
- Insufficient therapeutic response or recurrence of OSA symptoms following initial success in compliant patients.
- Cases of substantial weight gain with return of symptoms.

REMember:
Follow up PSG or PM-3 studies not routinely indicated for patients
on CPAP with continued resolution of symptoms.

- **Other tests:**
    - Cephalometrics or drug induced sleep endscopy to determine
      site(s) of obstruction if surgery contemplated.
    - Thyroid functions as indicated (not routinely recommended
      by AASM).
    - Pulmonary functions if co-morbid COPD or other
      pulmonary disorders suspected.
    - Echocardiogram if signs of pulmonary hypertension.

FYI:

**Diagnosis of Obstructive Sleep Apnea in Adults: A Clinical Practice
Guideline from the American College of Physicians.** (*Ann Intern Med* 2014;
161:210-220).

The American College of Physicians (ACP) recommends PSG in prefence to
HSAT's noting that:
- Compared with PSG, Types 2, 3, and 4 monitors have a "wide
  range of differences in AHI estimates."
- Data loss of 3% to 20% reported for Type 3 and Type 4
  monitors.
- "Inadequate data" resulting in "limited interpretation of
  results" reported in 13% to 20% of Type 3 monitors.

Key PSG data

- Overall RDI/AHI*: 5 - <15 mild; 15-30 moderate; >30 severe.
- Note presence of central apneas; if many CA's ↑ chance of
  central apneas occurring during CPAP titration (see CPAP-induced
  central apnea below).
- Position related RDI; may be of therapeutic importance.
- REM RDI; if high need to be particularly attentive to resolution of
  REM events during CPAP tritration.
- Oxygen nadir; if particularly low may recommend CPAP even if
  RDI in mild range.
- Arrythmias & whether related to events.
- Note desaturations unrelated to events; may indicate co-morbid
  cardiopulmonary pathology.

---

*RDI includes apneas, hypopneas and RERAs / hour of sleep (PSG).
AHI includes apneas and hypopneas / hour of sleep (PSG).
Note: MCR does not recognize RERAs and therefore neither the PSG-based
RDI. Remember too that MCR does not recognize 3% desaturation for scoring
hypopneas. See MCR definitions of AHI and RDI on page 143.

 *REMember:*

- O2 nadir usually seen *after* resolution of an apnea or hypopnea.

- Increase in BP also seen after the apnea event.

- REM events are generally longer and with more severe desaturations partly due to ↓ in hypoxic and hypercapnic ventilatory drives.

.• Degree of EDS not strongly correlated with AHI.

Impact of REM-dominant OSA

- Usually implies REM AHI ≥15 with normal or mild AHI or REMAHI/ NREMAHI > 2 with NREM AHI <15.

- ↑ risk metabolic syndrome and DM (*Euro Resp* J 2018).

- Early atherosclerosis (carotid intima thickness) in women with REM AHI ≥ 30 (*SLEEP* 2018).

- REM AHI ≥15 associated with ↑ incidence of nocturnal non-dipping of BP (i.e., < 10% ↓ from daytime BP) which is associated with future development of HT (*THORAX* 2015); REM AHI ≥ 20 associated with prevalent and recent onset HT (*CHEST* 2016).

- REM AHI ≥ 30 associated with recurrent CV events in patients with prevalent CV disease (AJRCCM 2018)

- Important take home message: since most REM sleep at end of sleep period, PAP therapy used only 4 hours / night may not be sufficient to prevent potential negative impact of REM-dominant OSA.

- REM-dominant OSA found to have no ↑ EDS compared with NREM-dominant OSA.

- No significant associations with REM - AHI and cognitive outcomes in middle aged/ older adults (*JCSM* 2019).

Management:

Details regarding management options are included in the 2009 *J. Clin Sleep Med* special article. An outline of an approach to management follows:

1. **Lifestyle changes** recommended for all patients:
   - Weight loss $\to\downarrow$ tongue size, $\downarrow$ lateral wall fatty tissue, $\downarrow$ abdominal fat: Wt $\downarrow$ 9-20% $\to$ $\downarrow$ AHI 30-74% (Strobel & Rosen, *SLEEP* 1996), Wt $\downarrow$ 10% $\to\downarrow$ AHI 26% (Peppard et al, *JAMA* 2000)
   - Weight loss $\to\downarrow$ tongue fat (Wang et al AJRCCM 2020; 201: 718-727)
   - Avoid sedation, alcohol close to bed-time.
   - Ideal BMI = $25\text{kg}/\text{m}^2$.

2. **Positional treatment:**
   - May be sufficient (with lifestyle changes) in certain patients with mild OSA without significant EDS or co-morbid disease.
   - Outcome monitored by reported compliance, symptom resolution, objective position monitor (e.g., actigraphy) or HSAT.
   - de Vries et al: Usage of Positional Therapy in Adults with OSA (*J Clin Sleep Med* 2015; 11(2): 131-137): PT devices (commercially manufactured or home-made) effective (AHI $\downarrow$ 14.5 $\to$ 5.9) but long-term compliance poor.

   Review article: Efficiency of the New Generation of Devices for Positional Therapy for Patients With Positional OSA. *J. Clin. Sleep Med* 2017; 13 (6): 813-824

3. **Positive airway pressure (PAP) devices:**
   - CPAP effective in mild, moderate, and severe OSA.
     - Treatment of choice for moderate and severe OSA.
     - Also indicated for mild OSA with cognitive impairment or co-morbid disease e.g., CHF, uncontrolled hypertension, cerebro-vascular disease.
   - BPAP indications:
     - Higher pressure requirements (>15cm H_2O).
     - Comfort at lower pressures.
     - Patients with chronic lung disease who need a higher IPAP to improve oxygenation.
     - BPAP with backup rate for hypoventilation syndromes (e.g., neuromuscular disorders).
     - If optimal BPAP not achieved during titration study, consider prescribing Auto-BPAP.
   - Auto-PAP.
     - Long-term treatment in appropriate patients, e.g., following a HSAT.
     - Could be used to establish an optimal pressure for ongoing CPAP use, e.g., in a patient on CPAP who may need a new pressure setting.
     - Not recommended for CSA, co-morbid conditions (e.g., CHF, COPD).

Note: Choice of interface crucial to success with PAP therapy. Pressure requirements usually lower with nasal compared to oronsal masks. The latter reserved for significant mouth breathing or ↑ nasal resistance. See *JCSM* 2019; 15(4): 673-4; *CHEST* 2019; 156(6); 1187-1194.

Official ATS Workshop Report: Importance of Mask Selection on CPAP Outcomes for OSA (*Annals ATS* 2020; 17(10): 1177-1185). Covers mask selection, mask fitting, dealing with adverse effects including leaks, patient participation.

2019 Practice Guideline

Treatment of Adult Obstructive Sleep Apnea with Positive Airway Pressure. An AASM Clinical Practice Guideline. *J. Clin Sleep Med* 2019; 15 (2): 335-343.

The statement strategizes PAP therapy recommendations as either STRONG or CONDITIONAL (lower degree of certainty of outcomes and of appropriateness for all patients).

In making recommendations, PAP therapy is compared to "no therapy" and is based on the AASM review and meta-analysis of evidence using PAP in adults with OSA reported in the same addition of the *JCSM* (2019; 15 (2): 301-334).

1. STRONG recommendations for PAP therapy (as opposed to no therapy) for treatment of OSA with EDS for (a) initiating treatment with APAP or with CPAP after an in-laboratory titration where no significant co-morbidities exist, (b) for using a CPAP or APAP for ongoing management, and (c) for educational initiatives at initiation of PAP therapy.

2. CONDITIONAL recommendations are (a) for PAP therapy use in OSA with impaired QOL or comorbid hypertension (as opposed to no therapy), (b) CPAP or APAP preferred over BPAP for routine OSA treatment and (c) behavioral/troubleshooting and telemonitoring interventions be employed during the initial period of PAP therapy.

Note:
  (i)   Absent co-morbidities where strong recommendation for PAP therapy made include CHF, CSA, COPD, opioid use, hypoventilation or neuromuscular disorders.
  (ii) QOL in conditional recommendation (a) includes snoring, am head-aches, nocturia, fatigue, disruption of bed partner's sleep, etc.
  (iii) In non-sleepy adults with OSA insufficient evidence exists regarding PAP therapy's ability to reduce cardiovascular events or mortality.

Summary: Clinical Guidelines for the Manual Titration of Positive Airway Pressure in Patients with Obstructive Sleep Apnea (*J Clin Sleep Med* 2008;4(2): 157-171).

Points to remember:
1. Recommended maximum CPAP pressure is 15 cm and recommended maximum IPAP pressure on BPAP is 20 cm for patients <12 years. In patients ≥12 years, maximum CPAP pressure is 20 cm, and IPAP (BPAP titration) is 30 cm.
2. Recommended minimum IPAP-EPAP differential is 4 cm H_2O and the recommended maximum IPAP-EPAP differential is 10 cm H_2O.
3. Switching from CPAP to BPAP may be done if:
   a. The patient is uncomfortable or intolerant of high pressures.
   b. There are continuous obstructive events at 15 cm H_2O.
4. Protocol for split night titrations is identical with full night titrations.
5. Add supplemental oxygen if:
   a. The patient's awake supine SpO2 on room air is ≤ 88%.
   b. If during the PAP titration, the SpO2 is ≤ 88% for ≥ 5 minutes in the absence of obstructive respiratory events.
   c. Begin oxygen at 1 L/min. and titrate upward to achieve a target SpO2 between 88 and 94%. The interval between increases in oxygen flow should not be <15 minutes.
6. For treatment emergent central apneas (complex sleep apnea), attempts may be made to down titrate pressures. If this is not successful, adaptive servo-ventilation (ASV) may be considered.

Effective Titration Criteria:

Optimal titration:
   a. reduces the RDI to < 5 for at least 15 minutes and
   b. includes supine REM sleep at the selected pressure.
Good titration:
   a. reduces the RDI to ≤ 10 or by 50% if the baseline RDI is <15 and
   b. should also include supine REM sleep at the selected pressure.
Adequate titration:
   a. does not reduce the RDI to ≤ 10 but reduces the RDI by 75% from baseline (especially in severe OSA patients), or
   b. a titration meeting criteria for optimal or good titrations, with the exception that supine REM sleep did not occur at the selected pressure.

Unacceptable titration does not meet any one of the above grades (repeat PAP titration should then be considered).

Medicare Policy for CPAP Treatment of OSA (Effective 01/01/2014).

- The patient has a face-to-face clinical evaluation by the treating physician prior to sleep test: PSG or covered home sleep test (HST).

- The patient has a medicare-covered sleep test which meets either of the following criteria for a diagnosis of OSA (ICD-10 code G47.33).

  a. AHI (apneas + hypopneas/hour of sleep) or RDI (apneas + hypopneas/hour of recording time during a HSAT) ≥ 15 with a minimum of 30 events, OR

  b. AHI/RDI is ≥ 5 and ≤ 14 events/hour with a minimum of 10 events and documentation of
     - EDS
     - Impaired cognition
     - Mood disorder
     - Insomnia
     - Hypertension
     - Ischemic heart disease
     - History of stroke

- Patient qualifies for BiPAP if cannot tolerate current pressure setting on CPAP unit despite properly fitted interface and if lower pressure settings failed to
     - adequately control OSA symptoms, OR
     - improve sleep quality, OR
     - reduce AHI/RDI to acceptable levels.

- MCR will continue PAP coverage beyond 90 days if clinical improvement documented and patient uses PAP ≥ 4hrs/night 70% of nights during 30 consecutive day period within first 3 months of usage. Face to face visit to document above occurs between 31 and 90 days of initiating PAP therapy.

Oral appliances:

- Snoring.

- Mild/moderate OSA. Not appropriate for initial treatment of severe OSA.

- CPAP non-responder or CPAP intolerance.

- OAs comparably effective compared with CPAP in mild OSA; less effective than CPAP in moderate or severe disease(*CHEST* 2011; 140(6): 1511-1516).

- Doff et al (*SLEEP* 2013;36(9):1289): OAs found to be "viable treatment alternative" to CPAP in mild to moderate OSA over 2 years with "substantial improvements in PSG and neurobehavioral outcomes." CPAP was more effective in lowering AHI and improving O2 saturations. In severe OSA, OAs reserved for CPAP non-responders or failures.

- Pliska et al: (*J Clin Sleep Med* 2014; 10(12):1285-1291): Mandibular advancement splints for OSA over 11 year study period caused clinically significant changes in occlusion. Changes were progressive.

- In a Clinical Practice Guideline for the **Treatment of OSA and Snoring with Oral Appliance Therapy** (OAT): an **Update for 2015**, the AASM and the AADSM recommend as STANDARD that OAT (as opposed to no therapy) be used for the treatment of primary snoring, for patients with OSA intolerant of PAP therapy or who prefer alternative therapy. GUIDELINE recommendations include the involvement of qualified dentists in delivering and providing ongoing care and that custom titratable appliances be utilized. Sleep physicians should also be involved in follow-up care and a follow-up sleep test is advised. (*J Clin Sleep Med* 2015; 11 (7); 773-827.)

- OAT in moderately sleepy patients with OSA reduced the AHI as well as symptoms of snoring, fatigue and sleepiness but did not affect BP or endothelial function as measured by the reactive hyperemia index despite satisfactory compliance. *Am J. Resp Crit Care Med* 2017; 195(9): 1244-1252. In review of CV benefits of OAT (*Journal of Dental Sleep Medicine* 2016) modest ↓ in BP (mean 4.2 mmHg) found in 7/8 studies.

- **Further reading/review articles:**
  - Oral appliances for the management of OSA. *CHEST* 2018; 153(2): 544-553
  - Update on OAT for OSA. *Curr Sleep Med Rep.* 2017; 3: 143-151
  - OAT for OSA: An Update. *JCSM* 2014; 10(2): 215-227. (± 1/3 patients recieved "no therapeutic benefit," CPAP more effective to reduce AHI but health outcomes "equivalent.")

Summary of Consensus Statement:
Definition of an Effective Oral Appliance for the Treatment of OSA and Snoring, *J Dental Sleep Med* 2014; 1(1):51.

- Oral appliance Therapy (OAT) indicated for mild to moderate OSA and primary snoring.
- Also indicated for patients with severe OSA unresponsive to or unable/unwilling to tolerate PAP therapy.
- OAT may be used as adjunctive therapy with PAP or other treatment approaches.
- Mandibular advancement devices are the most effective OAs.
- OAs should advance the mandible in increments of 1 mm or less with adjustment range of at least 5 mm.
- The OA should also have the ability to have the settings reversed.
- The OA should be custom made of biocompatible materials and should last for at least three years.

Complications of OAs (*CHEST* 2007;132:693-699)

SHORT-TERM	LONG-TERM
~ Salivation.	~Reduction in overjet.
~ Mouth Dryness.	~ Increase in facial height.
~Tooth pain.	~ Increase in degree of mouth opening.
~Gum irritation.	~ Changes in inclination of incisors.
~TMJ discomfort.	~ Increase in mandibular plane angle.

Pharmacologic: (Includes *JCSM* 2009 guidelines)
- Modafinil and armodafinil FDA approved for residual daytime sleepiness in patients on CPAP (important to instruct patients of continued need for CPAP).
- Solriamfetol (*Sunosi*). Inhibits dopamine and norepinephrine reuptake. FDA approval March 2019. (Approved dosing 37.5mg, 75mg and 150mg in OSA patients with EDS despite appropriate treatment).
- AASM does not recommend marijuana or medical cannibis for OSA treatment.
- Oxygen therapy is not recommended as primary treatment for OSA; may prolong apneas and potentially worsen nocturnal hypercapnia particularly in patients with comorbid respiratory disease.
- Treatment of associated hypothyroidism or acromegaly may improve AHI.
- SSRIs, protriptyline, theophyllines and estrogens are not recommended for the treatment of OSA.
- Short-acting nasal decongestants are not recommended.
- Topical nasal corticosteroids may be useful adjunct to primary therapies.
- Pitolisant (*Wakix*) shown to be effective and safe as adjunct to PAP for residual EDS in muticenter European study (*CHEST* April 2021; 159 (4): 1598). Currently only FDA approved for nacolepsy.

Desipramine in OSA:

Tricyclic antidepressants (TCA), e.g., protriptyline have been used in small studies to reduce the number of apneas and hypopneas during sleep (e.g., Brownell et al: *N Engl J Med* 1982; 307: 1037-42). The mechanism was thought to be the reduction in REM sleep. Taranto-Montemurro et al (Am *J Resp Crit Care Med* 2016; 194 (7): 878-885) have shown that desipramine is able to abolish the normal reduction of genioglossus activity seen in transition from wakefulness to non-REM sleep. TCA's by the ability to maintain oropharyngeal muscular tone during sleep, may therefore provide an alternative therapeutic approach in selected patients. TCA's however not approved for use in OSA.

Pharmacotherapy Research:

Studies involving the combination of atomoxitine (a norepinephrine reuptake inhibitor) and oxybutinin (an anti-muscarinic agent) taken prior to sleep and compared to placebo reduced the AHI by enhancing genioglossus activity and hence UA patency. The drugs were not effective when administered separately. The combination (called ato-oxy) may also slightly reduce the arousal threshold. (Taranto-Montemurra et al *AJRCCM* 2019 and *CHEST* June 2020).

Surgery: *(JCSM 2009)*

- Primary surgical treatment considered for patients with mild OSA who have severe obstructing anatomy that is surgically correctable.
- Surgery considered as secondary treatment for OSA where the outcome of PAP therapy (or an OA) is inadequate or where the patient is intolerant of PAP (or an OA), or if PAP (or an OA) is unable to eliminate OSA.
- Surgery considered as an adjunct therapy if obstructive anatomy or functional deficiency compromises other therapies. See case report *JCSM* 2020; 16(1): 149-151 where upper airway surgery enabled BPAP therapy to reduce the AHI from 90.1 to 1.3 events/hr (both values on BPAP at high presssures).

Summary: Practice Parameters for the Surgical Modifications of the Upper Airway for Obstructive Sleep Apnea in Adults (*SLEEP* 2010 33(10);1408-1413).

1. Standard recommendations include:

    With regard to specific surgical procedures, the only *standard* recommendation is that LAUP is NOT recommended as a treatment for OSA. (Failure rate 44%; Camacho et al *SLEEP* 2017).

2. All other surgical procedures have an *option* recommendation.

    a. Tracheostomy. Where other options have failed, or refused, do not exist, or indicated by clinical urgency.

    b. Maxillomandibular advancement (MMA): option in severe OSA for CPAP failures or where oral appliances in severe OSA have been "considered and found ineffective or undesirable."

    c. UPPP as a single procedure ± tonsillectomy is not a reliable procedure to normalize the AHI in moderate to severe OSA. Severe OSA patients should "initially be offered positive airway pressure therapy" and those with moderate OSA should "initially be offered either PAP therapy or oral appliances."

    d. Multilevel or step-wise surgery: option for patients with narrowing at multiple sites, particularly following UPPP failures.*

    e. Radiofrequency ablation (RFA): option for mild-to-moderate OSA patients unwilling or unable to adhere to PAP therapy, or in whom oral appliances are "ineffective or undesirable."

    f. Palatal implants: option in mild OSA patients who are unable or unwilling to tolerate PAP therapy or where oral appliances are "ineffective or undesirable."

        *Drug induced sleep endoscopy (DISE) may identify level(s) of obstruction.

Other surgical procedures

-   Nasal procedures for snoring or to enhance CPAP compliance. (Camacho et al *SLEEP* 2015; 38(2): 279 reported ↓ in CPAP pressures and ↑ CPAP use after nasal surgery)

- Base of tongue procedures (advancement, radiofrequency reduction, resection) e.g. genioglossal advancement ± hyoid suspension.
- Bariatric surgery
  -- BMI ≥40kg/m²
  -- BMI 35kg/m² with important comorbidities and dietary failure
  -- Remission rate 40% depending on amount of weight lost.

Review Article: Smith et al Surgical Management of OSA in Adults *CHEST* 2015; 147 (6): 1681-1690. Comprehensive; includes all levels of surgery.
- BMI > 30-32 predictor of poor surgical response.

Transcutaneous submental electrical stimulation of the genioglossus muscle (*CHEST* 2011; 140 (4): 998 - 1007, Strollo et al *NEJM* 2014; 370:139-149). Genioglossus the major dilator of the upper airway. In the pivotal study by Strollo et al:
- 126 participants, mean age 54.5 years, mean BMI 28.4.
- Patients eligible if baseline AHI 20-50 and intolerant of CPAP.
- Patients excluded if >25% central or mixed apneas, or BMI >32.
- AHI ↓29 →9 at 12m
- 66% participants had AHI <20 at 12m
- AEs included tongue soreness (21%), discomfort with stimulation (40%), and transient tongue weakness after surgery (18%).
- Follow up studies at 18 and 24 months demonstrated maintained improvement. *SLEEP* 2015; 38(10): 1593-1598. *J Clin Sleep Med* 2016; 12(1): 43-48.
- **Review Article:** UpperAirway Stimulation for Obstructive Sleep Apnea: Past, Present and Future. Dedhia et al *SLEEP* 2015; 38(6): 899-906.
- **Review Article:** Neurostimulation Treatment for OSA. *CHEST* 2018; 154(6): 1435-1447.

Summary from the Mayo Clinic website:
- Candidates should have mod - severe OSA with AHI 15-65/hr and have failed PAP therapy. BMI should be <33 kg/m²
- Absence of
  -- Significant comorbidities eg severe CP disease, NM disease, active psychiatric disease
  -- Pronounced UA abnormalities
- Anterior - posterior predominant retropalatal collapse demonstrated on drug induced sleep endoscopy.

From the Inspire® website
April 2020: FDA approved use of Inspire UAS in patients 18-21 yrs (previously only ≥ 22yrs) with - moderate - severe OSA
- failure or inability treat by tonsillectomy or post nasal soft tissue removal
- failure of PAP therapy

From the eXciteOSA® website:
Feb 2021: FDA approval to market eXciteOSA® neuromuscular tongue stimulator for snoring and mild OSA. Mouthpiece with 4 electrodes used during the day to improve tongue muscle function. Ages 18+. Needs Rx.

See also *JCSM* review of respiratory muscle therapy in OSA 2020; 16(5): 785-801. Includes speech therapy tongue and breathing excercises, and playing wind instruments to improve tongue and upper as well as lower airway muscle tone in order to enhance airway patency during sleep.

Note: Regarding Hypoglossal nerve stimulation...
- Lee et al (*J Clin Sleep Med* 2019; 15(8): 1165-1172) report that candidates for HGNS with PAP requirements <8cm had larger ↓ in AHI. Surgical success also more likely if baseline AHI <50/hr; BMI <32 kg/m^2 and where no complete contentric palatal collapse.
- *Genie* system's HGNS device validated in EU and undergoing multinational trials including the US, enables those with the implanted device to undergo MRI testing.
- Pilot study by Kent et al (*CHEST* 2021; 159(3): 1212-1221) involved stimulating the ansa cervicalis nerve (ACN) innervating the sternothyroid muscle. This causes caudal traction of cervical structures including the thyroid cartilage and hyoid bone thereby stiffening the upper airway supporting structures and enlarging airway patency. When combined with HGNS, the impact on enlarging UA patency is further enhanced (See also editorial comments on pages 912-4 of same *CHEST* edition).

Common Clinical Dilemmas: An Approach:

A. **Selection of a specific therapy:**
- Surgery for specific pathology (e.g., tonsillectomy, mandibular advancement procedure for severe retrognathia).
- Assess the <u>need</u> for CPAP. Indications for CPAP include the following:
  — Severe sleep apnea (RDI > 30).
  — Severity of EDS and other cognitive symptoms.
  — Severity of desaturations.
  — The presence of arrhythmias.
  — Comorbid conditions.
      - CAD, HT, cerebrovascular disease, CHF.
      - Morbid obesity.
- If mild (to moderate) OSA and no firm CPAP indication, patient preferences may help determine initial therapy.

B. *Persistence* **of EDS in CPAP** *compliant* **patients:**
- Prevalence reported 9-22% ↑ with ↓ use but EDS may be present even with 7hrs use. (Weaver et al *SLEEP* 2007;30:711)
- Causes may include:
  - Inadequate total sleep time; poor sleep hygiene.
  - Suboptimal pressure (machine malfunction or patient weight gain).
  - Medications causing sleepiness.
  - Comorbid conditions (e.g., depression, hypothyroidism).
  - CPAP itself disrupting sleep.
  - Long-term adverse effects of intermittent hypoxia and sleep fragmentation on sleep-wake promoting regions of the brain prior to initiating CPAP. (Imaging studies show structural changes associated with OSA).
  - Additional sleep pathology e.g., narcolepsy especially in younger patients, PLMD.
- Management
  - Correct or treat cause where possible.
  - Consider MSLT for suspected narcolepsy.
  - Modafinil (*Provigil*) or armodafinil (*Nuvigil*) or solriamfetol (*Sunosi*) as indicated. (FDA approved for residual EDS in OSA patients on appropriate therapy).

Further reading:
- Lal et al: EDS in OSA. Mechanics and Clinical Management. *Annals ATS*. Feb. 2021.
- Javaheri and Javaheri: Update on Persistent EDS in OSA. *CHEST* 2020; 150(2): 776.
- Lal et al: Excessive EDS in OSA. Discusses mechanisms and management. *Annals ATS* 2021; 18(5): 757-768.

C. *Recurrence* **of EDS (often after years) while on CPAP:**
- Check compliance.
- Check equipment.
  - Mask and tubing. ? Unintentional leaks (*CHEST* 2018; 153 (4): 834-842)
  - CPAP unit itself (check pressure).
- Check for weight gain. May need increased pressure.
- Review medications as cause of EDS.
- Evaluate for new co-morbid conditions (e.g., depression, hypothyroidism, anemia).
- Review for co-morbid sleep disorder (e.g., RLS, narcolepsy).
- Repeat PSG (?PLMD, ?OSA worse).
- Retitration study as indicated (split night study may be appropriate).
- MSLT, particularly in younger individuals (? co-morbid narcolepsy).
- Modafinil, armodafinil or solriamfetol as clinically indicated.

Further reading:

Clinical Guideline Summary for Clinicians: The Role of Weight Management in the Treatment of Adult OSA.
Billings et al, *Ann. Amer. Thor. Society* April 1, 2019; vol 16, No 4.
Discusses lifestyle interventions, reduced-calorie diet, exercise, weight-loss medications (phentermine/topiramate, liraglutide, orlistat, naltrexone/bupropion) and bariatric surgery.

Patel N et al : Split Night Polysomnography *CHEST* 2007 ;131: 1664-1671.

Javaheri et al: Sleep Apnea; Types, Mechanics and Clinical Cardiovascular Consequences. *J. Am. Coll. Cardiol* 2017; 69: 841-58.

Khan A et al: UPPP in the Management of OSA: The Mayo Clinic Experience *Mayo Clin Proc* 2009; 84(9): 795-800.

Quseem A, et al: Management of obstructive sleep apnea in adults: A clinical practice guideline from the American College of Physicians (*Ann. Int. Med* 2013; 159: 471-83).

Andrade et al Nasal vs Oronasal CPAP For OSA Treatment, a meta-analysis *CHEST* 2018; 153(3): 655-674.

A word about Upper Airways Resistance Syndrome (UARS).

- The term UARS traditionally applied to patients presenting with symptoms of OSA eg snoring, EDS/tiredness/fatigue, but PSG shows an AHI of <5/hour.
- Essence of condition is flow limitation in upper airways (UA) →↑ UA resistance →↑ work of breathing → recurrent arousals →sleep fragmentation →EDS.
- Neither ICSD2 nor ICSD3 recognize UARS as a separate clinical entity since the pathophysiology does not differ significantly from the rest of the OSA population.
- It has been suggested that in this subgroup of patients, there is increased sensitivity of the UA mechanoreceptors so that small increases in respiratory effort result in an arousal (low arousal threshold).
- Arousals are then termed RERAs and are included in the RDI (except for MCR patients). Patients in whom UARS previously regarded as separate entity now included under the OSAHS umbrella.
- While not recognized as a separate clinical entity, patients who fall into the end of the spectrum of OSA which UARS may represent may have some distinguishing clinical features:
    - Taller and thinner than typical OSA patients.
    - F =M (in OSA M > F).
    - Snoring frequent but occasionally absent.

- Systemic symptoms seen more often than in OSA
- Insomnia, headaches, cold extremities, IBS, myalgias, anxiety, mood changes.
- Low BP and postural hypotension.
- ↑BP seen in some patients.
- Weight gain in UARS patients may later result in development of OSA.
- Therapeutic approach for these patients patients does not differ from the rest of the group.
- Out-of-center testing using types 3 and 4 monitors do not detect RERAs. For those patients in whom the sleep disturbance is solely or predominantly due to RERAs, a diagnosis of sleep-disordered breathing will be missed.

REMember:

- Medicare guidelines for scoring respiratory events do *not* recognize RERAs. Only the AHI (average number of apneas and hypopneas per hour of sleep) is recognized by MCR for diagnostic purposes.
- Medicare definition of RDI = apneas + hypopneas/hour of *recording time*; usually applicable to type-3 or type-4 portable studies.
- AASM definition of RDI = apneas + hypopneas + RERAs/hour of *sleep* (PSG).
- AASM prefers term REI (respiratory event index) for scoring apneas and hypopneas/hour of monitoring time on a HSAT.

Further Reading:
Ballard, R.D. Upper Airway Resistance Syndrome, in Sleep: A Comprehensive Handbook. T. Lee-Chiong (editor), 2006, John Wiley & Sons, Inc.

Personalized/targeted therapy for OSA-the new frontier?

Multiple pathophysiological mechanisms involved in pathogenesis of OSA as described on page 127. To these may be added the effect of a low arousal threshold which, with UA obstruction, may cause frequent awakenings. Identification of these endotypes together with their clinical expression (phenotypes) may allow for the selection of an individualized therapeutic approach. Phenotypic manifestations may include patients who may be:

- Minimally Symptomatic
- Symptoms of UA obstruction
- Disturbed sleep (may have low arousal threshold and have more insomnia or less likely to tolerate CPAP)

- OSA with major cardiometabolic risk
- EDS: recent study found OSA patients (AHI ≥ 15) with severe EDS more likely to have incident CVD including CHF or be at risk for a future CV event than those with less severe daytime sleepiness (Mazzotti et al: *Am J Resp Crit Care Med* 2019; 200(4): 493-506. See also *AJRCCM* Editorial 2020; 202(12): 1622-4; PAP therapy → prevention of acute CV events in severe OSA or moderate OSA with EDS.)

Identification of endotypes at this time still in evolution. While anatomical abnormalities may be most important in determining therapy, the non-anatomical factors may help personalize treatment. These may include, for example:

- Prediction of CPAP induced CSA in high loop gain subjects.
- Low arousal threshold may contribute to EDS symptoms in a non-obese subject or in those without severe obstruction. If PAP therapy chosen, this sub-group may benefit from a non-myorelaxant hypnotic agent at least initially to improve CPAP compliance.
- PAP requirements <8cm H_2O → better prediction of success with hypoglossal nerve stimulation (*J Clin Sleep Med* 2019; 15(8): 1165-72). Individuals with a higher arousal threshold also had better outcomes with HGNS. (*AJRCCM* 2021; 203(6): 746-755).
- Desipramine shown to increase genioglossus muscle activity during sleep. May benefit those OSA subject with impaired UA dilator activity. Research also directed at additional pharmacological agents to enhance genioglossus activity (e.g. combination of atomoxetine and oxybutinin (*Am J Resp Crit Care Med* 2019; *CHEST* 2020).
- Polysomnographic endotyping to select patients for OAT. (*Annals ATS* 2019; 16(11): 1422-31 and editorial p1371-2.) Drug induced sleep endoscopy phenotyping may also assist in selecting patients for OAT (*JCSM* 2019; 15(8): 1089-1099).

Further reading

1. Eckert D. Phenotypic approaches to OSA - New Pathways for targeted Therapy. *Sleep Med Reviews* 2018; 37:45-49.

2. Eckert et al Defining Phenotypic Causes of OSA. *Am J Resp Crit Care Med* 2013; 188:996-1004.

3. Carberry et al Personalized Management Approach for OSA. *CHEST* 2018; 153 (3): 744-755.

4. Javaheri et al, Apneas of Heart Failure and Phenotype-guided Treatments *CHEST* 2020; 157(2): 394-402.

SLEEP DISORDERED BREATHING IN THE ELDERLY

- Studies in healthy elderly volunteers have shown an elevated AHI in the absence of cardiovascular disease and with normal cognitive performance:
- Knight et al *Am Rev Resp Dis* 1987;136:845-850: 10/27 healthy volunteers ave age 75.8 had an average AI 17.2/hr (6.6-37.6);
- 10% elderly had AI >10; 44% had RDI >20 (Review article by Ancoli-Israel & Coy *SLEEP* 1994;17:77-83)
- Therefore not always clear whether to treat ↑ AHI or RDI in absence of cardiovascular or cognitive abnormalities in the elderly population.
- The following table of **PSG Respiratory Abnormalities in Asymptomatic Individuals** (Pavlova et al *SLEEP* 2008;31) suggests a normal upward trend in the RDI with age:

PSG Respiratory Abnormalities in
Asymptomatic Individuals
(Pavlova et al *SLEEP* 2008;31 241-8)

	<35 (n=63)	35-49 (n=15)	50-65 (n=42)	>65 (n=43)
Ave age (yrs)	25.1	40.2	58	71.1
M/F	39/24	12/3	22/20	33/10
BMI	23.4	25.8	24.8	24.8
ESS	4.0	2.8	3.5	4.5
RDI	4.3	7.7	12.8	22.0

- An explanation as to why the elderly with OSA may have fewer consequences (see above) may be due to the presence of a lower loop gain compared to younger subjects; this may be protective by preventing large negative intrathortic pressure swings seen in younger OSA patients. (Kobayashi *CHEST* 2010 as reported by Owens et al *Chest Physician*, March 2018 page 12).

FYI.....Articles of interest in adult OSA over last few years:

OSA and Cardiovascular Complications:

- In patients with **congenital long-QT syndrome**, OSA may be associated with increased QT prolongation corrected for heart rate. OSA treatment may reduce QT prolongation and the risk of sudden cardiac death. Shamsuzzaman, et al *SLEEP* 2015; 38(7):1113-1119.
- Moderate-severe SDB with increased frequency of obstructive respiratory events and hypoxia had a two-fold increase in the odds of having any **nocturnal cardiac arrhythmia** after adjusting for age,

BMI, gender and cardiovascular diseases. This was felt to in part explain the increased risk in nocturnal sudden death in this group of patients. Selim, et al *J Clin Sleep Med* 2016; 12(6):829-837. Data from the DREAM study.

- Meta-analyses have shown that the **BP-lowering effect of CPAP** in hypertensive patients is approximately 2 to 3 mmHg. Even these small reductions in blood pressure may be associated with a 4-8% reduction in the risk of stroke and coronary heart disease (state-of-the-art review article *J Am Coll Card 2017*; 69(7): 841-858).

- Bouloukaki et al (*JCSM* 2020; 16(6): 889-898) found even mild OSA (e.g., AHI 11-15) had risk for HT. *JCSM* articles 2019; 15(2): 182-194 and 2020; 16(10): 1753-1760 point out that using the MCR 4% definition vs AASM criteria for scoring hypopneas will underestimate prevalence and severity of OSA and fail to identify individuals at risk from developing HT. Badhiraja et al (*JCSM* 2019; 15(9): 1261-1270) conclude that 4% desaturation requirement for hypopneas "too stringent and may deny treatment to some patients with OSA."

- Sapina - Beltran et al found 83.5% patients with resistant HT had OSA. Those with severe OSA had higher BP levels (*Annals ATS* 2019; 16(11): 1414-1421).

OSA and Mortality:

Apnea-Hypopnea Event Duration Predicts Mortality in Men and Women in the Sleep Heart Health Study. Butler et al *Am J. Resp Crit Care Med* April 1, 2019; 199(7): 903-912.

Eleven year follow-up of 5712 participants in the SHHS found that a shorter respiratory event duration was a predictor of all-cause mortality among men and women beyond that predicted by the AHI. The basis for this may be due to a low arousal threshold indicative of a phenotype associated with fragmented sleep and an increase in sympathetic tone. The risk associated was also stronger in those with moderate OSA (AHI 15-30). Short respiratory event duration may easily be determined from PSG analysis and identify those individuals at risk from adverse outcomes.

OSA and Nonalcoholic Fatty Liver Disease (NAFLD):

Mesarwi et al (*Am J Resp Crit Care Med*; Apr 1, 2019; 199(7): 830-841) review increasingly recognized association between OSA and NAFLD. Mechanism appears to be intermittent hypoxia → oxidative stress → mitochondrial dysfunction among other maladaptive consequences. Ng et al, however, failed to show improvement in NAFLD with CPAP (*Am J Resp Crit Care Med* 2021; 203(4): 493-501).

OSA and Cerebrovascular Disease:

- Review article (*J Clin Sleep Med* 2014; 10(1):103-108) evaluating the **impact of SDB in stroke or TIA patients on recurrence and death** indicated a dose-response relationship between the severity of SDB and the risk of recurrence and all-cause mortality. The impact of CPAP to lower the risk of these outcomes "remains controversial" indicating the need for additional studies.

- **25-40% of ischemic strokes are cryptogenic.** In this subgroup of patients, **a high clinical suspicion should be made for cardioembolic strokes and, in turn, this should lead to a search for the presence of OSA, which has a direct association with paroxysmal atrial fibrillation.** (Lipford, et al *SLEEP* 2015; 38(11):1699-1705)

- 50-70% of patients with acute ischemic stroke or TIA have obstructive sleep apnea of varying severity: AHI > 30 in 29% and > 40 in 14% patients. Most ischemic strokes occur while awake between 6:00 a.m. and noon, but there are a minority of acute ischemic stroke patients who fall under the category of so-called **"wake-up strokes"(WUS)**. Article by Siarnik, et al., (*J Clin Sleep Med* 2016; 12(4): 549-554) characterizes these patients as having a significantly higher AHI, desaturation index and arousal index compared with those who had non-WUS. (see also commentary on the above article: *J Clin Sleep Med* 2016; (12(4):463-465).

Review: Epilepsy and sleep related breathing disturbances (*CHEST* 2019; 156(1): 172-181. Incidence OSA ↑ in adults with epilepsy and increases with age. CPAP →↓ seizures compared to no treatment.

OSA and Depression:
- Edwards, et al *J Clin Sleep Med* 2015; 11(9):1029-1038 confirm the association between depression and OSA with a direct relationship to the severity of the SDB. 293 patients (who continued their usual anti-depressants) were treated with CPAP. 228 were compliant (mean nightly use > 5 hours) and were found to have a ↓in AHI from 46.7 to 6.5 and a significant improvement in the patient health questionnaire (PHQ-9) for depressive symptoms. The improvement on PAP therapy suggests a direct relationship between depressive symptoms and untreated OSA.

- Lang et al in *J Clin Sleep Med* 2017; 13(4):575-582 found that in an Australian study involving males 40-88yrs there was a significant association between undiagnosed OSA (AHI ≥30/hr) especially in those with EDS (Epworth Sleepiness Scale >10) and depression.

OSA and optic nerve function:
- Severe OSA may be responsible for **subclinical optic nerve dysfunction**. Study by Liguori, et al (*SLEEP* 2016; 39(1):19-23) found evidence of optic nerve dysfunction on electroretinography and visual evoked potentials in a group of OSA patients with an average AHI/time in bed ≥30/hr. Mechanism(s) thought to be hypoxia

causing increased vascular resistance or by elevated intracranial pressure during an apnea episode or by hypercarbia/acidosis.

- **Review article: Ocular Manifestation of Obstructive Sleep Apnea** *J Clin Sleep Med* 2017; 13 (11): 1345-8.

    - Floppy eyelid syndrome (FES)-upper eyelids easily evert with upward action. (Study: 27/50 patients with FES had OSA). 2-5% of OSA patients have FES – most with severe OSA. Present with ocular discomfort, dry eyes, redness, swelling of eyelid.

    - Non-arteritic ischemic neuropathy - Present with sudden painless visual loss. Ischemic basis. Increased risk with untreated OSA.

    - Central Serous retinopathy: idiopathic retinal detachment. OSA prevalence noted; 61% in one series.

    - Retinal vein occlusion: association with OSA 37-70%; symptoms often occur on waking. Possibly due to slow retinal bloodflow due to hypoxemia and intra-cranial pressure.

    - Glaucoma - both narrow angle and open angle glaucoma associated with OSA. Mechanism may be via hypoxic episodes (oxidative stress) causing optic nerve ischemia via effects on the retinal blood vessels, mitochondrial dysregulation and inflammation.

- **Progressive retinal arterial narrowing in severe OSA** (*JCSM* 2021; 17(5): 983-991).

OSA and pulmonary embolism:

There is a 30% chance of having a recurrence of PE. Alonso-Fernandez et al (*CHEST* 2016; 150 (6): 1291) indicate that OSA may be a risk factor for the recurrence because of its propensity for vascular endothelial impairment (via oxidative stress), decreased venous flow (sedentary lifestyle), and a tendency to increased coagulation. Secken et al (*JCSM* 2020; 16(7): 1029-36) report ↑ risk for acute PE and recurrances but found no ↑ in hospital mortality.

OSA and osteoporosis:

A case report and review of the literature (Chakhtoura et al *J Clin Sleep Med* 2015; 11 (5): 575-580) suggests that sleep apnea may be a risk factor for bone loss/osteoporosis. Possible mechanisms include hypogonadism (associated both with obesity and OSA), alterations in adrenergic tone (SNS known to play a role in regulation of bone remodeling), via increased inflammatory markers secondary to oxidative stress, the effect of hypoxia itself on bone formation (hypoxia increases formation of osteoclasts) as well as an increased prevalence of vitamin D deficiency in OSA. The authors do indicate that further studies are, however, needed to assess the incidence of bone loss and fractures in OSA patients.

White matter damage in OSA:
In a group of 20 patients with severe OSA (mean AHI 58.9; mean age 38.6; M18, F2) diffuse tensor imaging (an MRI sequence) detected impaired fiber integrity indicative of cerebral white matter damage and flow cytometry showed evidence of leukocyte apoptosis. The abnormal findings appeared to be correlated with increased OSA severity and hypoxia and could be mediated by systemic inflammation secondary to oxidative stress. Chen et al *SLEEP* 2015;38(3):361-70.

OSA and aging process:
Pinella et al found hallmarks of aging at the cellular level in younger OSA patients (median age <50yrs) with AHI $\geq$15, $\uparrow$ arousal index and O_2 saturation <90% (*Annals ATS* March 2021).

OSA and motor vehicle accidents; impact of CPAP:
In a Swedish study (SLEEP 2015;38(3):341-9) 1478 patients, 70.4% males; ave AHI 18; ODI 17, the following results were found when analyzing incidence of MVAs in the 5 years prior to CPAP therapy and comparing incidence to 5 years of CPAP:
    - MVA risk ratio 2.45 compared with controls (similar to other studies)
    - CPAP use >4hrs/night resulted in $\downarrow$MVA risk
    - Neither AHI nor ODI severity predicted risk
    - MVA risk correlated with age ($\uparrow$ in 65-80yr group), $\uparrow$ symptoms of daytime sleepiness (ESS >16), $\downarrow$TST, $\uparrow$hypnotic use and $\uparrow$total annual driving distance.

CPAP and Body Weight:
Studies have failed to demonstrate that CPAP treatment in itself is responsible for weight loss. Myllyla, et al (*J Clin Sleep Med* 2016; 12:519-528) demonstrated that the majority of CPAP compliant patients (mean age 55.6, mean BMI 33.5, mean AHI 33.7) failed to lose weight but gained at a slightly slower rate compared with an age-matched control population. High compliance did not prevent weight gain. Chen et al (*Annals ATS* 2021) report CPAP use <5hrs/night associated with $\uparrow$BMI whereas >5hrs/night "seems to be necessary in mitigation the risk for weight gain." A meta-analysis (*Thorax* 2015; 70:258-64) found that CPAP was associated with a 0.5 kg weight gain compared with controls over studies ranging from 1 to 48 months. The reports indicate that CPAP in itself does not cause weight loss and that specific measures for weight reduction need to be implemented.

Gut Dysbiosis and OSA:
Changes in the gut microbiome (GM) is an emerging concept in the pathogenesis of chronic disorders including OSA and HT. Intermittent hypoxia and hypercapnia may alter the GM. Reports suggest that gut dysbiosis may play a role in the pathophysiology of OSA-induced HT. (see Mashaqi and Gozal, *J Clin Sleep Med* 2019; 15(10): 1517-1527)

OSA variability: rostral fluid shifts.
OSA severity may vary from night to night. Cause is not always clear, but one possible explanation is that of **rostral fluid shifts**. Fluid which accumulates in the lower extremities due to gravity, shifts rostrally narrowing the upper airways and contributing to the pathogenesis of OSA. Variations in the amount of lower extremity fluid volume from day to day may subsequently affect the severity of sleep-disordered breathing on a night-to-night basis. (White et al *J Clin Sleep Med* 2015;11(2):149-156)

Epiglottic collapse (EC) and OSA: EC an uncommon cause of OSA and usually diagnosed during drug-induced sleep endoscopy. Patients have less severe OSA and mostly not overweight. Respond better to oral appliance therapy or positional therapy than PAP which could aggravate epiglottic closure. (Kim et al *J Clin Sleep Med* 2021; 17(3): 413-9).

State of Art Review: Sleep Apnea and Chronic Kidney Disease. Lin et al *CHEST* 2020; 157(3): 673-685. ↑ both OSA and CSA in CKD. OSA → more rapid progression of CKD.
Sleep Apnea and Insomnia. *CHEST* 2021; 159(5): 2020-2028. Focuses on management.

CENTRAL SLEEP APNEA SYNDROMES

PRIMARY CENTRAL SLEEP APNEA (CSA)

Prevalence:
Less common than OSA:
>- Prevalence in community studies 0.4-7.5% (highest in males > 65y)
>   Donavan and Kapur *SLEEP* 2016; 38(7): 1353-9.
>- 4-7% of sleep center referrals.
>- 17% in an apneic population.

CSA and OSA may overlap; CSA is primary diagnosis if >50% apneas are central.

Pathophysiology:
- Instability of CNS controller mechanisms play major role.
- CSA patients have ↑ respiratory drive due to ↑ peripheral & central ventilatory responsiveness to CO2 levels (high loop gain).*
- $PaCO_2$ levels are therefore relatively low and close to apneic threshold during wakefulness.
- With sleep onset, the apneic threshold rapidly rises above $PaCO_2$ levels leading to central apneas (see apnea threshold page 12).
- Sleep transitions are inherently unstable respiratory periods.
- Transitions are generally long in CSA thereby enhancing probability of central apneas.

> ***Loop Gain:** Describes stability of system controlled by feedback loops. In respiratory system, responsiveness to $PaCO_2$ plays key role. *High* loop gain results in *over-corrective* response to $PaCO_2$ levels, instability of the controller system (compared with low / damped loop gain) and a *propensity for central apneas.*

Clinical features
- Older than average OSA patient; M>F (?due to difference in testosterone levels).
- EDS (?less than OSA), poor concentration, morning headaches, irritability.
- Snoring (?less than OSA), often not obese, no cor pulmonale.
- More nocturnal awakenings, restless sleep & insomnia than OSA.
- Impact on BP , heart, cerebrovascular disease not as well defined as with OSA.
- CA reported to cause paroxysmal nocturnal dyspnea and nocturnal angina due to oxygen desaturations (Badr, S in *Central Sleep Apnea*, Up To Date, 2012).

Polysomnogram
- Increased N1 & N2 sleep, reduced N3.
- CA's uncommon in REM (? due to slightly higher $PaCO_2$).
- Oxygen desaturations milder than OSAS.
- OA's often seen too; generally diagnose CSA if 50%+ events are central.

Treatment approaches:
- PAP Therapy (generally regarded as first-line treatment, although very limited data available):
  - CPAP – generally regarded as initial therapeutic approach for primary CSA. (Mechanism unclear but may be due to end-expiratory loading causing mild CO2 retention).
  - BPAP-ST.
    - Caution: May induce hypocapnia and aggravate CSA.
    - Therefore use with backup rate (10-12 bpm).
  - Adaptive Pressure Support Servo Ventilation (APSSV or ASV).
    - ASV for primary CSA not as well studied as with CSB-CHF.
    - May be used as alternative to BPAP/ST after CPAP failure.
  - PAP and low concentration CO2 (Thomas, et al. *SLEEP* 2005; 28 (1), 69-77). AASM Guidelines for Treatment of CSA (*SLEEP* 2012) do not recommend CO2 as treatment option for Primary CSA. Alternative mechanism utilizing CO2 to prevent central apneas may be adding a dead space to the PAP circuit (rebreathing CO2 elevates the level above the apnea threshold).
- Supplemental oxygen as needed (with PAP therapy or where intolerant of PAP).
- Respiratory stimulants:
  - Acetazolamide. (Schmicki et al *CHEST* 2020; 158(6): 2632-2645. Acetazolamide for OSA and CSA. A systematic review. Short term improvement seen in CSA and OSA).

- Sedatives... Aim is to abolish arousals (no controlled studies):
  - Triazolam (one study: Bonnet, et al. *SLEEP* 1990; 13:31).
  - Zolpidem (Quadri, et al. *J Clin Sleep Med* 2009; 5 (2): 122-9).
- Transvenous stimulation of the phrenic nerve. Jagielski et al *Eur J Heart Fail* 2016; 18(11): 1386-93; Costanzo et al *Lancet* 2016; 388: 974-82. Both reports showed sustained improvement in AHI, central apnea index, oxygenation, sleep quality and QOL over 12 months. Additional studies report success rates up to 18 months; Javaheri & McKane, *JCSM* 2020; 16(12): 2099-2107.

Adaptive Pressure Support Servoventilation (APSSV or ASV).

- Provides variable amounts of ventilatory support depending on the subject's respiratory effort.
- Continuously monitors and records average ventilation (*Resmed* units) or average peak flow (*Respironics*) in 3-4 minute sampling periods.
- Continuously adjusts pressure support to achieve 90-95% of target ventilation (*Resmed*) or peak flow (*Respironics*).
- Backup rate: Auto mode (default frequency 15 breaths/min or fixed backup (usually 10-12 breaths/min depending on device used).
- End expiratory pressure adjusted for associated OSAS (usually determined during previous CPAP titration study). Newer ASV units have auto EPAP ability.
- Indications include
  - Opioid-induced sleep apnea especially where majority of events are central apneas.
  - Treatment-emergent CSA. ASV usually recommended if central apneas persist despite a trial of CPAP.
  - Caution in Cheyne-Stokes breathing associated with CHF. Avoid if EF $\leq$ 45% (See below).

Note:

(a) Central apneas may also occur as a result of brainstem pathology, classified ICSD3 as **Central Apnea due to a Medical disorder without CSB**. The brainstem pathology may be developmental (e.g. Arnold-Chiari malformation) or secondary to cerebrovascular disease, neoplasia, or other structural abnormalities, all of which may result in abnormalities of ventilatory control.

(b) Case reports of ticagrelor (*Brilinta*) causing CAs while on PAP therapy. (*JCSM* 2019; 15(8): 1179-1182, *Annals ATS* (Nov 2020). Mechanism may be $\uparrow$chemosensitivity to $\uparrow PaCO_2$.

(c) Positional primary CSA uncommon. Reported less frequently than with CSR-CSA in CHF. See case report *J Clin Sleep Med* 2013; 9(3): 265-8.

Further reading:
1. Javaheri et al: Positive Airway Pressure Therapy With Adaptive Servoventilation (part 1): *CHEST*; 2014; 146(2):514-523
2. Javaheri et al: Clinical Applications of Adaptive Servoventilation Devices (part 2): *CHEST*; 2014;146(3):858-868
3. Javaheri et al: Adaptive Servoventilation for Treatment of Opioid-Associated Central Sleep Apnea *J Clin Sleep Med*; 2014; 10(6):637-643
4. Eckert DJ et al: Central Sleep Apnea, Pathophysiology and Treatment *CHEST*; 2007; 131:595-607
5. Muza et al. Central Sleep Apnea - A Review. *J. Thor Dis.* 2015; 7(5): 930-937

CHEYNE STOKES BREATHING (CSA-CSB)

Diagnostic Features

CSB is a breathing pattern of recurrent episodes of *central apneas* alternating with hyperpneas , during which there is a crescendo- decrescendo pattern of tidal volume (Harrison et al, *Arch Int Med* 1934;53;89).

CSA-CSB is a *consequence* not the cause of the underlying condition (seen mainly in CHF; may occur in stroke syndromes; also less commonly reported in chronic renal failure).

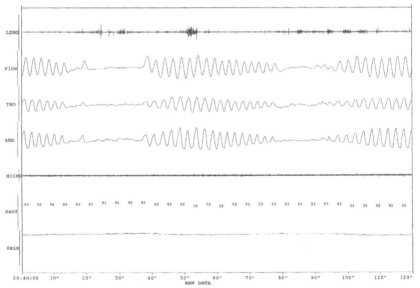

CSR: Note hyperpneas with crescendo- decrescendo pattern. Apnea duration relatively shorter.

Prevalence:

Reports vary:
- CSR 37% in CHF patients with EF <45%; 12% had OSA (Javaheri: *Int J Cardiol* 2006;106:21-28).
- Stable CHF & EF<45%:15% CSR; 53% OSA (Ferrier et al: *CHEST* 2005; 128: 2116-2122).

Pathophysiology of CSA-CSB in CHF

1. Apneas result from PaCO2 levels kept close to apneic threshold:
   - Hyperventilation due to venous congestion → stimulation of vagal afferents.
   - CHF patients may have increased ventilatory responses to rising PaCO2
   - Increased catecholamines stimulate hyperventilation
   - Arousals and sighs during sleep also→ ↑ventilation→ ↓$PaCO_2$
   - Apnea results when $PaCO_2$ falls below apnea threshold

2. Cresendo-decresendo breathing pattern of hyperpneas:
   - Very high correlation between ventilatory cycle length, LVEF & prolonged circulation time
   - Low CO → prolonged circulation time → delayed transmission of chemical signals from lungs and periferal tissues to central chemoreceptors → mismatch between arterial PaO2 and that of central controllers.

REMember:

- Apnea duration similar in length to idiopathic CSA (ICSA)
- Cycle time in ICSA 20-40 sec; in CSB 45-90 sec due to hyperpneas
- CSB uncommon in N3+REM

Risk factors for CSB in CHF:
- Males
- Age>60yrs
- Atrial fibrillation
- Severe LV dysfunction
- PaCO2 <38mmHg

Clinical features:
- Predominantly those of CHF (SOB,orthopnea, PND) and fatigue.
- Sleep fragmented (arousals due to apneas, orthopnea, PND).
- Poor prognosis with persistent CSB.

Treatment approaches:
- Optimize medical therapy (mainstay of Rx).
- Nocturnal oxygen (may ↓CSA but no improvement in cardiac function or QOL).
- CPAP –Canadian study showed improvement in nocturnal oxygenation, ejection fraction, lowered norepinephrine levels & distance walked in 6 minutes but **did not effect survival**. (Bradley et al *New Eng J Med* 2005; 353: 2025-2033).

- As a result of the above study there had been a concern by some in using CPAP in patients with a history of CHF and CSB (pro-con debate *J Clin Sleep Med* Oct 2006 p394). Post hoc analysis of the CANPAP study (Arzt et al *Circulation* 2007; 115(25): 3173-80) found that CPAP patients whose AHI was reduced to <15/hr at 3 months, had improved LVEF and heart transplant-free survival compared with the control group (i.e. no CPAP) while those CPAP patients whose AHI at 3 months was not reduced below 15 did not show a favorable outcome in these endpoints either. The results therefore suggest that "in heart failure patients, CPAP might improve both LVEF and heart transplant-free survival if CSA is suppressed soon after its initiation."
- CSB pattern may be difficult to eliminate on CPAP; may take weeks to resolve.
- In an earlier study ASV for SDB in CHF shown to be more effective than controls including CPAP and BPAP in improving AHI and LVEF (*CHEST* 2012; 142(5): 1211-1221). ASV in heart failure patients with a reduced ejection fraction (HFrEF) resulted in ↑mortality (*NEJM* 2015 - see below).
- Transvenous phrenic nerve stimulation for CSA (TPNS) found to be effective in CHF patients with CSA-CSR. ↓AHI ↑QOL reported. (Costanzo et al *Eur J. Heart Fail* 2018; 20(12): 1755-1759. See also Schwartz et al *JCSM* 2020; 16(5): 817-820.

Review Article: Update on Apneas of Heart Failure with Reduced Ejection Fraction. Javaheri et al *CHEST* 2020; 157(6): 1637-1646.

GUIDELINES FOR ASV IN CHF-ASSOCIATED CSAS:

Summary of Special Article regarding use of ASV in CSA associated with systolic heart failure: **Updated Adaptive Servo Ventilation Recommendations for the 2012 AASM Guideline: "The Treatment of CSA Syndromes in Adults."**
J Clin Sleep Med 2016;12(5)757-761.

As a result of a study published in the New England Journal of Medicine by Cowie, et al., (*NEJM* 2015; 373:1095-1105), in which 1325 patients with central sleep apnea and an ejection fraction of ≤ 45% were randomized to ASV therapy (together with medical therapy) or medical therapy alone, those in the ASV group were found to have a significantly higher all-cause and cardiovascular mortality. The mortality usually occurred as an out-of-hospital event, could occur without preceding hospitalization or worsening symptoms, did not diminish with amount of time on ASV, and was independent of patient's perceived response to ASV.

The new guidelines indicate that ASV should not be used for the treatment of moderate or severe central sleep apnea related to CHF when the ejection fraction is ≤ 45% (*standard recommendation*).
An *option recommendation* is given for ASV use where the there is mild CHF-associated CSAS or where the EF is >45%.
The manufacturers' recommendations (*Resmed & Philips*) include the same AASM guidelines outlined above, together with the recommendation that patients currently on ASV should be re-evaluated for continued use in light of the current guidelines.

Possible explanations for the increased mortality in the ASV group may include:
- decreased cardiac output with ASV.
- Cheyne-Stokes Respiration could be an adaptive rather than a pathologic response. (Shafazand and Badr, *J Clin Sleep Med* 2016;12(1):147-150.)

Summary of PAP therapy approach in CHF patients with CSR.

(a) If EF >45% some labs still begin with CPAP. May need supplemental O_2. If CAs persist treat with ASV (in preference to BiPAP S/T). Other labs will Rx with ASV preferentially over CPAP for severe CSA-CSR with EF >45%.

(b) If EF ≤ 45% recommendation is to avoid ASV. If CSA persists despite full medical therapy, options include CPAP, CPAP with O_2 or O_2 alone. BiPAP S/T avoided as effect may be similar to ASV in this population group. Costanzo et al in *J. Card. Failure* 2020; 26(10) supplement pS69 reported success with TPNS in CSA-CSB with reduced EF incl <45%. Fudim et al *JCSM* 2019; 15(12): 1747-1755 showed ↑ EF, ↑ QOL, ↑ sleep quality and ↓ CSA in CSB with EF≤ 45% over 12 months with TPNS.

REMember:

- **Periodic breathing** (PB) is a pattern of waxing and waning breathing in which hyperpneas alternate with hypopneas. This pattern is commonly seen at high altitude (usually > 8,000 feet) and most subjects are asymptomatic.
- Central apneas may also be present (**Central Sleep Apnea due to High Altitude Periodic Breathing**- ICSD3 p79).

TREATMENT-EMERGENT CENTRAL SLEEP APNEA:
(TE-CSA) (FORMERLY COMPLEX SLEEP APNEA)

1. Situation in which central apneas (CAs) emerge with increasing PAP.
   - Emergence or persistence of CAs on exposure to CPAP or BiPAP for treatment of OSA. CAs may ↓ as PAP decreases.
   - Reports of incidence very widely; 5.7% - 20% of CPAP titrations.
   - Risk factors:
     - CAs > 5/hr or mixed apneas on diagnostic PSG (Estimated that 7% - 8% of OSA patients will have a CA index > 5/hr).
     - Severe OSA.
     - History of cardiac disease.
     - M > F.
     - Opioid use.
   - Mixed apneas with long apnea duration and smaller ventilatory duration/cycle duration may predict TE-CSA. (Pavsic et al *AJRCCM* accepted for publication Nov 2020).

2. Possible Mechanisms:
   a. OSA patients have high upper airways resistance (UAR) which damps the ventilatory control system. PAP →↓ UAR →↓ $PaCO_2$ below apnea threshold → CA.
   b. CPAP/BiPAP may worsen sleep quality → arousals →↓ $PaCO_2$ below apnea threshold →CA. High loop gain may facilitate CA's.
   c. BiPAP also has pressure support component →↑ tidal volume →↓ $PaCO_2$ below apnea threshold →CA. If high loop gain present, may facilitate CA's.
   d. Overtitration → activation lung stretch receptors inhibiting central control.
   e. Hypopneas during diagnostic PSG may have had central and obstructive components. Elimination of obstructive element with PAP may unmask central component.
   f. Wash out CO_2 via mouth leaks or mouth breathing with ↑ PAP.

3. Treatment: Most cases (78% - 92%) CAs resolve within 2 - 3 months of regular CPAP therapy. Alternative treatment: ASV with EPAP set to control the OAs, or BiPAP *with* backup rate (BiPAP without backup rate may aggravate CAs).

4. Mogenthaler et al *SLEEP* 2014; 37(5):927 reported 65% success with CPAP and ~90% with ASV at 90 days (AHI 9.9 vs 4.4).

5. A therapeutic *approach* may be to initiate CPAP at "best" pressure for OSA. Repeat PAP study in 2 - 3 months with ability to initiate ASV if still significant CAs on CPAP.

6. Incidence of treatment emergent CSA using auto PAP uncertain.

Further Reading:
1. Javaheri S., et al: The Prevalence and Natural History of Complex Sleep Apnea. *J. Clin. Sleep Med* 2009; 5 (3): 205 - 211.
2. Lehman, et al: Central Sleep Apnea on Commencement of Continuous Positive Airway Pressure in Patients with a Primary Diagnosis of Obstructive Sleep Apnea. *J. Clin. Sleep Med.* 2007; 3 (5): 462 - 466.
3. Hoffman M. Schulman, M.D.: The Appearance of Central Sleep Apnea After Treatment of Obstructive Sleep Apnea. *CHEST* 2012; 142 (2): 517 - 522.
4. Brown S., et al: A Retrospective Case Series of ASV for Complex Sleep Apnea. *J. Clin. Sleep Med.* 2011; 7 (2): 187 - 195.

CENTRAL SLEEP APNEA DUE TO MEDICATION OR SUBSTANCE:

- ICSD-3 includes in this category central apneas due to chronic use of long-acting opioids, most commonly methadone, but also with other opioids including morphine and hydrocodone.
- Additional PSG findings include obstructive hypoventilation, Biot's (irregular or ataxic) breathing and periodic breathing. (If the predominant abnormality is hypoventilation then the diagnosis is that of sleep related hypoventilation due to a medication/substance).
- Prevalence CSA in chronic pain patients on opioids 20-33%. (Mubashir et al *J. Clin Sleep Med* 2020; 16(6): 961-9.
- Chronic opioid users may also have both OSA and CSA appearing simultaneously (*J. Clin. Sleep Med.* 2008; 4: 321-323.).
- CSA diagnosed when >50% events are central.
- Knowledge of pathophysiology of opioid-induced sleep apnea very limited. May be due to effect on μ receptors in medulla.
- Treatment with ASV generally successful in treating patients with opioid-induced central sleep apnea [Success rate approaching 70% in report by Ramar, et al (see reference below). ASV,however, generally unsuccessful in Farney et al's series. May have been due to the presence of irregular/ataxic breathing patterns in this group of patients].

Further Reading:
1. Walker J. M., et al: Chronic Opioid Use is a Risk Factor for the Development of Central Sleep Apnea and Ataxic Breathing. *J. Clin. Sleep Med.* 2007; 3 (5): 455 - 461.
2. Ramar K., et al: ASV in Patients with Central or Complex Sleep Apnea Related to Chronic Opioid Use and Congestive Heart Failure. *J. Clin. Sleep Med.* 2012; 8: 569 - 576.
3. Javaheri, et al: Adaptive Pressure Support Servoventilation; a Novel

Treatment for Sleep Apnea Associated with Use of Opioids. *J. Clin. Sleep Med.* 2008; 4: 305 - 310 (ASV successfully used in this series of patients.).

4. Farney, et al: ASV in Patients with Sleep Disordered Breathing Associated with Chronic Opioid Medications for Non-Malignant Pain. *J. Clin. Sleep Med.* 2008; 4: 311 – 319.

5. Van Ryswyk and Antic: Opioids and Sleep Disordered Breathing. *CHEST* 2016; 150(4): 934-944. Review article, "Currently available literature points to ASV for controlling CSA associated with chronic opioid use."

6. Mubashir et al: Prevalence of sleep disordered breathing in opioid users with chronic pain: a systematic review, *J Clin Sleep Med* 2020; 16(6): 961-9.

CENTRAL APNEAS IN HYPERCAPNIC DISORDERS
(NOT INCLUDED AS A SEPARATE SUBTYPE IN ICSD3)

- CAs may be seen in sleep in patients with chronic alveolar hypoventilation (Includes end stage lung disease or neuromuscular disorders).
- During sleep there is a progressive ↑$PaCO_2$ and ↓ PaO_2 leading to arousals.
- Brief returns to a wakefulness drive to breathe may drop the $PaCO_2$ below the elevated apneic threshold resulting in CAs.
- CAs in these situations are not primary manifestations of the underlying disorders.
- Treatment is directed to the underlying disorder with possible addition of BPAP (usually BPAP-ST).

Summary: **Practice Parameters Article: The Treatment of Central Sleep Apnea Syndromes in Adults** *SLEEP* 2012; 35 (1); 17 - 33.

Note: This guideline remains on the AASM website with the important 2016 update regarding ASV use (see above).

1. **Primary CSAS:** Limited studies; therefore limited evidence and all treatments regarded as *options* (as opposed to standard therapy).
   a. Positive airway pressure therapy.
   b. Acetazolamide (Side effects may include paresthesias, tinnitus, GI symptoms, metabolic acidosis, electrolyte imbalance, drowsiness).
   c. Hypnotics: zolpidem and triazolam.

---

2. **CSAS Due to Congestive Heart Failure (CHF) Including Cheyne-Stokes Breathing Pattern (CSBP) and Not Cheyne-Stokes Breathing.**
   a. CPAP therapy targeted to normalize the apnea hypopnea index is indicated for the initial treatment of CSAS related to CHF (_standard_ recommendation). CPAP treatment in CSAS due to CHF shown to have a positive effect on transplant-free survival if targeted to reduce AHI to < 15.
   b. Adaptive Servo-Ventilation (ASV) (_standard_ recommendation). Currently survival data not available but data does show improvement in AHI and LVEF "at least comparable, if not better, than the data supporting CPAP use." **See however updated guidelines for patients with EF ≤ 45% outlined above.**
   c. Oxygen therapy (_standard_). Studies have shown that oxygen therapy in CSAS associated with CHF may reduce the AHI and improve LVEF, but its effect on transplant-free survival has not been assessed. Consider O2 therapy where compliance with CPAP is poor.
   d. BiPAP therapy in the spontaneous timed (ST) mode only when there is no response to adequate trials of CPAP, ASV, and oxygen therapies (_option_).
   e. Acetazolamide and theophylline: (Data not strong; therapies are an _option_). Consider where central apneas persist despite optimization of standard medical therapy and PAP therapy is not tolerated.

3. **CSAS Due to Medical Condition Not Cheyne-Stokes:ESRD.**
   a. CPAP.
   b. Supplemental oxygen.
   c. Bicarbonate buffer during dialysis.
   d. Nocturnal dialysis.
   e. Level of evidence is very low and all of the above are regarded as _options_.

4. **CSAS Due to High-Altitude Periodic Breathing.**
   Pharmacologic agents used have included acetazolamide, theophylline, temazepam, zolpidem and zaleplon. Studies are limited and evidence is very low precluding a recommendation for any of these agents. All should be used for short periods of time.

5. **CSAS Due To Drug or Substance.**
   Limited studies regarding effectiveness of CPAP, BiPAP, or ASV. Results inconsistent and evidence very low precluding the formation of a recommendation.

Positional CSA – case reports
   • CSR and Supine Dependency, _Eur. RespJ_ 2005; 25: 829.
   • A case of positional CSA, _JCSM_ 2013; 9(3): 265-8.

SLEEP RELATED HYPOVENTILATION/ HYPOXEMIA SYNDROMES

Note: ICSD3 separates these into separate categories. Etiologies for disorders in both categories may be similar and differ only in the degree of severity. It may be necessary to reclassify a hypoxemic into a hypoventilation disorder as the condition deteriorates. Diurnal hypoventilation (chronic respiratory failure) may ultimately supervene.

- **Sleep-induced hypoventilation:**
  (a) $PaCO_2$ ↑ to ≥ 55 mmHg for 10 minutes, OR
  (b) ≥ 10 mmHg ↑ $PaCO_2$ above wake supine $PaCO_2$ to value > 50 mmHg for ≥ 10 minutes.

- **Sleep-induced hypoxemia:**
  SpO_2 ≤ 88% (≤ 90% in pediatric population) for ≥ 5 minutes; may be cumulative.

Examples of Sleep-Related Hypoventilation/Hypoxemia Disorders:

- Congenital Central Alveolar Hypoventilation Syndrome (see section 12).
- Idiopathic Central Alveolar Hypoventilation Syndrome.
- Obesity Hypoventilation Syndrome.
- Neuromuscular or chest wall disorders.
- COPD (section 11).
- Conditions associated with pulmonary parenchymal or vascular pathology (section11).

Mechanisms of Hypoxemia and Hypercapnia during Sleep in Lung Disorders and Neuromuscular Disorders.

- During sleep PaO_2↓ 3-9mmHg and $PaCO_2$ ↑ 2-6mmHg in healthy subjects (see section 2).
- In patients with lung disorders degree of deoxygenation. will depend on position of PaO_2 on the oxyhemoglobin dissociation curve.
- More severe desaturations occur if on or near the steep part of the curve.

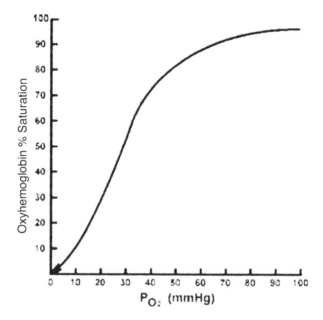

- **COPD, interstitial or vascular lung disease:** ventilation/perfusion (V/Q) mismatch is main cause of hypoxemia. CO2 retained as disease progresses and V/Q mismatch worsens.
- **Neuromuscular disorders:** CO2 retention occurs due to inability to maintain an adequate minute ventilation from muscular weakness.
    - Compensatory mechanisms including chemosensitivity responses and wakefulness drive which help to maintain PaO2 and PaCO2 levels during wakefulness are lost in sleep. Hypotonia in REM sleep further aggravates gas exchange.
    - Gas exchange becomes increasingly dependent on diaphragmatic activity which in itself may not in itself be able to sustain adequate alveolar ventilation.
- **In COPD,** the diaphragm is also compromised by flattening and therefore is at a mechanical disadvantage the extent of which depends on the degree of hyperinflation.

IDIOPATHIC CENTRAL ALVEOLAR HYPOVENTILATION SYNDROME.

Background:
- Patients have chronic alveolar hypoventilation (compensated respiratory failure; i.e., ↑ PaCO2 with normal pH) and **normal** pulmonary mechanics.

- Initially hypoventilation may be only sleep related; diurnal with disease progression.
- Uncommon; less frequent than secondary central alveolar hypoventilation due to pathological process affecting brainstem (e.g., poliomyelitis, brainstem infarction or tumors).
- Pathophysiology due to blunted chemoresponsiveness to PaO_2 and $PaCO_2$ levels.

Clinical features:
- Insomnia and EDS due to arousals.
- Morning headaches.
- Fatigue/dyspnea.
- With progressive disease; polycythemia, pulmonary hypertension, cor pulmonale, and RH failure.

PSG:
- Reduced tidal volumes lasting > 10 seconds (often >1min).
- Hypoxia/hypercapnia worse in REM sleep.
- Frequent arousals.
- OSA and CSA may coexist but not intrinsic features of the condition.

Treatment:
- Nocturnal ventilatory assist device (e.g., BiPAP/ BiPAP S/T).
- Oxygen, diuretics, respiratory stimulants.

OBESITY HYPOVENTILATION SYNDROME (OHS)
(Previously known as the Pickwickian Syndrome)

Essential features.
- Obesity
- Chronic CO_2 retention (PaO_2 >45mmHg) and hypoxia; worse in sleep
- 90% have associated OSA (AHI > 5/hr)

Pathogenesis: chronic CO_2 retention due to a combination of:
- central controller defect ($\downarrow$ chemoresponsiveness)
- associated OSA
- excessive mechanical load on respiratory system $\rightarrow\uparrow$ work of breathing aggravated during sleep by the supeimposed OSA.

Clinical features:
- Middle age; M>F
- Morning headaches, fatigue
- RHF (edema, ascites), plethora
- Snoring & other features of OSA
- EDS probably due to combination of CO2 retention and OSA

Laboratory testing:
- Elevated serum bicarbonate
- ABGs: compensated respiratory acidosis (elevated PaCO2 and normal pH) and chronic hypoxia
- PFTs....r/o COPD
- CBC (elevated HCT)
- EKG (RV hypertrophy), Echocardiogram(pulmonary hypertension)

PSG findings (*CHEST* 2007; 132 : 1322-1326)
- OSAS (90% cases; mean AHI 66/hour)
- SaO2 nadir 65%; 50% of the time spent with SaO_2 <90%
- Hypoxemia and CO_2 retention unrelated to obstructive events.

Treatment:
- CPAP successful in > 50% (average pressure 14 cwp, *CHEST* 2007; 132: 1322-1326).
- BPAP
  - Mean pressure 18/9 cwp
  - Some require additional inspiratory pressure for residual hypoxia once OSA resolved (8 - 10 cm above EPAP)
  - Supplemental oxygen needed in about 50%
  - ABGs often improve with regular PAP use
- Randomized controlled trial of CPAP vs BPAP for OHS: results were similar for overall improvement in ventilatory failure, QOL and adherance. Baseline $PaCO_2$ predicted persistent ventilatory failure on treatment. (Howard et al: *Thorax*: 11/15/2016)
- Medications:
  - Acetazolamide - caution if acidotic. No good study.
  - Medroxyprogesterone (Single study Sutton et al *Am J Int Med* 1975). Risk DVT — not recommended.
- Bariatric surgery.

Official American Thoracic Society (ATS) Clinical Practice Guideline:

Evaluation and Management of OHS. Mokhlesi et al. *AJRCCM* 2019; 200(3): 280-290. See also summary of above guideline *Annals of ATS* 2020; 17(1):11-15.

Note all recommendation conditional (i.e. not strong). Includes discussion with patients regarding individualized management choices.

1. Screening for OHS:
   (a) strong suspician: measure $PaCO_2$.
   (b) Low to moderate suspicion (<20% pretext probability): Measure serum bicarbonate. If <27 mmol/L, OHS unlikely; if >=27mmol/L may check PaCO2 to confirm or exclude OHS.

(c) Use of SpO2 to decide on whether to check PaCo, not recommended.

2. PAP treatment for OHS:
PAP recommended for stable ambulatory OHS patients.

3. PAP therapy also recommended in preference to non-invasive venti-lation (NIV) in stable ambulatory OHS patients with concommitant severe OSA and stable respiratory failure. (will apply to the majority of OHS patients, ≥ 70% having severe OSA). (See also *Annals ATS* 2019; 16(10): 1295-1303.

4. Hospitalized patients suspected with OHS: Treat and discharge on NIV. Evaluate within +/- 3 months in sleep lab for "outpatient workup and titration of PAP therapy."(Personal comment: PSG should include CO2 monitoring; may detect need for continued NIV).

5. Weight loss:
Should aim for 25-30% reduction in actual body weight to improve hypoventilation. If bariatric surgery considered, full discussion regarding risks and rewards essential. See also Weight Loss Inter-ventions as Treatment for OHS (*Annals ATS* 2020;17(4): 492 -502). Confirms target 25-30% ↓ body weight though evidence weak. Bari-atric surgery more effective in improving OHS and OSA.

REMember:

- OHS patients have higher ICU admission rates for respiratory problems and need for intubation compared with those who have similar degrees of simple obesity in similar circumstances.
- Also higher mortality compared to equally obese individuals without CO_2 retention.

Physiology Review Article: A Pickwickian Problem: How is Breathing Controlled? Lanks et al *Annals Am. Thorac Soc* 2019; 16(1): 138-143.

POSTPOLIO SYNDROME (PPS) — A NEUROMUSCULAR DISORDER

Background:
- Respiratory failure in acute polio due to anterior horn cell destruction or respiratory center involvement.
- PPS may occur 20 to 30yrs after the acute event; more often if with more severe involvement, older age and more complete recovery.

Symptoms include:
- Fatigue (80%) and concentration difficulties common.
- Swallowing and speech problems if bulbar involvement.
- Muscle weakness/atrophy,pain (focal or general)

PSG
- Nocturnal hypoventilation/hypoxemia
- OSA
- Central apneas may appear as the condition worsens.

Treatment may include CPAP or BPAP (with backup rate) $\pm$ O2.

Summary: **Best Clinical Practices for the Sleep Center Adjustment of Noninvasive Positive Pressure Ventilation (NPPV) in Stable Chronic Alveolar Hypoventilation Syndromes** (*J. Clin. Sleep Med.* 2010; 6 (5): 491 - 509).

- NPPV titrated during attended PSG for the following conditions associated with chronic alveolar hypoventilation (CAH):
  - ~ Obesity Hypoventilation Syndrome (OHS).
  - ~ Restrictive Thoracic Cage Disorders (RTCD).
  - ~ Central Respiratory Control Disturbances (CRCD), congenital or acquired.
  - ~ Neuromuscular Disease (NMD).

- BPAP should be able to deliver:
  - ~ Adjustable IPAP and EPAP to maintain upper airway patency; the IPAP-EPAP difference provides pressure support (PS) to augment tidal volume.
  - ~ In the spontaneous mode (S) setting, patient determines the time spent in IPAP and the respiratory rate.(Patient cycles device from IPAP to EPAP).
  - ~ Spontaneous - timed (ST) mode: Backup respiratory rate of minimum10 breaths/min for patients with central hypoventilation, significantly impaired respiratory drive,

frequent central apneas, or inability to trigger the device due to muscle weakness. Use if inadequate ventilation or persistent muscle fatigue despite maximum pressure support.
  ~ Timed mode (T) delivers IPAP-EPAP cycles at set respiratory rate; used where ST mode unsuccessful.

- Goals of NPPV titration.
  ~ Reduce sleep fragmentation and improve sleep quality.
  ~ $\downarrow$ work of breathing and provide respiratory muscle rest.
  ~ Normalize or improve gas exchange.
  ~ Improve nocturnal symptoms in patients with nocturnal hypoventilation.

- Parameters monitored include:
  ~ Airflow signal directly from NPPV device (not via thermal device or nasal pressure cannula).
  ~ $PaCO_2$ measured by arterial blood gas testing (most accurate), transcutaneous CO_2 or end-tidal PCO_2 monitoring.
  ~ Pressure settings:
    - minimum starting IPAP and EPAP is 8 cm H_2O and 4 cm H_2O respectively.
    - Minimum starting pressure support (PS)differences (between IPAP and EPAP) is 4cm; maximum PS difference is 20 cm H_2O.
    - Max IPAP is 20cm (for age <12 years) and 30 cm if $\geq$ 12 years.
    - $\uparrow$ PS by 1 - 2 cm H_2O at 5 minutes intervals for tidal volumes below 6 - 8 mL/kg.
    - $\uparrow$ PS by 1-2cm if PCO_2 levels remaining 10 mmHg above goal for 10 minutes or more (Goal is PCO2 level $\leq$ the awake PCO_2).
    - $\uparrow$ PS also for $SpO_2 \leq 90\%$ with low tidal volumes.

- If co-existing OSA, follow AASM Clinical Guidelines for PAP titration.

- Supplemental oxygen added if:
  ~ Awake supine SpO_2 on room air < 88%.
  ~ SpO_2 < 90% for > 5 minutes despite optimal PS and respiratory rate.
  ~ Begin oxygen at 1 L/min.; $\uparrow$ every 5 minutes until SpO_2 > 90%.

- Quality of NPPV titration.
  ~ Optimal titration includes:
    - RDI < 5/hour.
    - Absence of snoring.

- Minimum $SpO_2 > 90\%$ at sea level.
- Normalization/improvement of ventilation with PaCO2 (if measured) not >10 mmHg above treatment goal (see above).
- Reduction in excessive respiratory muscle activity.
- All above should occur for at least a 15 minute period including REM sleep in the supine position.

~ Good titration.
- All above criteria met but without REM sleep in the supine position (may include NREM sleep while supine or REM sleep in non-supine positions).

~ Adequate titration.
- Above goals met except RDI is < 10 per hour during a 15-minute sleep period, which includes NREM sleep while supine, or REM sleep in non-supine positions.

~ Unacceptable titration does not meet any of the above standards (should be repeated).

NOTE: Above guidelines do not apply for patients with COPD, Cheyne-Stokes Breathing or Primary Central Sleep Apnea.

Recent technology for patients with chronic alveolar hypoventilation including COPD, neuromuscular disease, or obesity-hypo-ventilation syndrome: **Volume-Assured Pressure Support Ventilation (VAPS)**.

Depending on the manufacturer, VAPS:
- Targets tidal volume or alveolar ventilation
- Uses variable pressure support to achieve target ventilation
- Able to set maximum pressure support, IPAP and EPAP levels
- Able to synchronize to patient's breathing pattern and to set inspiratory and rise times
- Has backup rate

Further reading/references:

Casey KR et al: Sleep-related Hypoventilation/Hypoxic Syndromes *CHEST* 2007;131:1936-1948

Ozsancak A & Hill N: Nocturnal Noninvasive Ventilation *CHEST* 2008;133;1275-1286

Sleep Disordered Breathing in Neuromuscular Disease *CHEST* 2017; 152(4): 880-892

SNORING

- Caused by vibration of soft tissue in the naso-, oro-, and hypopharynx.
- May occur as an independent condition ("primary" or "social"snoring) or part of a symptom complex associated with OSA.
- May be found secondary to other conditions such as nasal pathologies, adenotonsillar hypertrophy, craniofacial abnormalities, as well as conditions such as acromegaly or hypothyroidism.
- Alcohol and medications which relax the upper airways may precipitate or intensify snoring.
- Prevalence: ±20% of males snore > 50% of the night. (*Am. J. Resp. Crit. Care Med* 1995)
- Prevalence increases with increased body weight.
- Most common impact from snoring itself is disruption of the bed-partner's sleep.
- Impact of snoring, per se, on blood pressure and coronary artery disease uncertain. A study by Lee et al. (*SLEEP* 2008; 31:1207-13) suggested that snoring itself may be associated with carotid artery atherosclerosis. Also associated with ↑ carotid artery intima-media thickness and ↑ risk cerebral events (Li et al *CHEST* 2020; 158(5): 2146-2154).
- ↓ Palatal sensory function in untreated snorers. Svanborg et al *CHEST* 2020; 157(5): 1296-1303.
- Traumatic snoring vibrations and tissue stretch may cause axon degeneration of soft palate nerves resulting in swallowing dysfunction and ↑ risk for UA obstruction during sleep. *CHEST* 2018; 154(5): 1091-8.
- During pregnancy, the prevalence of snoring increases and may be a forerunner of sleep-disordered breathing which is associated with an increased maternal and fetal complication rate.
- Management:
  - Sleep testing (PSG versus HST) to exclude (or treat) OSA. Treatment of OSA will usually bring relief from snoring.
  - Lifestyle changes: Diet, smoking cessation, decreased alcohol consumption especially close to bedtime, avoid muscle relaxants including certain hypnotics e.g. BZDs.
  - Evaluate and treat for predisposing conditions: e.g. nasal problems, adenotonsillar hypertrophy, clinically significant retrognathia, hypothyroidism.
  - Positional therapy as appropriate.
  - External or internal nasodilators (usually purchased OTC). Variable success.
  - Oral appliances (OTC or custom made).
  - Empiric use of CPAP.

- Surgical procedures:
    (a) For underlying pathological processes (see above).
    (b) Modified UPPP procedures e.g. Laser-assisted uvuloplasty (LAUP).
    (c) Radio frequency ablation to soft palate or tongue base.
    (d) Injection snoreplasty.
    (e) Palatal implants (Pillar procedure).
- Feb 2021: FDA approval for marketing of eXciteOSA®, a neuromuscular tongue simulator for snoring and mild OSA for patients 18+ years . Needs physician Rx.

SLEEP RELATED GROANING (CATATHRENIA)

Clinical features:

- Clusters expiratory groaning almost exclusively in REM in 2nd half of night.
- Deep inspiration followed by long expiration with groan-like sound.
- May end with change in sleep position.
- Onset usually in childhood; often initial physician encounter is prior to leaving home for camp, college, etc.
- Subject unaware; bedpartner concerned and his/her sleep disrupted.

PSG indicated to exclude sleep disordered breathing; may show arousals.

Treatment:

- Treatment often unsatisfactory.
- ?empiric CPAP (positive result reported in Case Book of Sleep Medicine *AASM* 2008 but failure in one case report discussed in *Principles and Practice of Sleep Medicine* 4th edition pp 917-918).

See also:
State-of-Art Review Article: Alonso et al: Catathrenia *J. Clin Sleep Med* 2017; 13(4): 613-622.

Test Your Memory (Section 10):

1. Risk factors for OSA may include all except:

    a. Hypothyroidism.
    b. Polycystic ovarian syndrome.
    c. COPD.
    d. Pregnancy.
    e. Acromegaly.

2. Untreated OSA is a risk of motor accidents that is higher than controls by a factor of about:

    a. 2.5 - 3.
    b. 4 - 5.
    c. 5 - 6.
    d. 6 - 7.
    e. 8 - 10.

3. The STOP screening questionnaire aims to obtain responses for all of the following except:

    a. Hypertension.
    b. Cognitive symptoms such as sleepiness.
    c. Witnessed apneas.
    d. Weight.
    e. Loud snoring.

4. In what has been traditionally known as the UARS, which of the following statements is correct?

    a. Blunted sensitivity of UA mechanoreceptors may contribute to the syndrome.
    b. Arousals are directly caused by oxygen desaturation.
    c. Airflow limitation associated with desaturations of 3%.
    d. Systemic symptoms often reported.
    e. Nasal pressure transducer is the definitive diagnostic test.

5. Absolute contraindications to CPAP include:

    a. Bullous emphysema.
    b. Recurrent sinus infections.
    c. Recurrent ear infections.
    d. Severe asthma.
    e. None of the above.

6. The "cut off" ejection fraction below which ASV should not be used in patients with CSR:

    a. 55%.
    b. 50%.
    c. 45%.
    d. 40%.
    e. 35%.

7. ASV has been typically used in the treatment of the following conditions except:

    a. Cheyne-Stokes breathing.
    b. Complex sleep apnea syndrome.
    c. Obesity hypoventilation syndrome.
    d. Opioid-induced sleep-disordered breathing.

8. Obesity hypoventilation syndrome (OHS) reported to be associated with all except:

    a. Restrictive pulmonary mechanics.
    b. OSA.
    c. Polycythemia.
    d. Carbon dioxide retention found only during sleep.
    e. Positive response to CPAP.

9. Which of the following is considered not to be a risk factor for treatment-emergent CSA?

    a. Frequent central apneas on diagnostic PSG.
    b. Underlying hypertension.
    c. History of cardiac disease.
    d. Severe sleep apnea.
    e. Methadone use.

10. Which of the following statements is/are correct?

    a. AASM definition of RDI = number of apneas, hypopneas and RERAs/hour of sleep.
    b. Medicare definition of RDI = number of apneas and hypopneas/hour of monitoring time for home sleep testing.
    c. AASM defines respiratory event index (REI) as number of apneas and hypopneas/hour of monitoring time for home sleep testing.
    d. All are correct.

11. What serum bicarbonate level could trigger a suspician for OHS in the appropriate setting?

    a. > 20 mmol/L.
    b. < 27 mmol/L.
    c. > 27 mmol/L.
    d. none of the above.

Answers: 1c, 2a, 3d, 4d, 5e, 6c, 7c, 8d, 9b, 10d, 11c

Section 11:

SLEEP IN OTHER DISORDERS

Section includes sleep associated with

Epilepsy Syndromes
Psychiatric Disorders
Neurodegenerative Disorders
Respiratory Disorders
Fibromyalgia
Pregnancy
Cancer and Sleep

EPILEPSY AND SLEEP:

Background:

Definitions:
- A *seizure* is the clinical manifestation of an excessive hypersynchronized discharge of neurons in the cerebral cortex.
- *Epilepsy* is the clinical disorder resulting from recurrent seizures.
- *"Ictal"* refers to a seizure event which may be generalized (tonic-clonic),absence, myoclonic, partial (simple or complex).
- Transient abnormal EEG discharges between seizure events are referred to as *"interictal."*
- *"Epileptiform"* refers to the pattern of EEG waves similar to that seen in patients with epilepsy but alone does not make the diagnosis of epilepsy.

REMember:
- Not all epileptiform activity is an indication of clinical epilepsy.
- Not all patients with epilepsy have epileptiform discharges on EEG.

Seizure Activity and Sleep:
- 70% of patients with epilepsy have seizures both awake and asleep.
- 10 to 20% of seizures may occur only during sleep.
- Nocturnal seizures have two peaks: ± 2 hours after sleep onset and a second peak between 4 and 5 a.m.
- Sleep deprivation and the sleep state may facilitate seizure activity.
- Certain seizure disorders occur preferentially during sleep (see below).
- Nocturnal seizures in NREM > REM sleep (especially in N2).
- On a PSG, frontal lobe seizures may be seen in the eye leads and temporal seizures may be seen in the mastoid electrodes.
- Most seizures are brief, lasting 60-120secs

EPILEPSY SYNDROMES MANIFESTING ONLY OR PREDOMINANTLY DURING SLEEP

A. Nocturnal frontal lobe epilepsy (NFLE).

- Autosomal dominant condition
- Seizures usually stereotyped sensory-motor manifestations which may be violent and may include:
    - "Fencing posture" with arm abducted at shoulder, flexed at elbow, and with the head turned towards the abducted arm.
    - Cycling motions of the legs.
    - Flailing or dystonic movements of arms and legs.
    - Screaming and fear may be displayed .
    - Usually minimal postictal confusion.
    - Complex behaviour may cause injury & death.
- Episodes are usually brief (seconds or a few minutes) and may be repetitive.
- Surface EEGs both ictal and interictal often normal as seizure focus may be deep seated; → misdiagnosis of parasomnia.
- Daytime seizures, if present, often brief with variable change in consciousness and little postictal confusion → misdiagnosed as "pseudoseizures" or "psychogenic seizures."
- Average onset 12 to 14 years; subjects have ↑ incidence of parasomnias.

B. Benign Epilepsy of Childhood with Central Temporal Spikes (BECT) (Rolandic Epilepsy).

- Rare; may be inherited; usually starts between the ages of 3 to 12 years and outgrown by late teens.
- 70 - 80% occur during drowsiness and sleep.
- Perioral or hemifacial numbness progressing to clonic jerking of face, lips, tongue, and pharyngeal muscles typical.

- Atypical nocturnal symptons accompanying seizure include
  - Apneas (obstructive or central)
  - Coughing, choking, stridor
  - Chest pain, cardiac arrythmias
  - Autonomic symptoms (flushing,night sweats)
- Subject may be conscious during the episode and complain of difficulties with speech and swallowing or a feeling of suffocation.
- Interictal rolandic spikes typically seen in paracentral area.
- May need antiepileptic drugs (AEDs) but the prognosis ultimately good.

C. Juvenile Myoclonic Epilepsy (JME).

- Bilateral, often massive, myoclonic jerks of limbs and occurring especially soon after waking.
- Some patients may develop generalized tonic-clonic seizures or absence seizures usually within 1 - 3 years of presentation of myoclonic jerks.
- Average age of presentation is 12 - 18 years; genetic predisposition may be present.
- Treatment may be lifelong (valproate drug of choice; if contraindicated alternatives include lamotrigine, topiramate, levetiracetam).

REMember:
Isolated myoclonic jerks may mimic PLMS.

D. Continuous Spike Waves During Non-REM Sleep (CSWS).

- 85 - 90% of NREM occupied by continuous spike-and-wave pattern.
- The abnormal EEG pattern may not be accompanied by abnormal movements.
- Generalized tonic-clonic, focal, or absence seizures may occur while awake.
- Condition often accompanied by cognitive impairment which may persist after the disorder abates (usually by teenage years).

E. Temporal Lobe Epilepsy (TLE).

- Most common focus for partial seizures.
- May occur only during sleep.
- TLE may be
  a. Simple partial
    - Brief, usually no impairment of consciousness.

- May have motor or sensory symptoms.
- Typically no aura or post ictal state.
  b. Complex partial
    - Altered or impaired consciousness.
    - May occur only in sleep.
- Clinical presentations include:
  - Déjà Vu or out of body experiences.
  - Olfactory or auditory hallucinations.
  - Unpleasant taste or nausia.
  - Automatisms (e.g., lip smacking).
  - Staring/vacant appearance without any other obvious activity.
  - Post-ictal confusion common.

F. Nocturnal Paroxysmal Dystonia.

- Repeated dystonic or dyskinetic movements during the night.
- May involve single or all extremities.
- Occurs in NREM sleep.
- May not show surface EEG abnormalities (seizure activity generated in deep frontal cortex).
- Age onset from childhood to adult.
- Episodes may be short (less than 1 minute) or long (up to 60 minutes) duration.
- Short duration episodes respond better to AEDs.

G . Absence Seizures (formerly "Petit Mal")

- Often arises clinically out of REM; only seizure type to do so.
- Onset usually 5-9yrs;outgrown by early 20's.
- Brief (<20secs); typically no post-ictal state.
- No loss of posture or bladder/bowel control.
- Responds to divalproex sodium (*Depakote*) or lamotrigine (*Lamictal*).

EEG Recognition of Epileptiform Waves

"Interictal epileptiform discharges are those with distinctive waves or complexes, distinguished from background activity and resembling those recorded in a proportion of human subjects suffering from epileptic disorders." (International Federation of Societies for Electroencephalography and Clinical Neurophysiology).

The interictal epileptiform discharges should be:
- Paroxysmal.
- Transient.
- Distinct from normal background activity.

- Exhibit an abrupt change in polarity (usually negative).
- Morphologic descriptions include:
  - Sharp waves: pointed peak at conventional paper speeds and duration 70 - 200 milliseconds (msec).
  - Spikes: Same as sharp waves but duration 20 -70 msec.
  - Spike-and-slow-wave complex: Spike followed by a slow wave which is usually of higher amplitude than the spike, typically delta or theta frequency.
  - Multiple spike-and-slow-wave complexes: Two or more spikes associated with one or more slow waves.
  - Rhythmic focal slowing.

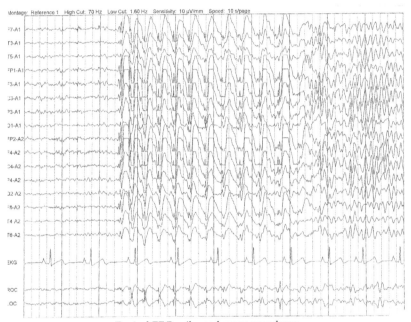

Typical EEG spike and wave complexes

REMember:

- Parasomnias may mimic epilepsy.
  - Epilepsy more likely if history of epilepsy or similar events during wakefulness.
  - Full seizure montage with simultaneous video recordings or ambulatory monitoring may be necessary.
  - The presence of seizure-associated phenomenon such as automatisms, tongue biting, urinary incontinence, and postictal confusion should be documented by the technologist to aid in diagnosis.
  - Therapeutic trial of AEDs may be useful in doubtful cases.

- Comorbid OSAS may increase seizure activity, possibly by frequent arousals causing sleep deprivation.
  - Treatment of OSAS may improve seizure control.
- Impact of selected AEDs on sleep pattern (see section 4, page 41).
  - BZDs - ↓ sleep latency, ↓ SWS, ↑ REM latency.
  - Gabapentin (*Neurontin*) - ↑ SWS, may ↑ REM.
  - Tiagabine (*Gabitril*) - ↑ SWS.
  - Phenobarbital - ↓ REM.

Review Article: Sleep-Disordered Breathing and Spinal Cord Injury. *CHEST* 2019; 155(2): 438-445.

PSYCHIATRIC DISORDERS AND SLEEP

Classification

- Standard classification of psychiatric disorders found in the American Psychiatric Association's Diagnostic and Statistical Manual of Mental Disorders Fifth Edition, (DSM-5).

- Most common psychiatric disorders seen in sleep centers (ICSD-2, Appendix B):

  1. Mood disorders.

     - Major Depressive Episodes (last ≥2 weeks).
     - Major Depressive Disorder (MDD) ≥2 major depressive episodes.
     - Dysthymic Disorder - chronically depressed mood most days 2+ years.
     - Bipolar disorders.

  2. Anxiety disorders.

     - Panic Disorders (recurrent panic attacks).
     - Posttraumatic Stress Disorder (PTSD).
     - Acute Stress Disorder - follows exposure to a traumatic event.
     - Generalized Anxiety Disorder (GAD) - difficult-to-control anxiety and worry for at least six months.
     - Obsessive Compulsive Disorder (OCD).

3. Somatiform Disorders; physical symptoms unexplained by medical condition.

    -   Somatization Disorder - c/o pain, GI symptoms, sexual or neurological dysfunction etc.
    -   Hypochondriasis - over concern of a serious disease despite medical reassurance.

4. Schizophrenia (a psychotic disorder; symptoms of unreality).

DEPRESSION AND SLEEP

*   The vast majority of patients with depression complain of insomnia: 40-55% of outpatients and up to 90% of inpatients with MDD.
*   Insomnia associated with depression should be regarded as "comorbid" rather than "secondary" (NIH State of the Art Conference 2005).
*   Chronic insomnia may precede mood disorder (in contrast to an anxiety disorder where insomnia usually occurs concurrently or following the onset of anxiety).
*   Insomnia may predict relapse of MDD.
*   Chronic insomnia may contribute to the persistence of depression.
*   Insomnia often last of depressive symptoms to resolve with treatment.

PSG

*   ↑ sleep latency.
*   ↑ wake after sleep onset (WASO) time, ↓ TST, ↓ sleep efficiency.
*   ↓ SWS.
*   ↓ REM latency (generally < 65 minutes), ± ↑ % REM. 1st REM period may be prolonged.
*   ↓ REM latency and ↓ SWS may persist while in remission.

REMember:
Other causes of short REM latency on PSG:
*   Narcolepsy.
*   Following cessation of REM suppressing medications (REM rebound).
*   Following chronic sleep deprivation.
*   OSAS after initiation of CPAP therapy.
*   In association with circadian rhythm disorder.
*   Schizophrenia.
Above conditions may also cause SOREMs on MSLT.

REMember:

- Sleep changes in depression may be due to relative increase of cholinergic vs. monoaminergic activity.
- Neurotransmitter receptor dysfunction of the monoaminergic systems regarded as the main cause for MDD.

PSG in Other Mood Disorders

- PSG changes in manic patients similar to those found in MDD.
- PSG in dysthymia similar to normal controls.

REMember:

- If poor response to AD therapy, consider comorbid sleep disorder (e.g., OSA). Successful CPAP treatment may result in improvement in depression.
- Successful management of co-morbid insomnia (e.g., with a BzRA) may hasten resolution of depression symptoms. (Fava M et al; *Biol Psychiatry* 2006; 59(11):1052-1060)
- ADs may induce or ↑ the frequency of RLS and PLMS (see Sections 4 & 9).
- RBD may be precipitated by ADs including TCA's, SSRIs, venlafaxine (*Effexor*) and mirtazapine (*Remeron*). Bupropion (*Wellbutrin*) is an exception. *JCSM* Review Article (2010:6(1):79-83) indicates, that the strongest evidence for drug-induced RBD is for clomipramine (*Anafranil*) and phenelzine (*Nardil*).

BIPOLAR DISORDERS AND SLEEP

- Episodes may be manic, hypomanic, depressed or mixed.
- In manic or hypomanic phases ↓ need for sleep (e.g., rested after 3hrs sleep).
- In depression phase, similar PSG changes as in major depression.
- Treat with mood stabilizers (see p.48).

REMember:
- Lithium → ↑ SWS, ↓ ↓ REM;
- Other mood stabilizers → little effect on sleep architecture; most sedating.

GENERALIZED ANXIETY DISORDER (GAD)

Essential Features(DSM-5)
- Excessive difficult-to-control anxiety/worry for ≥ 6 months causing:
  - feeling of restlessness, "on edge"
  - fatigue
  - concentration difficulty
  - irritability

Sleep associations
- Insomnia found in up to 80% with patients with GAD.
- PSG changes include:
  - ↑ sleep latency and WASO.
  - ↓ sleep efficiency and TST.
  - No significant changes in REM.

Treatment includes:
  - SSRIs: e.g., escitalopram (*Lexapro*), paroxetine (*Paxil*).
  - SNRIs: e.g., duloxetine (*Cymbalta*), venlafaxine (*Effexor*).
  - BZDs.

POST-TRAUMATIC STRESS DISORDER (PTSD)

Essential features (DSM-5)
- Exposure to event(s) involving serious harm or death or sexual violence.
- Responses include emotions such as fear, horror, helplessness.
- Subsequent distressing recollections of event(s); (images, thoughts, dreams) "flashbacks."
- Psychological distress on exposure to cues resembling event(s).

Sleep associations:
- Insomnia (onset &/or maintenance).
- Disturbing dreams and nightmares common.
- Panic and fear on awakening from disturbing dreams/nightmares.

Treatment of sleep related PTSD symptoms:

(*JCSM* 2010; 6 (4): 389-401).

- Psychotherapy as appropriate.
- Pharmacotherapy for PTSD nightmares:
    - Prazosin (*Minipress*) - level A recommendation.
    - Clonidine (*Catapres*) - level C recommendation.
    - Other level C recommendations (low grade & sparse data): trazodone, atypical antipsychotics (olanzapine, risperidone), topiramate, fluvoxamine, BZDs (triazolam and nitrazepam), gabapentin, cyproheptadine, TCAs, phenelzine.
    - Venlafaxine (*Effexor*) - produced <u>negative</u> results; not recommended.
- SSRI medication, e.g., Sertraline used as adjunctive to psychotherapy.
- See also nightmare disorder p99 and pp101-2.
- Propranolol reported to be useful for PTSD including nightmares associated with PTSD.

OBSESSIVE COMPULSIVE DISORDER (OCD)

Essential features (DSM-5)

- Recurrant and persistant irrational thoughts,impulses,images.
- Repetitive compelling behaviors (e.g., hand washing) or mental acts (e.g., praying, counting).
- Behaviors/mental acts aimed to reduce or prevent anxiety or distress.
- Obsessions and compulsions cause distress,are time consuming and interfere with normal routine; usually recognized as unreasonable.

PSG changes:

- ↓ sleep efficiency.
- ↑ WASO.

Medications used:

- SSRIs: fluvoxamine, fluoxetine, sertraline, paroxetine.
- TCAs, e.g., clomipramine (*Anafranil*).

SCHIZOPHRENIA

Essential features (DSM-5)

- Distortions of reality including delusions and hallucinations.
- Disorganized speech and behavior; catatonic behavior.
- Negative symptoms including a flat affect, paucity of thought, and speech (alogia), or of goal-directed behavior (avolition).
- Social/occupational dysfunction.

PSG changes:

- ↑ sleep latency.
- ↓ sleep efficiency and TST.
- Effects on SWS and REM variable.

Pharmacotherapy:

i. First generation antipsychotics (phenothiazines):
    - Most cause sedation and extrapyramidal side effects.
    - Act by blocking dopamine receptors.

ii. Second-generation antipsychotics:
    - Act by blocking dopamine and serotonin receptors.
    - May cause sedation but less extrapyramidal side effects.

    Examples include:
    Clozapine (*Clozaril*)
    -   Sedating ($\downarrow$ sleep latency), $\downarrow$ N3, little effect on REM.
    -   Restricted distribution in USA.
    Olanzapine (*Zyprexa*)
    -   Sedating, $\uparrow$ N3, $\downarrow$ REM.
    Risperidone (*Risperdal*)
    -   Less sedating, $\uparrow$ N3, $\downarrow$ REM.
    Quetiapine (*Seroquel*)
    -   Sedating, little effect on N3, $\downarrow$ REM.

(For extended list of antipsychotic medications see section 4, pages 47-49.)

Review Article

Gupta M, Simpson F: **Obstructive Sleep Apnea and Psychiatric Disorders: A Systematic Review**, *J Clin Sleep Med* 2015;11(2):165-175

- $\uparrow$ OSA in MDD and PTSD
- OSA not found to be more prevalent in psychoses, bipolar disorders and anxiety(panic) disorder
- Treatment of OSA may improve both OSA related symptoms and psychiatric symptoms
    - Consider PSG in treatment-resistant MDD & PTSD patients
    - May be able to $\downarrow$ psychopharmaceuticals

Additional reading:

- Sateia MJ: **Update on Sleep and Psychiatric Disorders**, *CHEST* 2009;135:1370-1379.

- El-Solh et al, Sleep Disorders in Patients with PTSD, *CHEST* 2018; 154(2): 427-439. Addresses OSA, insomnia and nightmares including treatments.

Appendix: Table of Commonly Used Antidepressants

Generic Name	Brand Name	Class	Mode of Action (MOA)	Other uses
amitriptyline	*Elavil*	TCA	inhibits NE, 5-HT reuptake	Chronic pain
clomipramine	*Anafranil*	TCA	inhibits NE and 5-HT reuptake	OCD
fluoxetine	*Prozac*	SSRI	Selective serotonin reuptake inhibitor	OCD, panic disorder, depressive bipolar disorder
sertraline	*Zoloft*	SSRI	as above	OCD, panic disorder, PTSD, premenstrual dysphoric disorder, social anxiety disorder
paroxetine	*Paxil*	SSRI	as above	as above + GAD
escitalopram	*Lexapro*	SSRI	as above	GAD
citalopram	*Celexa*	SSRI	as above	
fluvoxamine	*Luvox*	SSRI	as above	OCD
vilazodone	*Viibryd*	"other," SSRI	Inhibits 5-HT reuptake and partially agonizes 5-HT 1A receptors	
venlafaxine	*Effexor*	SNRI	Inhibits NE, 5-HT and DA reuptake	GAD
duloxetine	*Cymbalta*	SNRI	Inhibits NE and 5-HT reuptake	GAD, fibromyalgia, diabetic neuropathy
levomilnacipran	*Fetzima*	SNRI	as above	
desvenlafaxine	*Pristiq*	SNRI	inhibits NE and 5-HT reuptake	
bupropion HCl	*Wellbutrin*	"other" (tetra-cyclic)	inhibits NE and DA reuptake	Smoking cessation (Zyban)

bupropion HBr	*Aplenzin*	As above	as above	
mirtazapine	*Remeron*	"other"	antagonizes alpha-2 adrenergic and 5-HT2 receptors	
vortioxetine	*Trintellix*	"other"	Selectively inhibits 5-HT reuptake; antagonizes 5-HT5—HT3 receptors; agonizes 5-HT1A receptors	
nefazodone	*Serzone*	SARI	inhibits NE and 5-HT reuptake; antagonizes 5-HT2 receptors (risk of severe hepatotoxicity)	
trazodone	*Desyrel*	SARI	Inhibits or antagonizes various 5-HT receptors	Used more often for insomnia (off-label) than depression

Abbreviations: TCA = tricyclic antidepressant; SSRI = selective serotonin reuptake inhibitor; SNRI = serotonin and norepinephrine reuptake inhibitor; SARI= Serotonin Antagonist and Reuptake Inhibitor; 5-hydroxytryptamine (5-HT) = serotonin; NE = norepinephrine; DA = dopamine

NEURODEGENERATIVE DISORDERS AND SLEEP

ALZHEIMER'S DISEASE AND OTHER DEMENTIAS:

- Insomnia, circadian rhythm changes.
- ↓ Sleep efficiency, TST, spindles, K-complexes, N3 and REM.
- ↑ Arousals, WASO
- Daytime hypersomnolence due to fragmented sleep.
- With disease progression and cognitive decline; *sundowning* (less nocturnal sleep with increased night-time agitation, confusion, restlessness and wandering) and ↑ daytime sleepiness.
- ↑ Cortical amyloid plaque deposition in AD may be due to various sleep disruptions including melatonin production (melatonin inhibits amyloid generation and formation of fibrils in vitro, *CHEST*, 2017; 151; 1375-86)
- Mechanism may be loss of SCN cells containing neurotensin and vasopressin (*CHEST* 2012; 141 (2): 528 - 544; *CHEST* 2017; 151(6); 1375-1386).

- Management sundowning:
  - Sleep hygiene with planned activities.
  - Light therapy may be useful though timing (morning or evening), is still uncertain.
  - Caution with psychoactive medications: potential adverse events.
- Research suggest OSA may be a risk factor for AD. AASM Health Advisory (June 2018) suggests screening for and treating OSA and other sleep disorders "may prevent or delay AD."

PARKINSON'S DISEASE (PD):

- Up to 90% of PD patients may have sleep-related problems.
- Insomnia, both sleep onset and maintenance, very common.
- Vivid dreams, nocturnal hallucinations, RBD.
- Sleep fragmentation, ↑ arousals/awakenings → daytime hypersomnolence.
- Biochemical mechanism for EDS in PD may be degeneration of dopaminergic neurons in the substantia nigra and of cholinergic cells in the basal forebrain (*CHEST* 2012; 141 (2): 528 - 544). Studies also report on loss of hypocretin (orexin) neurons in the hypothatamus (*CHEST* 2017; 151(6); 1375-1386)
- Bradykinesia/rigidity → inability to turn in bed → respiratory problems including aspiration, atelectasis and SDB.
- ↑ association with RLS, PLMS and RBD. RBD may precede PD.
- PSG: ↑ sleep latency, ↓ sleep efficiency, ↑ WASO, ↑ arousals/ fragmented sleep, ↓ N3, ↓ REM.
- In cases of RBD with PD: ↑ EMG activity and absence of muscle atonia in REM.
- SDB in 20-50% PD patients (*CHEST* 2017, 151(6); 1375-1386)

Review: The spectrum of sleep disorders in PD. *CHEST* 2021; 159(2): 818-827

MULTIPLE SYSTEM ATROPHY

Sleep related features may include:
  - fragmented sleep; insomnia; EDS
  - RBD
  - stridor (failure of vocal cord abduction); may be fatal
  - central sleep apnea, central neurogenic hypoventilation.
  - obstructive sleep apnea (*J. Clin Sleep Med* 2018; 14(5); 893-895) likely due to impaired input from upper airway sensory fibers compromising UA patency and resulting in abnormally long obstrutive apneas. (See case report *JCSM* 2018; 14(5): 893-5 documenting an OSA lasting 233 seconds in a patient with autonomic dysfunction).

Review Article: Pillai JA, Leverenz JB: Sleep and Neurodegeneration *CHEST* 2017; 151(6); 1375-1386 Discusses possible mechasims responsible for sleep disruption (neuronal, neurotransmitter, neuroendocrine) together with clinical features and areas for further research.

RESPIRATORY DISORDERS AND SLEEP

NOCTURNAL ASTHMA:

Mechanisms:
- Enhanced parasympathic tone.
- Hormonal (cortisol ↓ , histamine ↑).
- Inflammatory: ↑ total leukocyte count (neutrophils, eosinophils, lymphocytes) on broncho-alveolar lavage.
- 33% ↓ beta adrenergic density on neutrophils and mononuclear leukocytes at 4am.
- Circadian changes: lowest PFR, FEV1: 4 a.m. with ↑ lower airway resistance.
- Effect of airway cooling.
- Allergen exposure.
- Supine posture (↑ airway resistance).
- GERD (up to 80% asthmatics may have abnormal esophageal pH studies).
- Co-morbid OSA.

PSG:
- ↑awake time, ↓ sleep efficiency.
- ↑ N2 ↓ N3 sleep.
- no change REM cycles.
- Hypoxemia relatively uncommon (cf COPD).

REMember:
Equal frequency of asthma attacks in NREM and REM sleep

Relationship between OSA and asthma:

a. Mechanisms by which OSA may aggravate nocturnal asthma:

- ↑ Parasympathetic activity in OSA.
- Inflammatory: Local and systemic (oxidative stress).
- Cardiac dysfunction: OSA→ LV dysfunction→ ↑ bronchial hyperresponsiveness to cholinergic stimuli and downregulation of pulmonary ß-receptors.
- GERD: Direct cause asthma; higher prevalence in OSA.
- Leptin hypothesis: Leptin (anti-obesity hormone) is pro-inflammatory. May promote airway inflammation. Levels are markedly increased in obesity (leptin resistance) but also in male asthmatic children independent of BMI. Obese males with OSA have 50% higher leptin levels than obese males without OSA.

- Weight gain: Obesity per se may be a risk factor for asthma; OSA promotes weight gain (? via insulin & leptin resistance and inactivity).
- Chronic intermittent hypoxia → airway inflammation and tissue remodeling.

b. Does Asthma promote OSAS?

- Higher prevalence of OSA in unstable asthmatics receiving frequent bursts of oral corticosteroids (OCS).
- Mechanisms may include
  - Decrease in upper airway cross sectional area due to chronic mucosal inflammation and lateral pharyngeal wall fat deposits.
  - Sleep fragmentation may increase upper airway collapsibility (Series et al; *Am J. Resp Crit Care Med* 1994).
  - Increased frequency of nasal problems.

c. CPAP and Asthma control :

- CPAP improves asthma control (Chan; *Am Rev RespDis* 1988;137:1502).
- CPAP shown to be safe in asthma.
- Mechanisms for improvement include abolishing upper airway irritation/collapse which may have negative vagal and inflammatory influences, and also by improving GERD.

Further reading:
Alkhalil M et al: Obstructive Sleep Apnea and Asthma: What are the Links? *J Clin Sleep Med* 2009; 5(1):71-78.
Prasad et al: Asthma and OSA overlap. *Am J Resp Crit Care Med* 2020; 201(11): 1345-1357.

COPD AND SLEEP:

- Nocturnal oxygen desaturation (NOD) is main PSG abnormality due to COPD per se; most marked if hypoxic while awake (on steep part of oxyhemoglobin dissociation curve).
- Virtually all patients with daytime $SpO2 < 92\%$ had nocturnal desaturations; none if $SpO2 > 95\%$ (Douglas et al *Lancet*; 1979; 1: 1-4).
- Desaturations most severe in REM sleep (intercostal muscle hypotonia).
- Main cause is V/Q mismatch; aggravated by diaphragmatic flattening.
- With progressive disease, chronic hypoxia and CO_2 retention occurs (also most marked during REM).
- Hypoxia may cause ↑ pulmonary artery pressures, ectopy and ↑ mortality.

- Sleep fragmented with ↓ sleep efficiency,↓ TST,↑ WASO,↓ N3 and ↓ REM.
- COPD medications may contribute to fragmented sleep (steroids, beta adrenergics, theophyllines).
- ↑ prevalence RLS in COPD patients (*Sleep Med* 2009;10:572).

COPD AND OSA.

Coexisting COPD and OSA known as the "overlap syndrome" (Weitzenblum: *Proc Am Thor Soc* February 15, 2008). 74% of COPD patients at intermediate to high risk of undiagnosed OSA (Donovan et al *J. Clin Sleep Med* 2019; 15(1): 71-77).

Features of overlap syndrome:

- Lower and longer nocturnal O_2 desaturations.
- More severe pulmonary hemodynamic disturbances including cor pulmonale than the rest of the COPD or OSA populations for a given PFT or OSA severity.
- Diurnal hypercapnia more frequent at lower BMI and AHI levels than in OSAS without COPD.
- Lower all cause five-year survival. ↑cardiovascular morbidity.
- Itermittent hypoxia (as opposed to sustained hypoxia) responsible for activation of proinflammatory pathways and systemic inflammation. Hypoxemia severity most important cause of ↑ CV morbidity.
- Treatment may include CPAP or BPAP ± supplemental oxygen. PAP → ↑ Survival (*J Clin Sleep Med* 2020; 16(2): 267-277).

PSG indicated in COPD patients if

- Typical clinical features of OSAS
- Pulmonary hypertension disproportionate for level of PaO2.
- Polycythemia with relative well preserved PaO2 (>60mmHg).
- Disproportionately abnormal ABGs for PFTs.
- Suggestive overnight pulse oximetry (superimposed cyclical/ sawtooth pattern of desaturations in addition to those due to COPD which show less fluctuations).

REMember:
- Same incidence of OSA in COPD as in the general population.
- Co-morbid COPD and severe OSA increases the risk of acute respiratory failure during COPD exacerbations leading to increased ICU admission rates (Fletcher et al *Crit. Care Med.* 1991; 19; 1158).

Further Reading:
1. Budhiraja et al: Sleep Disorders in Chronic Obstructive Pulmonary Disease: Etiology, Impact and Management. *J. Clin Sleep Med* 2015; 11(3):259-270.
2. Editorial: Does Associated COPD increase Morbidity and Mortality in OSA: *Annals ATS* 2019; 16(1): 50-52
3. OSA / COPD convergence on a theme: *J. Clin Sleep Med* 2019; 15(1): 171-77. Commentary stresses importance of screening for overlap syndrome in view of increased morbidity and mortality.
4. Xu et al: Risk of cardiovascular and cerebrovascular disease in overlap syndrome. *J. Clin Sleep Med* 2020; 16(7): 1199-1207.

SLEEP IN INTERSTITIAL LUNG DISEASES

- Fragmented sleep:↓ sleep efficiency,↑ arousals,↓ TST,↑ WASO
- ↑ N1, ↓ N3 and ↓ REM
- Desaturations mainly in REM

SLEEP IN PULMONARY HYPERTENSION (PH)

Limited studies; variable results:

Minic et al: Sleep-Disordered Breathing in Group 1 Pulmonary Arterial Hypertension. *J Clin Sleep Med* 2014;10(3):277-283. 52 consecutive subjects with Group1 PAH were found to have SDB. In this study OSA was more prevalent than CSA. Older age and ESS score > 10 were predictive of SDB.

Rafanan A et al : Nocturnal hypoxemia is Common in Primary Pulmonary Hypertension *CHEST* 2001;120:894-899
- 13 patients with PPH (idiopathic pulmonary hypertension):
- 10(77%) had nocturnal hypoxemia with >10% TST having saturation <90%
- Mean RDI only 4.6
- Desaturations not related to apneas or hypopneas

Ulrich S et al: Sleep-related Breathing Disorders in Patients With Pulmonary Hypertension *CHEST* 2008;133:1375-1380)
- 38 patients (F:M 27:11)
- Ave age 61y
- PH classification
    Idiopathic 17 (45%)
    Connective tissue disease 5 (13%)
    Congenital heart disease 1 (3%)
    Chronic PTE disease 15 (39%)
PSG results
- 15 had ≥10 CSR/CSA events/hr.
- 4 had ≥10 obstructive events/hr.
- 68% patients spent ≥10% of the night with a oxygen saturation<90%.
- No difference between those with CSR/CSA and those with no SDB

in terms of severity of PH and NYHA class of dyspnea.
- EDS not significant; mean ESS 8/hr in CSR/CSA group.
- Samhouri et al (*JCSM* 2020; 16(8): 1231-9) - positive association with PHT and TST with SaO_2 <90%; not with AHI.

GERD AND SLEEP

- Gastric acid secretion peaks around midnight.
- Reflux common postprandially but uncommon in sleep.
- GERD associated with ↓lower esophageal sphincter pressure (LES); hiatal hernia may be present.
- Daytime reflux associated with relatively rapid acid clearance time, night-time reflux episodes fewer but *last longer*.
- GERD complications more likely with prolonged mucosal contact time (e.g., severe esophagitis, ulcerations, stricture, Barrett's esophagus).
- Symptoms may be more pronounced in sleep: dyspepsia/heartburn (may be mistaken for nocturnal angina), unexplained cough, or wheezing. These symptoms may also disrupt sleep and cause *insomnia*.
- Nocturnal reflux symptoms may be due to lifestyle issues (e.g., eating/drinking late at night, including caffeine-containing products and alcohol) and also failure to elevate the head of the bed during sleep.
- GERD & OSAS:
  Increased upper GI symptoms and prevalence of GERD in OSA patients (5/6 patients in study by Kerr, et al., *CHEST* 1992; 101: 1539; about 60% in two other studies; Valipour, *CHEST* 2002; Green, *Arch Int Med* 2003).
  - Mechanisms:
    - Apneas → autonomic dysfunction → transient LES relaxation.
    - Increased ↑ Respiratory effort →↑ pressure gradient across LES.
    - Large negative intrapleural and increased transdiaphragmatic pressures swings facilitate GER.
    - Lifestyle factors in OSA patients – obesity.
  - Improvement in GERD symptoms on PAP therapy.
- GERD & NOCTURNAL ASTHMA:
  -GERD may cause nocturnal asthma: wheezing &/or cough
  -Unexplained cough, nocturnal or diurnal, may be due to GERD
  -GERD may be main overall cause of patient's asthma
  -Mechanisms may be microaspiration &/or vagally mediated
- **Review Article:** Sleep and Nocturnal GER *CHEST* 2018; 154(4): 963-971 (good update/review).

FIBROMYALGIA AND SLEEP

Sleep-related symptoms common (± 75%).
- Insomnia (either sleep onset or sleep maintenance).
- Nonrestorative sleep.
- Daytime fatigue, tiredness, and sleepiness.

Polysomnogram
- ↑ sleep latency, ↑ fragmented sleep, ↑ arousals, ↑ WASO, ↓ sleep efficiency.
- ↑ N1, ↓ N3.
- Alpha intrusions in NREM sleep; correlated with the sensation of nonrestorative sleep.
- Alpha intrusions not pathognomonic for fibromyalgia; may be seen in:
  - ~ Rheumatoid arthritis.
  - ~ Osteoarthritis.
  - ~ Sjögren's syndrome.
  - ~ Psychiatric disorders.
  - ~ Postinfectious and posttraumatic conditions associated with fatigue and pain.
  - ~ Patients with insomnia.
  - ~ Chronic fatigue syndrome.
  - ~ Healthy individuals.

References:
Lineberger, M.D. et al.; Sleep Disturbance in Fibromyalgia. Sleep Med. Clinics 2007; 2: 31 - 39).

Drewes, AM; Pain and Sleep Disturbances with Special Reference to Fibromyalgia and Rheumatoid Arthritis (editorial) Rheumatology 1999; 38: 1035 - 1038.

FYI: Jackson M and Bruck D; Sleep Abnormalities in Chronic Fatigue Syndrome/ Myalgic Encephalomyelitis: A Review. *J Clin Sleep Med* 2012; 8(6): 719-728 Article indicates that CFS patients may have long sleep onset latency but that sleep architecture and TST show little difference from healthy controls. CFS patients may report unrefreshing sleep and daytime sleepiness but MSLT does not confirm pathologic daytime sleepiness.

PREGNANCY AND SLEEP

Sleep disturbances in pregnancy:

78% women report ↑ sleep disturbances in pregnancy than at other times (National Sleep Foundation).

1st trimester:
↑ Fatigue
↑ Daytime sleepiness
↑ Urinary frequency → sleep disruption

2nd trimester
Nocturnal sleep improves; less urinary frequency
Less EDS
30% report onset snoring(nasal congestion due to estrogens)

3rd trimester
>95% have sleep disturbances, especially insomnia.
Insomnia due to
Nocturia-85%
Leg cramps 75%; RLS 25%
GERD 30-50%
Fetal movements; general discomfort
Anxiety re upcoming labor, relationship problems with partner

Post partum period
↑ insomnia (demands of baby)
Disrupted sleep→ daytime napping
↑ N3 sleep in women who breast feed (?prolactin effect)
Post partum depression in up to 20%

Sleep architecture in pregnancy
Most studies suggest ↑ N1, ↓ N3 and only slight ↓ REM
↑ Awakenings and ↑ WASO

Hormonal effects on sleep
Estrogen
↓ REM
Edema nares & upper airway → snoring
Progesterone
↑ NREM (N1)
↑ Respiratory drive
- May be protective for development of OSA
- May cause sleep onset central apneas and insomnia

Sleep Disorders in Pregnancy

Restless Leg Syndrome
- ±25% prevalence.
- Associated with low ferritin, iron and folic acid levels .
- Drugs traditionally used for RLS treatment not generally recommended in pregnancy. Check individual drug formulary. See also article by Miller et al referenced below.

Insomnia
- Impact of hormonal, mechanical or emotional influences (see above).
- Maximum in 3rd trimester.
- Hypnotics in pregnancy generally avoided. See also article Miller et al referenced below.
- Poor sleep → screen for depression (*Obstet Gynecol* 2018; 132: e208-212).

Snoring
- 25% by 3rd trimester; edema of nares and upper airway (estrogen).
- Associated with ↑ incidence of HT, pre-eclampsia, fetal growth retardation and higher APGAR scores (Franklin et al *CHEST* 2000; 117(1);137-141), O'Brein et al, *SLEEP* 2013;36(11):1625-32.

OSA
- Prevalence uncertain.
- ↑ Risk with obesity during pregnancy. (Wilson DL et al: *J. Sleep Res* Oct 2018.
- Protective factors may include:
  - ↑ respiratory drive due to progesterone
  - Adopting lateral sleep position in 3rd trimester
  - ↓ REM sleep in 3rd trimester
- OSA in pregnancy associated with:
  - Gestational hypertension
  - Pre-eclampsia, eclampsia
  - Gestational diabetes mellitus (GDM). (see also *CHEST* Jan 2021: ↑ incidence SDB with GDM).
  - Fetal growth retardation & low birth weight infants
  - Cardiomyopathy and pulmonary embolism
  - ≥ 5-fold increased odds of in-hospital mortality (Louis et al: *SLEEP* 2014).
- CPAP safe & effective in pregnancy.
- Withdrawal of CPAP post pregnancy:
  a. If severe OSA, obtain PSG to assess residual severity after appropriate weight loss before withdrawing.
  b. For mild or moderate OSA in pregnancy, could withdraw CPAP and monitor clinically (?HSAT); if symptoms recur → PSG or HSAT.

Parasomnias
No increased incidence in pregnancy.

Further reading (pregnancy):

Pien GW Schwab RJ: Sleep Disorders in Pregnancy *SLEEP* 2004; 27(7): 1405-1417.

Miller et al- Sleep Pharmacotherapy for Common Sleep Disorders in Pregnancy and Lactation *CHEST* 2020: 157: 184-197. (Good review and reference with useful tables).

Pamidi and Kimhoff. Maternal Sleep Disordered Breathing *CHEST* 2018; 153(4): 1052-1066.

Izci-Balserak et al: A Screening Algorithm for OSA in Pregnancy. Age, BMI and tongue size useful screening tools. *Annals ATS* 2019; 16(10): 1286-1294.

Edward N, Sullivance CE: Sleep - Disordered Breathing in Pregnancy, *Sleep Medicine Clinics* 2008; 31(1): 81-95.

Louis, et al., Obstructive Sleep Apnea and Severe Maternal-Infant Morbidity/Mortality in the United States, 1998-2009. *SLEEP* 2014; 37 (5): 843-849).

Further reading (general):

Parish, James M: Sleep Related Problems in Common Medical Conditions. *CHEST* 2009 135: 563-572. (Discusses sleep in pulmonary problems, GERD, renal disease, endocrine disorders, infectious diseases including HIV, fibromyalgia, menopause and cancer.)

Dyken, ME et al: Sleep-Related Problems in Neurologic Diseases *CHEST* 2012; 141(2).

ASSOCIATION BETWEEN CANCER AND SLEEP

Sleep Deprivation and Cancer

- Men with insomnia: twice as likely to develop prostate cancer
- Less than 6 hours sleep: 50% ↑ risk of colorectal cancer
- Lack of sleep: more aggressive form of breast cancer
- Shift work disorder: the ↑ risk of breast cancer

Obstructive Sleep Apnea (OSA) and Cancer:

- 80% head and neck cancer patients have OSA, most commonly oropharyngeal squamous cell carcinoma.
- Severe OSA: 65% increased risk of cancer reported
- Results of prevalence studies inconclusive and some studies report on ↑ prevalence of particular cancers with OSA (e.g., increase pancreatic, kidney, melanoma – Gozal et al *SLEEP* 2016. ↑ lung cancer report by Cabezas Warmisher et al *Eur Resp J.* 2018). ↑ mortality in stages III and IV Lung cancer with severe OSA (Huang et al *J. Clin Sleep Med* 2020; 16(7): 1091-8).
- ↑Aggressive cutaneous melanoma reported by Martinez-Garcia in *CHEST* December 2018.
- Cyclical intermittent hypoxia in OSA (vs sustained hypoxia) may affect microenvironment at primary or metastatic site altering impact of killer immune cells. ↑ all-cancer incidence with ↑ ODI and time $SaO_2 < 90\%$ *CHEST* 2020; 158(6): 2610-2620.

Most Common Sleep Complaints in Cancer Patients

- Insomnia
- Restless leg syndrome: associated with chemotherapy, medications (e.g. antidepressants, Benadryl), neuropathy and anemia
- Excessive daytime sleepiness (secondary to sleep deprivation, insomnia, specific sleep disorders, etc)
- Fatigue

Causes of Fatigue in Cancer Patients

- Underlying cancer itself
- Secondary to sleep disorders
- Radiation
- Chemotherapy
- Weight loss
- Anemia
- Stress / depression / anxiety
- Biochemical / hormonal changes

Insomnia in Cancer Patients

- 30-50% in cancer patients (10-15% general population)
- 20-40% persist 2-5 years after treatment
- Contributing factors:
  - Pain
  - Anxiety / psychological distress
  - Radiation
  - Chemotherapy
  - Hot flashes (hormone therapy)
  - Medications, e.g., steroids, opioids
  - Hospitalization
  - General symptoms like nausea / vomiting, coughing, nocturia
  - Sleep disorders, e.g., restless leg syndrome, sleep apnea

Further reading:

Davidson JR et al, Sleep Disturbances in Cancer Patients *Social Science and Med.* 2002; 54: 1309-1321.

Gavidia et al, OSA in patients with head and neck cancer: a systematic review. *JCSM* 2021; 17(5): 1109-1116.

1. In Nocturnal Frontal Lobe Epilepsy, which of the following statements is correct?

   a. Fencing posture typical.
   b. Violent movements rare.
   c. EEG always diagnostic.
   d. Seizure episodes are generally prolonged.
   e. Condition usually begins in early childhood and resolves by age 10 to 12 years.

2. PSG in depression may show a relatively short REM latency. In which of the following conditions may one also see a short REM latency?

   a. Schizophrenia.
   b. Certain circadian rhythm disorders.
   c. OSA after initiation of CPAP therapy.
   d. Following chronic sleep deprivation.
   e. All of the above.

3. Treatment considerations for PTSD may include all except:

   a. prazosin (Minipress).
   b. clonidine (Catapres).
   c. venlafaxine (Effexor).
   d. benzodiazepines.
   e. Risperidone (Risperdal).

4. PSG in depression may show all of the following features except:

   a. Prolonged sleep latency.
   b. ↓ sleep efficiency & ↑WASO.
   c. Shortened REM latency and ↑ slow wave sleep.
   d. Shortened REM latency and ↓ slow wave sleep.
   e. ↓ REM latency may be present in remission.

5. Alpha intrusions in NREM sleep may be seen in:

   a. Rheumatoid disease.
   b. Fibromyalgia.
   c. Healthy individuals.
   d. a & b.
   e. a, b & c

6. The most frequent PSG abnormality seen in Primary Pulmonary Hypertension:

   a. Central apneas.
   b. Oxygen desaturations
   c. Obstructive hypopneas.
   d. Cardiac arrhythmias.
   e. Snoring.

7. Which seizure disorder is usually associated with REM sleep?

   a. Temporal lobe epilepsy.
   b. Nocturnal frontal lobe epilepsy.
   c. Nocturnal paroxysmal dystonia.
   d. Absence seizures.
   e. Juvenile myoclonic epilepsy.

Answers: 1a, 2e, 3c, 4c, 5e, 6b, 7d.

Section 12:

PEDIATRIC CONSIDERATIONS AND DISORDERS

This section includes the following:

A. Development of sleep patterns.

B. Sleep scoring.

C. OSA in children.
1. Clinical manifestations.
2. Points of differentiation from adults.
3. Respiratory scoring in children.

D. Other respiratory disorders occurring in infants and children.
1. Congenital Central Alveolar Hypoventilation Syndrome (CCAHS).
2. SIDS.
3. Acute Life-Threatening Event (ALTE).
4. Primary Sleep Apnea of Infancy.

E. Insomnias in childhood.
1. Behavioral insomnia of childhood.
    * Sleep onset association type
    * Limit setting type
2. Other childhood insomnias

F. Points of differentiation in sleep disorders occurring commonly in adults (other than OSA).
1. Narcolepsy.
2. RLS.

Note: Other sleep disorders commonly found in children are found in the appropriate sections of this book (e.g., night terrors, narcolepsy, bedwetting (parasomnias), delayed sleep phase syndrome (circadian rhythm disorders).

DEVELOPMENT OF SLEEP PATTERNS

Sleep development preterm.

- 24 weeks - EEG activity emerges.
- 28 weeks - sleep and wakefulness differentiated.
- 32 weeks - active sleep appears (equivalent of adult REM).
    - REMs.
    - Body movements.
    - Grimaces and twitches.
    - Irregular respiratory pattern and irregular heart rate.
    - EEG is irregular, low voltage.
- 34 weeks - quiet sleep identified.
    - Opposite of active sleep (no REMs, $\downarrow$ body movement, regular respiratory rate and heart rate, $\uparrow$ EEG voltage).

Tracé discontinue (TD) and tracé alternant patterns (TA):

- TD consists of alternating segments of EEG activity separated by 20 to 30 seconds of inactivity with a nearly isoelectric background.
    - TD usually appears by about 28 weeks.

- TA consists of bursts of high amplitude slow waves lasting 4 - 5 seconds alternating with low amplitude EEG waves also lasting 4 - 5 seconds.
    - Usually appears by about 36 weeks.

- Both TD and TA usually disappear 4 - 6 weeks post-term. Sleep EEG becomes more "mature" with a contiguous pattern of SWS.

Sleep Architecture and age

- Various sleep stages recognizable by 4 - 6 months.
- Sleep onset usually through REM sleep in neonates; progressively declines to ±20% sleep onset REM by 6 months.
- 50% sleep in neonates is REM, decline to ± 30% at about 1yr & adult levels (20 - 25%) by 10 years.
- Adult pattern of sleep manifests by ages 5 - 10 years; prominent SWS in first third to half of nocturnal sleep time.

Sleep cycles.

Sleep cycles lengthen progressively:
- 50 - 60 minutes during the first year.
- ± 75 minutes by two years.
- ± 90 minutes at 5 -6 years.

Sleep Duration.

Consensus Statement from the AASM: Recommended amount of sleep for the Pediatric Populations *J Clin Sleep Med* 2016; 12(6):785-6

Recommended amount of sleep in a 24 hour cycle (includes naps at appropriate ages):

- No recommendations for infants <4 months; wide variation in sleep duration & patterns
- 4-12 months: 12-16 hours
- 1-2 years: 11-14 hours
- 3-5 years: 10-13 hours
- 6-12 years: 9-12 hours
- 13-18 years: 8-10 hours

Insufficient sleep at various ages may give rise to attention, memory, behavioral and learning problems as well as ↑ risk of accidents/injuries.. Too little sleep as well as longer than recommended sleep on a regular basis may include ↑ risk of hypertension, diabetes, obesity and mental health problems. Insufficient sleep in teenagers has been associated with depression and suicidal tendencies.

REMember:
- "Settling" with nighttime sleep consolidation lasting 6 -8 hours begins between the ages of 3 - 6 months and is present in most children by 12 months.
- Night feeding on nutritional basis not needed after 6m of age.
- Napping progressively decreases from 4/day in infants through preschool years and disappearing by about age 5yr .

SLEEP SCORING IN CHILDREN

Reference: AASM Manual for the Scoring of Sleep and Associated Events (Version 2.6, 2020).

General comments:
- Rules apply for children two months post-term or older.
- N1, N2, and N3 sleep usually recognized 5 to 6-months post-term (occasionally at 4 months).
- Spindles usually seen 6 weeks-3 months post-term; present in all normal infants 2 - 3 months post-term.
- K-complexes usually present 3 - 6 months post-term.
- Slow wave activity (≥ 75 µV; 0.5 - 2 Hz) usually present 4 - 5 months post-term.

- **Rule of thumb:** Score N1, N2, and N3 whenever recognizable. If cannot recognize spindles, K-complexes, or SWS, then score as stage N (NREM).
- In children, the **posterior dominant rhythm (PDR)** replaces the term "alpha rhythm" for the purposes of scoring W and NREM stages.

Stage W:
- Recognized by PDR of relaxed wakefulness with eyes closed.
- PDR has frequency of 3.5 - 4.5 Hz at 3 - 4 months post-term, 5 - 6 Hz by 5 - 6 months, and 7.5 - 9.5 Hz by 3 years.
- PDR amplitude > 50 μV.
- PDR best recognized over the occipital regions.
- Stage W scored when > 50% of epoch has age-appropriate PDR over the occipital region; or alpha rhthm (8-13Hz) in older children.
- If no age-appropriate PDR or alpha rhythm, then score epoch as stage W if ANY of the following are present for > 50% of epoch.
   a. Eye blinks.
   b. Reading eye movements.
   c. Irregular, conjugate REMs associated with normal or high chin muscle tone.
- Note: Most children have mean alpha frequency of 9 Hz by 9 years and 10 Hz by 15 years. Average amplitude of PDR in children is 50 - 60 μV.

Sleep onset period:
- The first epoch other than stage W.

Stage N1:
- Score stage N1 when PDR attenuates or replaced by low amplitude mixed frequency for > 50% of the epoch.
- If PDR not generated, score N1 if any of the following occur:
   - 4 - 7 Hz activity with slowing of background frequency by $\geq$ 1 - 2 Hz.
   - Slow eye movements.
   - Vertex sharp waves (usually maximally seen over central regions).
   - Rhythmic anterior theta activity (4 - 7 Hz).
   - Hypnagogic hypersynchrony (bursts of high amplitude waves maximal over frontal and central regions).
   - Diffuse or occipital-predominant high-amplitude rhythmic 3 - 5 Hz activity.

Stages N2, N3, and R:
- Same rules as adults.

For Sleep Staging Rules for infants 0-2 months please refer to AASM Scoring manual V 2.6, 2020.

Note: Home sleep testing in infants (mean 1.1yr) provided technically adequate reference data for the group. OAs and CAs rare (mean OA index 0.0, mean CA index 2.5 *Annals ATS* Oct 2020, v 17, pp 138-146) PSG testing in healthy neonates (before 30 days of age) showed lower sleep efficiency (71%) and higher AHI (14.9/hr mainly CAs). *JCSM* 2019; 15: 437-443.

RESPIRATORY SCORING RULES FOR CHILDREN

Reference: *AASM Manual for the Scoring of Sleep and Associated Events (Version 2.6, 2020).*

Background physiology:

- Respiratory rates decline from neonate (40/min) to toddler (30/min) to adult (12/min).
- Apneas present if two cycles skipped (equivalent to 10 seconds/2cycles in adults).
- In children, apnea is scored when two breaths are missed or duration of two missed breaths as determined by the baseline-breathing pattern.
- Sleep specialist may choose whether to use childhood or adult criteria between the age of 13 and 18 years.

Recommended Sensors:

- Oronasal thermal airflow sensor for **apnea** during **diagnostic** study. (If oronasal thermistor is not functioning or the signal is not reliable, use an alternative sensor: nasal pressure transducer or RIP are recommended alternatives. End-tidal PCO_2 acceptable alternative).
- Nasal pressure transducer for identification of **hypopnea** during **diagnostic** study. (If nasal pressure transducer is not functioning or the signal is not reliable, recommended alternatives are oronasal thermal airflow sensor or RIP).
- During **positive airway pressure titration study**, use **PAP device flow signal t**o identify both apneas and hypopneas.
- Esophageal manometry or RIP belts to monitor respiratory effort.
- Pulse oximetry for **oxygen saturations** (signal averaging time ≤ 3 seconds).
- **Snoring** monitored using an acoustic sensor (e.g., microphone), piezoelectric sensor, or nasal pressure transducer.
- **Hypoventilation** detected by $PaCO_2$, transcutaneous PCO_2, or end-tidal PCO_2 during diagnostic study;(during PAP titration use $PaCO_2$ or transcutaneous PCO_2).

Apnea Rules:

- Apnea scored when:
  a. ↓peak signal excursion by ≥ 90% of pre-event baseline AND

b. ≥ 90% drop lasts at least the equivalent of two breaths during baseline breathing (No minimum O_2 saturation required to score apneas).
- Apnea scored as **obstructive** when respiratory effort is present in the absence airflow.
- **Central** apnea is scored when there is no inspiratory effort throughout the apnea and
  a. Event lasts ≥ 20 seconds, **OR**
  b. Event lasts at least duration of two breaths during baseline breathing and is associated with an arousal or ≥ 3% oxygen desaturation, **OR**
  c. Event is associated with a ↓ in heart rate to < 50 bpm for at least 5 seconds or < 60 bpm for 15 seconds in infants < 1 year of age.
- **Mixed** apnea scored if during event there is absent respiratory effort during one portion and inspiratory effort present in another portion independent of order.

Hypopnea Rules:
- Hypopnea scored if *all* of the following present:
  a. ≥30% ↓ in airflow using appropriate sensor,
  b. duration of the ≥30% ↓ in signal excursion lasts at least 2 breaths, and
  c. event associated with ≥ 3% oxygen desaturation from pre-event baseline, or an arousal.
- Hypopneas scored as **obstructive** if occurs with *any* of the following:
  a. Snoring
  b. Inspiratory flattening of the nasal pressure or PAP device waveform
  c. Thoracoabdominal paradox.
- **Central** hypopneas are scored when no criteria associated with an obstructive hypopnea are present during the event.
- Scoring hypopneas as being either central or obstructive is optional.

Hypoventilation Rule:
- Score if > 25% of TST is spent with a PCO_2 >50 mmHg.

Hypoxemia Rule:
- Scored when saturation ≤ 90% for ≥ 5 minutes (ICSD3 p.134).

Periodic breathing (PB) rule:
- PB scored if 3+ central apneas lasting > 3 seconds are separated by no more than 20 seconds of normal breathing.

RERA Arousal Rule:
- RERA scored where 2 or more breaths (or the equivalent duration of 2 breaths) are associated with ↑ respiratory effort, flattening of

the inspiratory portion of the NP transducer, snoring, or ↑end-tidal PCO$_2$ *results in an arousal from sleep.*
- Breaths preceding the arousal can not meet criteria for an apnea or a hypopnea.
- Scoring of a RERA is *optional.*

Consider including comment regarding presence of airway protective measures in PSG report, e.g. mouth breathing, neck extention or avoiding supine sleep.

PEDIATRIC OBSTRUCTIVE SLEEP APNEA

Differences from adult OSA

Pediatric OSAS has clinical similarities but also significant differences from that seen in adults. Noteworthy differences include the following:

1. **Demographics:**
   - ± 2% - 5% prevalence.
   - No gender difference in children.
   - Peak age 2 - 6 years (i.e. preschool).
   - Failure to thrive (decreased weight) not uncommon. Weight, however, may also be normal or increased.
   - Obesity prominent in adolescents.

2. **Etiologic differences:**
   - Major cause is adenotonsillar hypertrophy.
   - Nasopharyngeal pathology (e.g. allergies) more common as a cause than in adults.
   - Congenital abnormalities causing craniofacial abnormalities and / or ↓ upper airway (UA) muscle tone:
     - Pierre Robin Syndrome (micrognathia).
     - Achondroplasia (midface hypoplasia).
     - Down Syndrome (midface hypoplasia, micrognathia, macroglossia as well as UA hypotonia).
     - Mucopolysaccharoidoses.
     - Prader-Willi Syndrome (neonatal and infantile hypotonia which may cause feeding problems, delayed milestones, characteristic facial features, and excessive weight gain between ages 1 and 6 years).
     - Crouzon Syndrome (craniofacial dysostosis).
   - Orthodontic abnormalities (eg high arched narrow palate)
   - SDB highly associated with malocclusions in children age 7-8 yrs (*JCSM* July 2020) and malocclusion responsible for persistent SDB in children (mean age 8.8 yrs) following adenotonsillectomy (*JCSM* Aug 2020).

Clinical manifestations.

- History from parents (rather than bed partner) who may report:
  - Loud continuous snoring may be most significant risk factor (with or without apneas, gasping, etc).
  - Nocturnal diaphoresis and enuresis.
  - Sleep very restless.
  - Paradoxical breathing with retractions; (may lead to pectus excavatum).
- Daytime symptoms reported by parents or teachers.
  - Hyperactivity/ADD-like symptoms.
  - Behavioral or emotional problems.
  - Lack of attention/day dreaming (due to "microsleep" episodes).
  - Poor school performance owing to the above problems (may be the presenting issue).
  - EDS in older children.
- Complications may include hypertension and LV & RV hypertrophy.

PSG findings (ICSD3).

- AHI ≥ 1 per hour (obstructive or mixed apneas or hypopneas) or,
- Hypoventilation (25% of TST with $PaCO_2 > 50mm\ Hg$) associated with snoring or flattening of the inspiratory portion of the nasal pressure transducer waveform or paradoxical breathing.
- Events mainly in REM sleep.
- Sleep architecture may be fragmented but more often normal (high cortical arousal threshold in children).

NOTE: The AASM does not endorse a HSAT for OSA diagnosis in children. (Position Paper *JCSM* 2017; 13(10): 1199-2013)

Suggested Classification of severity

- No universally accepted classification for OSA severity in children.
- Assessment of severity takes into account AHI or RDI, impact on child's health and degree of functional impairment.
- Following guideline (after Roland et al , *Otolaryngol Head Neck Surg* 2011) is referenced in *UpToDate*, Feb 2021:
  - Mild OSA=AHI or RDI 1-4.9/hr
  - Moderate OSA =AHI or RDI 5-9.9/hr
  - Severe OSA= AHI or RDI >10/hr

Treatment:

- Adenotonsillectomy main surgical approach (70 - 90% success). Postoperative complications more common in following

high-risk patients:
- < 3 years.
- Severe OSA (AI >10/hr).
- SaO_2 <80% on PSG.
- Morbid obesity.
- Failure to thrive.
- Cor pulmonale.
- Craniofacial abnormalities.
- Neuromuscular weakness/hypotonia.

- CPAP successful in pediatric OSA; used mainly in moderate-to-severe OSA not amenable to surgical treatment or where surgery has failed.
  - In *JCSM* 2020; 16(6): 871-8, Khatin et al report on effective use in pediatric population with mean age 13.
  - In *CHEST* 2021; 159(2):810-817, Cielo et al report on successful PAP treatments in infants.

- UPPP, dental appliances not recommended with the exception of **rapid maxillary expansion** by experienced orthodontists for maxillary constriction (orthotic appliance exerts lateral pressure to upper molars). (Cristulli et al. Treatment of OSAS by Rapid Maxillary Expansion. *Sleep*; 1998; 21(8): 831-835)

- Antiinflammatory agents (intranasal corticosteroids and/or montelukast) reported to improve AHI in mild pediatric OSA (*Pediatrics* 2008; 122:149 - 155, *Pediatrics* 2006; 117: 61 - 66; *CHEST* 2014; 146(1)88-95). Not effective in adults to ↓AHI (*JCSM* 2019; 15(7): 979-983.

- Maxillofacial surgery as indicated for craniofacial abnormalities.

- Weight reduction, particularly in absence of underlying anatomic/pathologic abnormalities may be successful.

- Obese children have high rate of persistent disease despite T&A or medical treatment (Gokdemir and Ersu: *Eur Respir Rev* 2016; 25: 48-53.

REMember:
- High-risk patients should be monitored overnight following surgery.
- Follow-up PSG to confirm resolution in moderate to severe OSA, and with co-morbidities including obesity, Down syndrome, craniofacial abnormalities.
- Following reported deaths in children treated with codeine for pain control following tonsillectomy and adenoidectomy (T&A) for OSA, the FDA on 2/20/2013 posted a warning to include the contraindication to the use of codeine post-operatively following T&A in children.

Summary of Practice Parameters for the Respiratory Indications for Polysomnography in Children (*SLEEP* 2011; 34(3): 379-388).

A. **Standard recommendations:**
- Clinical suspicion of OSA.
- Following adenotonsillectomy in mild OSA for children who have residual symptoms of OSA after surgery.
- Following adenotonsillectomy in children with preoperative moderate-to-severe OSA, obesity, craniofacial anomalies, and neurologic disorders contributing to OSA.
- For positive airway pressure titration.

B. **Guideline Recommendations:**
- For congenital central alveolar hypoventilation syndrome or sleep-related hypoventilation due to neuromuscular disorders or chest wall deformities.
- Following an apparent life-threatening event (ALTE) where there is evidence of a sleep-related breathing disorder.
- Prior to adenotonsillectomy as treatment for OSA.
- In children on long-term PAP to determine whether there are any growth and development-related changes in pressure requirements or if symptoms recur while on PAP.

C. **Option recommendations.**
- To assess efficacy of rapid maxillary expansion for OSA.
- To assess the efficacy of oral appliance therapy.
- For noninvasive positive pressure ventilation titration therapy with other sleep-related breathing disorders.
- To adjust ventilator settings in children treated with mechanical ventilation.
- Prior to decannulation in children treated with tracheostomy.
- In children with asthma, cystic fibrosis, pulmonary hypertension, bronchopulmonary dysplasia, or chest wall abnormalities, PSG is indicated only where there is a suspicion of an accompanying sleep-related breathing disorder.

FYI..... Articles of interest in Pediatric OSA over last several years:

- Recent studies presented evidence that mild and moderate OSAS in middle childhood (ages 5 to 9 years) frequently **remit spontaneously**, often as early as within 7 months. Polysomnographic remission was generally more frequent than symptomatic improvement in at least one of the studies. (*CHEST* 2015.) In the study reported by Spilsbury et al (*SLEEP* 2015), there was a 91% remission of middle childhood cases. Reasons include changes in airway size, regression of lymphoid hyperplasia and alterations in BMI. A case may be made for carefully observing this group of patients providing that the symptom burden is not severe. (See *CHEST* 2015;148(5):1204-13; *New Eng J Med* 2013;368:2366-76; *SLEEP* 2015;38: 23-29.)

- In *CHEST* 2019; 156(1): 120-130, Chan et al report that 30% children (mean age 9.8 yrs) had complete remission and 69% had OAHI <5/ hr after mean 10 yr follow up. More often in females. Obesity and male sex ↑ risk for persistence.

- In an editorial in *Eur Respir J* 2016;47:1310-1312,Campos-Rodriguez & Martinez –Garcia express concerns in a watchful waiting approach to OSA in middle childhood. They point out that (a) other studies have shown lesser rates of remission and some cases of mild OSA have been shown to become more severe over time. Spontaneous remission should therefore not be taken for granted. (b) SDB in children may result in permanent sequelae and the "watchful waiting " period before intervention is therefore unclear. (c) OSA of mild severity and even snoring may permanently affect cognition, growth and cardiovascular function. Uncertainty exists as to whether reduction in AHI accompanies symptom remission and the challenge is to try and identify those children who may need early surgery and those in whom a conservative approach is justified.

- Since most childhood OSA cases are secondary to adenotonsillar hypertrophy, adenotonsillectomy is usually regarded as the first line of treatment. Domany et al present evidence that in nonobese children under the age of 7 years and with moderate OSA and smaller tonsils, **adenoidectomy** alone may prove to be a reasonable surgical option (*J Clin Sleep Med* 2016;12(9):1285-1291).

- **High flow nasal cannula** therapy at 5 to 10 L/min using room air was found in a pilot study to significantly improve the apnea/hypopnea index in a group of 5 children ages 2 months through 15 years. These children did not have adenotonsillar hypertrophy and for one reason or another (including some with neurological deficits) were unable to tolerate PAP therapy. (*J Clin Sleep Med* 2015;11(9):1007-1010.)

- OSA is a risk factor for cardiovascular disease via **endothelial dysfunction**. This phenomenon may be identified even in pediatric OSA. Similar observations may be found in simple childhood obesity. A key mediator of vascular function (exosomal microRNA) may identify the propensity for endothelial dysfunction and subsequent cardiovascular disease risk in these groups of patients. (Khalyfa, et al., *Am J Resp Crit Care Med* 2016;194(9):1116.) Kontos et al (*AJRCCM*, Dec 2020) identify ↑ platelet aggregation, a marker of endothelial dysfunction, in children with SDB.

- Tzeng et al (*JCSM* 2019:15(2):275-284) found ↑ major adverse cardiovascular events in children and adolescents with untreated OSA.

- Barreto et al in *Sleep Medicine* 2018 reports on ↑ exhaled levels of 8 - isoprostane (an oxidative stress bio-marker) in children with OSA on waking compared with primary snoring and controls.

- **Review Article:** OSA and Cardiovascular Risk in Pediatrics. Smith and Armin: *CHEST* 2019; 156: 402-413. Includes discussion of inflammatory changes leading to CV risk.
- OSA in children with **sickle cell disease** →↑ risk neurological complications *SLEEP* 2021; vol 44(2).
- In article The Falling Asleep Process in Adolescents (*SLEEP* 2020) De Zambotti et al demonstrated an inefficient sleep initiation in young females perhaps indicative of a risk factor for insomnia.

OTHER RESPIRATORY DISORDERS OCCURRING IN INFANTS AND CHILDREN

Congenital Central Alveolar Hypoventilation Syndrome (CCAHS).

- Most case severe; present in early infancy with cyanosis, respiratory failure, tachycardia, bradycardia, diaphoresis, or feeding difficulties.
- Other cases may present later in infancy as ALTE or with respiratory failure during activity or with cyanosis, cor pulmonale, or delayed development due to hypoxic neurological damage.

Associated conditions may include:
- Hirschsprung's disease.
- Esophageal dysmotility.
- Neural crest tumors.
- Arrhythmias (e.g., heart block).
- Ocular problems (e.g., strabismus).

Laboratory data:
- ↓ PaO_2, ↑ $PaCO_2$, ↑ HCO_3.
- ↑ hematocrit.

Polysomnogram:
- Hypoxia and hypercapnia; primarily due to severe hypoventilation (tidal breathing 1-2ml/kg compared to normal of about 6ml/kg).
- Changes seen in REM>NREM; central apneas may be seen.

Pathogenesis:
- failure of automatic respiratory control.
- genetic mutation found in most cases (PHOX2B gene).

Primary Central Sleep Apneas of Prematurity and of Infancy.

Primary Central Sleep Apnea of Prematurity.
- Infants < 37 weeks gestation.
- Central apneas of ≥ 20 seconds or periodic breathing >5% TST.
- Apneas associated with bradycardia, hypoxemia (cyanosis) or an intervention such as stimulation or resuscitation.
- May be seen in 25% of infants weighing < 2,500 gm at birth; 84% < 1,000 gm at birth.
- 98% resolve by 40 weeks after conception.

Primary Central Sleep Apnea of Infancy:
- Similar events in an infant ≥ 37 weeks gestation.
- Apneas due to immaturity of respiratory control center in both categories.
- Events may be precipitated or aggravated by comorbid conditions such as GERD, infections, hypoxia, metabolic changes, large temperature swings (Also with apneas of prematurity).
- **Management** includes treating the underlying comorbid condition, supplemental oxygen, respiratory stimulants such as theophylline, ventilatory support as needed.

Sudden Infant Death Syndrome (SIDS).
(Not synonymous with an ICSD3 sleep disorder).

- Sudden unexplained death in an infant < 1 year, despite forensic investigation of death scene & medical investigation with autopsy.
- SIDS commonest cause post-neonatal infant death (incidence has however ↓ from 2/1000 live births to 1/1000 in US with the "Back to Sleep" campaign by the AAP promoting supine sleeping).
- Highest prevalence in winter.
- M > F (60%).
- No relationship to OSAS or ALTE (see next page). (Note: term "near-miss SIDS" no longer used).
- Risk factors:
  - Lower socioeconomic groups.
  - Parent smokers.
  - Preterm birth.
  - Soft sleep surfaces.
  - Prone sleep (may cause upper airway occlusion, CO_2 rebreathing).
  - Hyperthermia.

Note: SIDS included in syndrome of Sudden Unexpected Infant Death (SUID) which encompasses sudden infant death from all causes (suffocation, infection, ingestions, metabolic disorders, trauma, SIDS).

REMember:

"Safe" infant sleep:
- Position infant supine; keep face uncovered.
- Firm mattress; tight-fitting sheets.
- Sleep in sleeper rather than blanket.
- No pillows or soft toys in crib.
- Crib slats should be $< 2\,^3/_8''$ apart.
- Avoid overheating and passive smoke exposure.
- Only one infant per crib.
- No bed-sharing with parents.

Apparent Life-Threatening Event (ALTE).
(Not synonymous with an ICSD3 sleep disorder).

- Sudden frightening change in infant's condition.

- Clinical disturbances may include:
    - combination of apnea with change in color and/or tone.
    - gagging and choking.
    - change in consciousness.

- Underlying cause found in only 40 - 50% of cases:
    - Pneumonia or respiratory infection (especially RSV).
    - GERD.
    - Seizure.
    - Cardiac cause (e.g., rhythm disturbance).
    - "Breath-holding."

- Management of ALTE.
    - Admit for evaluation and to observe for recurrent episode.
    - Treat underlying cause if identified
    - Consider home apnea/bradycardia monitoring (with recording capability).
    - CPR teaching to parents.
    - Prognosis generally good with no sequelae.

REMember:

R/o child abuse, especially if repeated events or where events witnessed and reported by only one caregiver.

INSOMNIAS IN CHILDHOOD

In ICSD2, Behavioral Insomnia of Childhood was an independent subtype in the classification of insomnias. **In ICSD3, insomnias in childhood subsumed within the broader category of chronic insomnia when occurring at least three times per week for at least three months.** However, since pediatricians or pediatric sleep specialists are those who primarily deal with the problem of childhood insomnia, this category remains in the current chapter dealing with pediatric sleep disorders.

Behavioral Insomnia of Childhood.

- May be sleep onset or maintenance or both.
- Due to inappropriate sleep related behavior / activities.
- Occurs ≥ 3x / week for ≥ 3 months.

Two main varieties:

1. Onset association type.
- Sleep onset dependent on specific activities or objects in environment (e.g., rocking, reading, bottle, or parents' room).
- These activities / objects are soothing and sleep inducing.
- Insomnia becomes a disorder when activities are excessively prolonged, demanding and disrupting to parents' sleep.

2. Limiting-setting type.
- Child stalls or refuses to go to bed.
- Child may awaken and refuse to return to sleep in own bed.
- Parents often do not institute appropriate limits, thus promoting the insomnia.
- May occur when transitioning from crib to bed.
- May occur after long-term sharing of parental bed (precipitates anxiety about sleeping on own).

Clinical associations:
- Behavior insomnia of childhood usually diagnosed > age 6m.
- May persist until preschool years (3 - 5 years).
- 10 -30% of this age group affected.

- Condition may be associated with:
    - Daytime behavioral problems.
    - Parental poor sleep, daytime irritability.
    - Family tensions and conflicts.

Two main treatment approaches:

> **1. Extinction** - ignoring negative behaviors occurring with the insomnia.
>
> **2. Gradual extinction** - scheduled brief (a few minutes) parental checks permitted.
>
> **Caution:** Parents should be able to observe unobtrusively for needs such as diaper change or emesis during above treatment approaches.

Summary: Practice Parameters for Behavioral Treatment of Bedtime Problems and Night Awakenings in Infants and Young Children (*SLEEP* 2006; 29(10): 1277-1281).

Effective and recommended therapies include:

1. Parent education/prevention (standard recommendation).

2. Unmodified extinction and extinction of undesired behavior with parental presence (standard).
   - Unmodified extinction: Parents put their child to bed at a designated bedtime and do not respond to the child's undesired behavior.
   - Extinction with parental presence: Some parents may prefer to remain in the child's room at bedtime during the extinction procedure.

3. Graduated extinction ("sleep training") (guideline).
   - Parents ignore bedtime crying and tantrums for a specified period according to a fixed schedule for progressively longer intervals and avoid reinforcing protest behavior.

4. Bedtime fading/positive routines (guideline).
   This recommendation includes the following:
   - Temporarily delaying the child's bedtime to approximate actual sleep onset time.
   - Removal from the bed if sleep onset is not achieved in a prescribed time.
   - Institution of pleasurable/calming activities preceding bedtime.

5. Scheduled awakenings (guideline).
   - Preemptive waking of the child prior to the expected wake time and subsequent fading out of the awakenings over a period of time.
   - Studies suggest this technique may be less acceptable to parents and may have less utility in very young children.

AASM Advisory:
Behavioral interventions primary approach for childhood insomnia, cause of which often lying in parent-child interactions. Hypnotics for short term use if necessary or in special situations, e.g., where cognitive impairment.

Other Childhood Insomnias:

1. Night-time fears.
    - Usually in preschool years (3 - 5 years).
    - May be associated with a dark room or imaginary "scary" creatures.
    - Usually disappear by the age of 5 or 6 years.
    - Parental tensions may aggravate/perpetuate by increasing child's anxiety level.
    - Parental counseling: balance reassurance and limit-setting.

2. Nightmares (see also section 8 ; Parasomnias).
    - Features in children may include:
        - Imagery content may include "scary" creatures.
        - Medications often used in children may be precipitating factor e.g., sedatives, stimulants, leukotriene modifiers, erythromycin
        - Withdrawal of REM suppressants e.g., clonidine, antidepressants or anxiolytics.
        - Treatment includes withdrawal of responsible medication(if appropriate), parental reassurance, counseling for PTSD.

3. Sleep hygiene issues e.g., excess caffeine, television (especially disturbing/violent programs), internet use.
    May occur in school age children (6 - 12 years) as well as adolescents.

4. In adolescents, additional causes of insomnia may include:
    - Delayed sleep phase syndrome.
    - Drug/alcohol abuse.
    - Depression (estimated that at least 50% of adolescent insomnias may be comorbid with a psychiatric problem).

5. Restless leg syndrome (see below).
    Estimated to occur in 2% of children over the age of 2 years.

- Fernandez-Mendoza et al report only 30.3% full remission of insomnia syptoms from childhood (mean age 8.8 yrs) to adolescence (mean age 17 yrs). Risk factors include females, minority groups, lower SE status, psychiatric/behavioral/neurologic disorders, obesity and smoking as well as evening chronotype. (*SLEEP* 2021; v.44(3).
- Inkelis et al (*JCSM* 17 (4): 675-683) report an ↑ risk of depression including suicidal ideation in adolescents with sleep disorders especially insomnia.

Summary of Review Article **Pediatric Insomnia** (Brown and Malow, *CHEST* 2016; 149(5):1332-1339).

This is a very good review which addresses insomnias of infancy as well as those of older children. The latter group includes children with autism spectrum disorders (ASD) in whom there may be dysregulation of multiple neurotransmitters including GABA, melatonin and serotonin. Also reviewed are medical causes of insomnia such as asthma or OSA, neurologic disorders such as epilepsy, psychiatric problems such as depression and PTSD as well as circadian rhythm disorders (e.g. delayed sleep phase syndrome). Sleep hygiene issues may be similar to those in the adult, e.g. use of electronic devices or caffeine close to bedtime also need to be considered.

Treatment will depend on the underlying cause and may include sleep hygiene and behavioral approaches similar to the adult if appropriate. Pharmacological therapies are not approved for pediatric insomnia, but in the ASD group, melatonin 0.75 to 6 mg taken 30 minutes before bedtime has been used with some success; mild side effects (morning sleepiness and increased enuresis) may occur infrequently. Gabapentin, which has been shown to increase SWS and sleep efficiency, has been used in children with neurodevelopmental or neuropsychiatric disorders.

SLEEP DISORDERS OCCURRING IN BOTH ADULTS AND CHILDREN: POINTS OF DIFFERENTION

Narcolepsy:

- Rare <5 years of age. May present with recurrence of daytime naps.
- 1/3 narcoleptic patients are symptomatic before the age of 15 but only 4% diagnosed in this age group.
- Narcolepsy mistaken for:
    - Laziness or inattentiveness, behavioral problems, depression, ADD, schizophrenia because of hypnagogic hallucinations, seizures because of cataplexy.
    - In children, narcolepsy may be associated with conditions such as Prader-Willi Syndrome, CNS trauma, or CNS tumors.
- MSLT may not show SOREMs; may need repeat study when older.
- Cataplexy, hypnagogic hallucinations, and sleep paralysis may also occur later in the course of the illness.
- Mean sleep latency for MSLT in *normal* prepubertal children longer than in adults (16 - 18 min); not validated in children <8yrs.
- CSF hypocretin levels low in narcolepsy with cataplexy and may predate the appearance of cataplexy, may become a useful diagnostic test when more widely available.

REMember:

- The most common causes of short mean sleep latency and SOREMs on MSLT in pre-pubertal children and adolescents are:
  - Chronic sleep deprivation.
  - Delayed sleep phase syndrome.

- Narcolepsy may be precipitated by the combination of genetic susceptibility (DQB1*0602) and a stressful event such as systemic illness, head injury, or bereavement ("two-hit hypothesis").

- Dextroamphetamine/amphetamine (*Adderall*) and dextroamphetamine (*Dexedrine*) are approved for pediatric narcolepsy ages ≥ 6 years.

- Other stimulants, modafinil, armodafinil or solriamfetol not FDA approved for narcolepsy in children.

- Xyrem (Sodium Oxybate) now FDA approved for pediatric use ages 7yrs & older. Dose, also split as in adults, is weight related 20-29kg: 2-6gm, 30-44kg: 3-7.5gm, >45kg: 4.5-9gm.

- Xywav (Ca, Mg, K, Na Oxybate) also approved ages 7+ yrs. Dose also weight based.

- **Intravenous immunoglobulin therapy**: French study in 22 children <18 yrs; improvement no better than standard therapy but occurred more rapidly in a subset of patients (*J. Clin Sleep Med* 2017; 13(3): 441-453).

Restless leg syndrome.

- 2% prevalence for RLS in children.
- If PLMS present →↑ sleep disruption and ↑ EDS.

Diagnostic criteria depend on age

For children ages 2 to 12 years:

- Child meets all 4 adult criteria.
  - Urge to move legs, usually associated with uncomfortable sensations.
  - Occurs mainly during periods of inactivity.

- Urge to move or unpleasant sensations relieved by movement.
- Symptoms occur or worsen in the evenings.
- Essential criteria should be associated with the child's own description of discomfort (terms used may include "creepy/crawly, spiders, wiggly").
- If child cannot give a description of sensations then the essential diagnostic criteria should be associated with 2 of the following 3 supportive criteria:
  - Sleep disturbance for age (sleep onset and/or sleep maintenance insomnia).
  - The presence of definite RLS in a biologic parent or sibling.
  - Child has PLM index of ≥ 5/hr on overnight polysomnogram.

For children/adolescents (ages 13 to 18):
All four essential adult diagnostic criteria.

Associated clinical features:
(Kotagel S, Silber MH *Ann Neurol.* 2004 56(6):803-7)
- Insomnia (onset or maintenance) 87%.
- Inattentiveness 25%.
- Family history RLS especially mothers 72%.
- Serum ferritin <50 mcg/L 83%.
- 2/3 children (mean age 10.6y) with RLS had co-morbid psychiatric disorders (ADD, anxiety, mood disorders and behavior disturbances. (Pullen et al; *JCSM* 2011; 7(6): 587-596).

Periodic Limb Movement Disorder (PLMD)

- PLM index ≥ 5/hr. in children (cf > 15/hr. in adults).
- Diagnose PLMD only if there is a clinical sleep disturbance in the absence of an alternative primary sleep disorder.
- 72% of 39 children with PLMS had serum ferritin <50mcg/L (*SLEEP* 2003; 26: 735-8).

- **Treatment RLS/PLMD**
  - Sleep hygiene.
  - Supplemental iron for serum ferritin level <50 mcg/L.
  - Medications used in adult PLMS/RLS if used are used "off-label."
  - **Comment:** Most pediatricians use supplemental iron for up to 3 months. Polysaccharide-based preparations have fewer side effects and are better absorbed.

REMember:

- RLS and ADHD appear to occur co-morbidly as separate and distinct diagnostic entities. One condition may, however, aggravate the other and treatment of one may impact positively on the other.

OTHER SLEEP DISORDERS COMMONLY FOUND IN CHILDREN/ADOLESCENTS:

Delayed Sleep Phase Syndrome:
Section 5.

Parasomnias:
Section 8.
Sleep terrors, confusional arousals; sleepwalking, sleep enuresis.

Further reading/reference:

Moore M et al A Review of Pediatric Nonrespiratory Sleep disorders
CHEST 2006;130:1252-1262

FYI:

Del Rosso et al define a condition Restless Sleep Disorder (RSD) -- not included in ICSD3 -- where children display large body movements during sleep (>5/hr) and are associated with daytime impairments such as EDS, hyperactivity, irritability. Serum ferritin <50mcg/L found in cohort of RSD children. Response shown to iron supplements but less side effects with IV compared with oral iron. (*SLEEP* 2021; v.44 No 2).

Summary of Practice Parameters Article: **Practice Parameters for the Non-Respiratory Indications for Polysomnography and Multiple Sleep Latency Testing for Children.** (*SLEEP* 2012; 35 (11): 1467 - 1473).

Additional Comments From: **Non-Respiratory Indications for Polysomnography and Related Procedures in Children: An Evidence-Based Review.** *SLEEP* 2012; 35 (11): 1451 - 1466.

1. MSLT, preceded by nocturnal PSG, is indicated in children as part of the evaluation for suspected **narcolepsy** (STANDARD).
    *   MSLT in narcoleptic children as young as five years and in adolescence is usually abnormal: Mean sleep latency <8 minutes (often <5 minutes) with 2 or more SOREMPs. Sensitivity 79-100%.
    *   PSG to exclude other major sleep disorders as the cause of EDS and to assure that the subject had at least six hours of sleep prior to the MSLT.

2. MSLT preceded by nocturnal PSG indicated in children suspected of having **hypersomnia from causes other than narcolepsy** to assess excessive sleepiness and to aid in differentiation from narcolepsy (OPTION).

Note:

*   MSLT technically feasible in developmentally normal children ≥ 5 years.
*   Developmentally normal prepubertal and early pubertal children rarely fall asleep during standard 20-minutes daytime nap opportunities.
*   Mean sleep latencies longer in children and adolescents than adults.
*   Some researchers modify standard MSLT protocol by affording 30-minutes nap opportunities to avoid underestimating mild degrees of sleepiness.
*   1 - 2 SOREMPs fairly common in adolescents; interpret MSLT with caution.
*   Small % of prepubertal narcoleptic patients may have <2 SOREMPs.

3. **Parasomnias.**

    *   PSG usually unnecessary in children with typical parasomnias.
    *   Consider PSG with expanded EEG montage and video to differentiate atypical parasomnias from nocturnal seizures or to confirm the diagnosis of an atypical or potentially injurious parasomnia (OPTION).
    *   PSG useful to rule out SDB or PLMD as comorbid disorders in children with frequent NREM parasomnias (GUIDELINE); SDB found in >50% of children with parasomnias (mainly sleepwalking).

4. **Epilepsy.**

   - Consider PSG to r/o SDB or PLMS in children whose seizures are not well controlled by medications (GUIDELINE).
   - SDB in children with epilepsy and sleep complaints ranged 27% - 80%.

5. **Nocturnal enuresis.**

   - Consider PSG to r/o co-morbid OSA if child with enuresis is obese and/or failed standard treatments for enuresis (GUIDELINE).
   - Enuresis may improve or resolve after adenotonsillectomy in children with habitual snoring and/or OSA.

6. **Sleep-related movement disorders.**

   - Reports support a relationship between RLS and increased prevalence of PLMS on PSG which is then used as an additional diagnostic criterion for RLS in children.
   - PSG therefore indicated in children suspected of having RLS who require supportive data for diagnosing RLS (OPTION).
   - PSG indicated in children suspected of having PLMD to confirm diagnosis (STANDARD).
     - PLMD diagnosed if PLMS index ≥ 5/hour with complaints of sleep disturbance and/or daytime fatigue.
     - 72% of 39 children in one study with PLMS had serum ferritin levels < 50 mcg/L. and 3/4 of these improved with supplemental iron therapy.

7. **Bruxism.**

   - PSG not routinely indicated (STANDARD).

8. Children with **chronic pain syndromes** including fibromyalgia and rheumatologic disorders: limited use for PSG. Studies in this group of patients done to evaluate cause of sleep disturbance and not for diagnosis of underlying pain disorder.

Test Your Memory (Section 12):

1. Active sleep in utero usually seen by:

    a. 24 weeks.
    b. 28 weeks.
    c. 32 weeks.
    d. 34 weeks.
    e. 36 weeks.

2. Which of the following has a known association with SIDS?

    a. Breastfed infants.
    b. Prematurity.
    c. Supine sleep.
    d. Older parents.
    e. Sibling with OSA.

3. OSA in children differs from adults by which of the following?

    a. F > M prevalence.
    b. Having a congenital abnormality as the most frequent cause.
    c. Snoring not usually audible.
    d. ADD more frequently seen.
    e. UARS less frequently seen.

4. Regarding central sleep apnea of infancy, which statement is correct?

    a. Seen < 37 weeks postconception.
    b. No relationship to birthweight.
    c. <50% resolved by 40 weeks post-conception.
    d. Co-morbid conditions may play a role in presentation.
    e. Caused by upper airway muscle hypotonia.

5. Regarding childhood insomnia, recommended treatment approaches may include all of the following except:

    a. Extinction approaches.
    b. Calming routines prior to bedtime.
    c. Very small doses of antihistamines.
    d. Keeping the child awake until approximate usual sleep onset time.
    e. Ignoring bedtime crying.

Answers: 1c, 2b, 3d, 4d, 5c.

APPENDIX:

The AASM website includes clinical as well as public awareness statements -- many of which are based on position statements published in *J. Clin Sleep Med*. The following summarizes these statements.

OSA
- Neither marijuana nor synthetic medical cannabis should be used in OSA treatment.

- Annual screening (e.g., STOP-BANG or Berlin) for righ risk patients:
    H - heart failure
    E - elevated blood pressure
    A - atrial fibrillation
    R - resistent hypertension
    T - type 2 diabetes
    S - stroke

Pediatrics
- Infant sleep environment (see "safe sleep" section 12.)

- Insomnia in children -- behavorial interventions first-approach. Sleep physian evaluation for failure to respond or complex cases.

- School start times -- 8:30 am for middle school and high school to account for natural pupertal shift of circadian clock toward a late-night bedtime.

Public awareness
- Adult sleep ≥ 7 hours per night to promote optimal health, productivity and alertness.

- Measures to counter drowsy driving including education at government and commercial levels, work shift scheduling and screening drivers for OSA.

- **Daylight savings time** (DST) may disrupt sleep/wake patterns which may last 5-7days and may affect daytime alertness and function. Ensuring ≥ 7 hours of nightly sleep before and after DST changes and gradually adjusting sleep and wake times a few days before DST may be beneficial.

The AASM also advises:
(1)   No PSG for
        (a) Chronic insomnia unless a comorbid sleep disorder present.
        (b) Diagnosis of RLS except where diagnosis unclear or need to document PLMS.

(2) No re-titration for patients stable on PAP therapy. Consider re-titration if symptoms recur despite good compliance or if significant weight gain. Could do PSG if weight loss to assess for improvement in AHI and continued PAP use.

(3) Adult insomnia should be initially managed with CBT. Hypnotics reserved for adjunctive therapy where necessary.

(4) Behavioral interventions primary approach for childhood insomnia, cause of which often lying in parent-child interactions. Hypnotics for short term use if necessary or in special situations, e.g., where cognitive impairment.

AASM position statements regarding current/topical sleep issues

(1) J. Clin Sleep Med 2020; 16(10): 1781-4. Regarding Daylight savings time (DST)
- DST occurs when clocks set one hour ahead of standard time (starts 2 a.m. 2nd Sunday in March - "spring forward"; ends 2 a.m. first Sunday in November- "fall back").
- Adds to circadian misalignment.
- May contribute to CV disease risk, metabolic syndrome as well as public health and safety risk.
- AASM therefore *against* DST and *for* fixed natural standard time.

(2) *JCSM* 2020; 16(4): 605-7. Re: **Artificial Intelligence (AI)**: AI useful to argument PSG scoring. May identify cardiovascular risk phenotype, for example, and guide treatment. Data from PAP devices useful for enhancing management and compliance.

(3) *JCSM* 2020; 16(5): 803-5. AASM identifies a "critical need to evaluate the role of sleep disruption, sleep deprivation, and circadian misalignment in physician well-being and burnout" and "for the development of effective countermeasures."

(4) *JCSM* 2015; 11(10): 1187-1198. AASM position paper regarding **Telemedicine** covers many aspects including patient interactions, prescription medication and diagnostic studies. See also AASM update on use of telemedicine incorporating lessons learned during the COVID-19 pandemic *JCSM* 2021; 17(5): 1103-7.

AASM website has a very useful **telemedicine template** for adult comprehensive sleep evaluation; also includes components of physical examination which may be possible to detect remotely.

INDEX

A

AASM Practice Parameters
actigraphy 35
Central Sleep Apnea 168
insomnia (adult)..............................71
insomnia (pediatrics)....................224
nightmare disorder 101-102
OSA 135,141,147
NIPPV for hypoventilation...........175
PAP titration...................................141
PSG in pediatrics (SDB)................218
PSG/MSLT in pediatrics 230
RBD 95
RLS/PLMD 114
Surgery for OSA 147
Acetylcholine 2,4
and REM..4
Actigraphy 35
Adjustment sleep disorder...................65
Advanced sleep phase syndrome ... 55,58
AHI defined 138
Alcohol, effects on sleep......................45
Alpha intrusion — causes...................202
ALTE 222
Alzheimer's disease 195
Amphetamines (mode of action) 5
Antidepressants, (tables)...............47, 194
effect on sleep/REM..................40-44
Antihistamines, effect on sleep 41
Antipsychotics (table)............................47
Anxiety disorders.................................191
Apnea, defined 27-28
Apneic threshold 12
Arousal rule 31
Armodafinil..81
ASV 161
ASV in CHF..164
Asthma and sleep..................................197
Augmentation & RLS 113, 116

B

Benzodiazepines, mode of action 42
effect on sleep 40
Beta blockers,sleep disruption 42
Bruxism...121
(scoring)..30

C

Cancer and Sleep...................................205
Catathrenia(groaning).........................179
Cataplexy...79, 83
Central sleep apnea syndromes 159
Cheyne Stokes Breathing, definition ... 29
Cheyne Stokes Breathing/CHF.........162
Chronic obstructive lung disease
(COPD), and sleep..............................198
Circadian physiology........................5,53

Circadian rhythm disorders 54
CRDs treatment.............................57ff
Complex sleep apnea..........................166
Confusional arousals 89

D

Delayed sleep-wake phase syndrome.. 54,57
Depression...189

E

Eating disorders and sleep...................93
Endocrine changes in sleep..................13
EEG and sleep staging......................22,24
Elderly sleep pattern, SDB 8, 154
Endocrine physiology............................13
Enuresis 103
Epilepsy and sleep 184
Epworth sleepiness scale......................18
Excessive daytime sleepiness,
evaluation..17
Exploding head syndrome.................107

F

Ferritin levels 111
Fibromyalgia and sleep 202
Flumezenil for I.H. 85
Free running CRD 56

G

GABA..4
Genito-urinary changes in sleep 15
Gabapentin in RLS 112
Growth hormone in sleep 14
GERD 201
Ghrelin 7, 14

H

Hallucinations in narcolepsy...............79
Histamine as neurotransmitter 2
HLA typing in narcolepsy....................78
Hypersomnia, idiopathic 84
Hypnotics, (table)...................................70
Hypocretin 2
in narcolepsy..............................78, 80
Hypopnea, definition............................28
Hypoventilation syndromes...............170
Hypglossal nerve stimulation 148

I

Idiopathic/primary CSA......................161
Insomnia, clinical approach.................19
Insomnia, causes and management.. 66ff
Insomnia, pediatric 223ff
Irregular sleep wake cycle 56, 59

J

Jet lag 55, 58

K

K complex defined 24
Kleine-Levin Syndrome 85

L

Lemborexant 70

Leptin...7, 14
Lithium as REM suppressant 44, 48
Loop gain...160

M
Mallampati classification 132
Medicare policies
    scoring respiratory events 152
    CPAP/BPAP therapy.....................143
Medications causing
    insomnia...42
    nightmares 99
    RBD 96
    REM sleep effects 44
    RLS, PLMS 111
    sedation 40
    sleepwalking...................................91
Melatonin and sleep-wake cycle.......5,53
Modafinil, armodafinil 81
MSLT..32
MWT...33
Multiple System Atrophy....................196

N
Narcolepsy 77
Narcolepsy, pediatric...........................226
Neurotransmitters of sleep 4
Neurotransmitters of wakefulness 2
Nightmare disorder 99
Nocturnal frontal lobe epilepsy 184
Neonatal sleep 210
Non-24hr SWRD....................................56

O
Obesity hypoventilation syndrome...172
Obsessive compulsive behavior
    disorder 192
Obstructive sleep apnea, adult........126ff
Obstructive sleep apnea, pediatric 215
Ocular manifestations OSA 156
Oral appliance therapy.................144-145
Orexin/hypocretin................................2
    in narcolepsy 80
Overlap syndrome 199
Oxygen-hemoglobin dissociation
    curve 171
OSA severity 137

P
Parkinson's disease 196
Periodic limb movements 30, 118
PLMD, pediatric....................................228
Personalized therapy for OSA............152
Pitolisant...82
Polysomnography 21-32
Post polio syndrome 175
Pregnancy and sleep............................202
Post-traumatic stress syndrome.........191
Prolactin..14
Propranolol, as cause of insomnia.......42
"Prozac eyes" 43
Peseudospindles and BZDs.................46
Psychiatric disorders 188ff

Psychoactive medications (table).........47
PTSD 191
Pulmonary hypertension 200

R
REM-dominant OSA.............................139
REM sleep, defined 26
RBD 95
Respiration in sleep..............................11
RDI, defined.................................138, 143
Renal changes in sleep..........................15
Restless leg syndrome 109
RLS, pediatric.......................................227
RLS treatment 112ff
Respiratory Scoring Rules
    adults 27ff
    pediatrics.......................................213ff

S
Sexsomnias 105
SIDS...221
Sleep physiology 11
Scoring rules, adults 24ff
    pediatrics.......................................211ff
Shift work disorder..............................56
Sleepiness, clinical evaluation..............17
Sleep deprivation 6
Sleep hypoxia-hypoventilation
    defined...170
Sleep paralysis, isolated 98
Sleep paralysis in narcolepsy 79
Sleep related eating disorder...............93
Sleep spindles 24
Sleep stages sequence 9
Sleep staging 24ff
Sleep terrors 92
    differentiation from nightmares...101
Sleepwalking...90
    differentiation from RBD 92
Snoring...178
Sodium oxybate (Xyrem) 82
Sodium oxybate in children...............227
Solriamfetol 82
SSRIs, and sleep disruption 42
SSRI (in table of psychoactive
    medications)....................................47
STOP-BANG questionaire 131
Suprachiasmatic nucleus 5
Suvorexant 70

T
Thermoregulation in sleep..............15,54

U
UARS..151
UPPP, ...147

V
Violent parasomnias 104
VLPO..3-4
Volume assured pressure
    support ventilation 177

W
Wakefulness physiology 1-2

Made in the USA
Las Vegas, NV
28 December 2023

83669436R00138